LOW-CARBON EUROPE

80 INSPIRING & SUSTAINABLE NO-FLY TRAVEL ITINERARIES

Contents

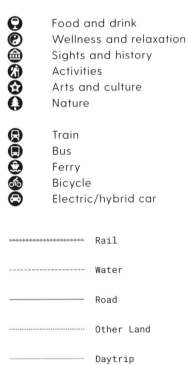

KEY

🍽 Food and drink
🅿 Wellness and relaxation
🏛 Sights and history
🏃 Activities
✪ Arts and culture
🌲 Nature

🚆 Train
🚌 Bus
⛴ Ferry
🚲 Bicycle
🚗 Electric/hybrid car

⋯⋯⋯⋯⋯ Rail

‒ ‒ ‒ ‒ ‒ Water

——————— Road

⋯⋯⋯⋯⋯ Other Land

——————— Daytrip

Bag a window seat as your French TGVs (Train à Grande Vitesse) speeds across the country

Introduction

by Tom Hall, London 2019

Waking up on a train somewhere in Europe must be one of the great pleasures of travel. Out the window the outskirts of Rome or Edinburgh or Vienna roll by. After a short stroll along a platform you emerge into the morning of one of the world's most iconic cities. Just like that — no airport security lines, little stress, and with the warm glow of travelling by a more climate-friendly form of travel.

It's only recently that flying short-haul in Europe became anything like the norm. Generations of post-war travellers got to know Europe — and each other — by inter-railing or taking longer independent trips across the continent by bicycle or even hitch-hiking. Since the rise of low-cost carriers we've been able to inexpensively and more quickly get to more places.

Recently though it feels like we might have lost some things along the way. The joy of slow exploration, watching the landscape gradually change from a bicycle, ferry or train window feels a long way from the whistle-stop weekend away. Certain undoubtedly beautiful places have become victims of their own popularity, with many cities still trying to get to grips

with having too many people in the same places. And in these climate-conscious times, the impact of aviation on carbon dioxide (CO_2) emissions can, for many travellers, no longer be ignored.

Happily Europe remains a wonderful place for low-carbon travellers. An ever-growing network of fast high-speed trains rivalling planes for end-to-end journey times complements inter-city, regional and local services to form a network reaching from northern Norway to Morocco, from the west of Ireland to the point where European Russia meets Asia, and beyond. Where the rails run out, there are buses and ferries. And across the continent cycling and hiking paths, combined with hostels, guesthouses and social accommodation, make doing your own thing easy. There's no need to fly from London to Amsterdam, Madrid to Barcelona or from Paris to Zurich. And to spend a week or more cruising the cycle lanes of Denmark or the Netherlands is a wonderful window on a whole different take on getting from A to B.

This book is an important project for Lonely Planet. All of us here are

Milan's central station beats most airport architecture

passionate travellers and believe that, practised responsibly, travel is a force for good in the world. It's impossible to ignore the impact all of us have when travelling, and the importance of making changes where we can. For us, this is not about stopping travelling but about looking at what we can all do differently. We hope we're giving some food for thought about travel in Europe with the places we list here. There remain, of course, places that require a flight to get to – and for those we'd advocate staying longer and pursuing ground travel while there. We continue to offset the emissions from our own travel, while recognising that's not a solution in itself. And we'd add our voice to those looking to reduce the carbon footprint of flying, and indeed of the travel industry as a whole.

How to use this book

Each itinerary, whether it features a ferry journey to the Faroe Islands or a train ride along the French Riviera, suggests ways of getting to the start of the itinerary from different cities in Europe, typically north, south, east or west of the itinerary's first stop. Then each itinerary is plotted, stop by stop, with day trips from some stops also suggested. The transport logistics of how to get to the next stop are detailed in bold. Most itineraries use Europe's excellent rail network, from 400km/h high-speed, long-distance services to slower local trains. But you'll also find ferry trips, journeys by hybrid vehicles, bicycle rides and hikes.

Duration: We have suggested the average amount of time each itinerary might take, always erring on the shorter rather than the longer side. To extend many of these itineraries, simply stay longer in the places you like the most. Similarly, families might need to factor in more time to make connections or complete cycling routes.

Carbon counts: We've used Resurgence's carbon calculator to total the kg of carbon dioxide for each itinerary (per person) from the first stop to the last but not including how you get to the start (this depends on where you live). The calculator allows for different modes of transport. However, some itineraries have varying options for some legs (taking a train instead of cycling).

The rules of low-carbon travel

Know when to book: Many fast train services go on sale 90 days in advance. The cheapest tickets tend to go first. If you're flexible with timings you can often find bargains even quite close to travel time.

Pack light: Whether on two wheels or on fast trains you'll be grateful for shedding a kilogram or two from what you're carrying. There's nothing that you'll need that you can't pick up along the way.

Book accommodation ahead: While you'd be unlucky not to be able to get on a particular train or ferry as a foot passenger, accommodation in summer months is best reserved ahead, even dormitories.

Expect to pay (a little) more: Some travellers are put off by the cost of rail journeys versus flying. Before you write it off though consider the total end-to-end cost of getting to and from the airport, baggage fees and food and drink. It will bring the difference down considerably.

The journey's part of the fun: Airports are not fun. But a boat or train journey is part of the experience. Bring some food to share with fellow passengers too as the scenery rolls by.

Tips

Cycling: Some itineraries have the option of cycling part of the route. Many trains have restrictions on how and when you can take a bicycle on board. One tip to pack your bicycle for train travel without putting it in a heavy-duty bag or box (which may exceed the permitted dimensions) is to take a large lightweight bag. Remove the front and rear wheels, remove or turn the handlebars to one side, slot the wheels beside the frame, then slide into the bag. Alternatively, you can ask local bike shops for spare cardboard boxes or use a bike bag and store it at the start of your trip at accommodation or by using a service such as www.nannybag.com.

Trains: In peak season and on popular routes it's always advisable to book train tickets as far in advance as possible. Mark Smith (www.seat61.com) shares a lot of tips about whom to book train tickets for specific journeys with and how.

ABOUT ONE WEEK

Art trail to Amsterdam

Paris · Lille · Antwerp · Amsterdam

This short route artfully combines engaging cities with world-class galleries, disembarking the train to meet French Impressionists and the masters of the Dutch Golden Age.

Departure points

This trip makes the most of high-speed rail links between Paris and Amsterdam. It's very easy to link up with this itinerary from the south, with services to Paris Gare de Lyon from Lyon Part Dieu (2h), Marseille's Gare St-Charles (3h) and Milan Centrale (7h). Alternatively do the route in reverse, departing Hamburg Hauptbahnhof for Amsterdam (5h) or intercept half way, travelling direct from London St Pancras to Lille Europe station (1h30).

❶ Paris

Paris is a titan of art – from Renoir's visions of the city in the Musée d'Orsay, to a certain person's enigmatic gaze in the Louvre. For something different, head to the Musée Picasso: it's spread over a 17th-century mansion in the Marais district. Works chronicle the artist's life in the city, during which he was accused of stealing the Mona Lisa.

🚊 **Around 20 daily services run from Paris Gare du Nord to Lille stations (1h). www. sncf.com**

🏨 **Hotel tip: Hotel Gavarni**

The Musée d'Orsay in Paris

Fact box

Carbon (kg per person) 10

Distance (km) 513

Nights 6+

Transport budget (€) 300

Rembrandt's The Night Watch in the Rijksmuseum

❷ Lille

An industrial city at a crossroads of the Low Countries and France, Lille punches well above its weight when it comes to the visual arts. Founded on the instructions of Napoleon, the Palais des Beaux-Arts was built to introduce Old Masters to the masses, housing works from Raphael to Rembrandt. Fast forward to the present and those masses also flock to LaM, Lille's contemporary art museum and sculpture park, with a proud pedigree displaying weird and wonderful installations.

🚆 **SNCF operates direct services from Lille Flandres to Antwerp Centraal (1h30). www. sncf.com**

🔄 Day trip

Louvre-Lens

A northern cousin of the famous Parisian pyramid, this striking glassy structure opened in 2012 with a mission to provide a new home to a sizeable chunk of the Louvre's vast collection and to help regenerate the former mining town of Lens in the north of the country.

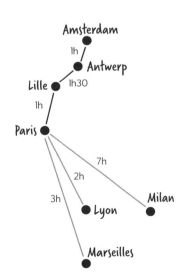

🚊 **More than 50 trains a day travel from Antwerp to Amsterdam stations (1h). www. thalys.com**

❹ Amsterdam

Amsterdam's holy trinity of art galleries cluster around the Museumplein – a grassy expanse beloved of picnickers. There's the distinctive 'bathtub' design of the contemporary Stedelijk Museum, and the iconic towers of the reinvigorated Rijksmuseum. But if you want to reflect back on your trip, step inside the Van Gogh Museum – the world's largest collection of his art includes works from his career in Antwerp, and depictions of the cafes and boulevards of Paris.

Returning home

It's very easy to return to Paris, with 11 daily direct Thalys trains to Gare du Nord (3h30).

🚊 **Around 50 trains a day travel from Lille Flandres station to Lens (0h30). www.sncf.com**

❸ Antwerp

The prosperous port of Antwerp was the home town of baroque master Peter Paul Rubens – his house and workshop are open to the public, while the nooks of Antwerp's soaring cathedral are adorned with his works. If the written word is more your thing, head to the remarkable Museum Plantin-Moretus – a medieval building housing the world's first industrial printing works, dating back to an age when the Low Countries disseminated books and ideas across Europe.

The new atrium of Amsterdam's Rijksmuseum

Beer pilgrimage to Belgium

Paris · Brussels · Antwerp · Bruges

Starting from Paris, hop into the heartland of Belgian beer to tour breweries and visit cavernous bars amid the canals and cobbled squares of Flanders.

Departure points

Geneva has connections to Paris Gare de Lyon on TGV Lyria services (3h). You could also start the itinerary from London St Pancras, travelling by Eurostar to Paris Gare du Nord (2h30) or skipping France and heading straight to Brussels Midi/Zuid (2h). Alternatively, there are direct trains to Brussels from Cologne Hauptbahnhof (2h), a route travelled by both German ICE and Thalys trains.

❶ Paris

Start your odyssey in Paris – a city not traditionally well known for its brewing scene, though a flurry of taprooms has opened in recent years. Toast your departure at Le Triangle, a microbrewery

that's a 20-minute walk from Gare du Nord, close to the Canal St Martin.

🚆 **About 30 daily trains connect Paris Gare du Nord with Brussels Midi/Zuid station (1h30). www.thalys.com**

🛏 **Hotel tip: Le Citizen**

❷ Brussels

The de facto capital of the EU, Brussels is nonetheless a surprisingly compact city. A 15-minute walk from the station

Fact box

Carbon (kg per person) 10
Distance (km) 500
Nights 5+
Transport budget (€) 200

There are more than 800 Belgian beers to try

❸ Antwerp

Antwerp has perhaps Europe's most ornate station, with gilded clocks, soaring ceilings and monumental staircases. The city was: one of Europe's richest ports during its 16th-century heyday, Antwerp has a spring in its step thanks to its fashion industry and regenerated docks. While away a morning in Rubenshuis – the home and studio of Old Master painter Peter Paul Rubens (1577-1640), adorned with his canvases. Then make for a cafe in the Grote Markt – the medieval square – for a *bolleke*, the distinctive rounded glass typically filled with the city's De Koninck beer.

🚆 **Up to 40 trains each day travel from Antwerp Centraal to Bruges (1h). www. belgiantrain.be**

❹ Bruges

Though blighted by overtourism, Bruges is an archetypal fairy-tale city: belfries, little windmills, serene canals and cobblestone alleys. Those same cobbles become more challenging once you've sampled its famous export – delicious Belgian beer. Wait until the midday crowds have abated and head to De Halve Maan brewery to try the town's signature Brugse Zot (Bruges Fool). Otherwise set out on a quest to find De Garre, a well-hidden, multistorey tavern where the house beer is so potent they will only serve you three glasses (so you can safely navigate the stairs).

❸ Day trip

Ghent

Set midway between Bruges and Brussels, Ghent is another postcard-perfect Flemish city – albeit with a gritty industrial fringe, and where tourists are mercifully thinner

brings you to its iconic fountain statue (of a peeing boy!), the Manneken Pis – walk another five minutes and you'll be amid the baroque guildhalls of the Grand Place, lauded by some as the most beautiful in Europe. A highlight for beer lovers is the Cantillon Brewery, which uses 19th-century equipment to create distinctive lambic brews. It's in the neighbourhood of Anderlecht, about a 20-minute walk from the town centre.

🚆 **About 70 trains a day link Brussels Nord with Antwerp Centraal (0h30). www. belgiantrain.be**

Explore Bruges' waterways by boat

on the ground than Bruges. You could easily spend a day browsing its historic churches, galleries and cloth hall – and lose an evening in its bars. Het Waterhuis aan de Bierkant has a riverside terrace.

🚆 **Over 80 trains a day travel to Bruges, the fastest in under 30 minutes. www. belgiantrain.be**

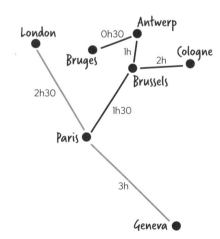

Returning home

From Bruges, roughly 60 trains a day depart for Brussels (1h). From Brussels change for onward connections to Paris and all points south.

© S-F / Shutterstock

A Basque food adventure

Portsmouth · Bilbao · Logroño · Vitoria-Gasteiz · Donostia-San Sebastián
Tour one of Europe's gastronomic heartlands on this itinerary, which also takes in bustling ports and stately cities, world-class art centres and accomplished vineyards.

Departure points

The itinerary begins with one of the UK's few ferry connections to Spain, departing Portsmouth – accessible by train from London (1h30), Edinburgh (8h) and Cardiff (3h) – and arriving in Bilbao some 24 hours later. It's also possible to connect to Bilbao and San Sebastián (Donostia) from Paris, boarding TGV Duplex services at Montparnasse and changing on the border at Hendaye for direct services to San Sebastián, and onward buses to Bilbao (a fiddly travel route). Five trains travel from Madrid Chamartín to Bilbao Abando station daily (5h).

❶ Portsmouth–Bilbao

If you're travelling from the UK, begin your adventure as a foot passenger on the Portsmouth-Bilbao cruise ferry. Sailing on the MV Cap Finistère, highlights include pulling out of Portsmouth Harbour – with Lord Nelson's flagship HMS *Victory* on the port side – and hauling into the Estuary of Bilbao with the surfing beach at Playa de Arrigunaga visible in the distance.

Fact box
Carbon (kg per person) 151
Distance (km) 1500
Nights 8+
Transport budget (€) 450

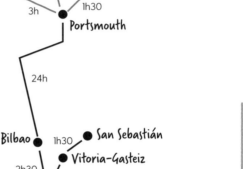

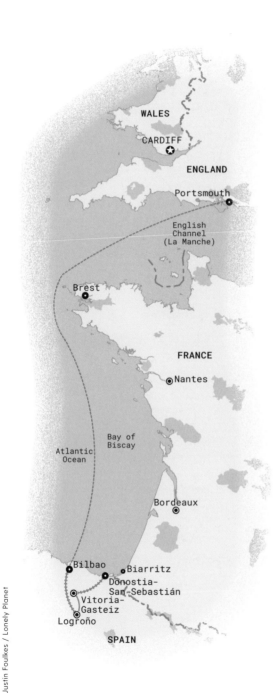

Mix and match your pintxos in San Sebastián

⊗ **Departures on the Portsmouth-Bilbao route (24h) vary erratically throughout the year, from up to three times a week in high summer to once a week in winter. www.brittanyferries.co.uk**

❷ Bilbao

Few European cities have reinvented themselves quite like Bilbao, once synonymous with heavy industry but today one of the continent's artistic centres. As well as the Museo Guggenheim, get acquainted with Iberian masters in the Museo de Bellas Artes. Museum-hopping will whet your appetite for the local *pintxos* (Basque tapas) – for atmosphere, Cafe-Bar Bilbao has been hard to beat since it opened in 1911.

🚆 **Twice daily direct trains connect Bilbao Abando to Logroño (2h30). www.renfe.com**

Left, Bilbao's River Nervión;
right, San Sebastián's Bahía
de la Concha

❺ San Sebastián

San Sebastián is the holy city at the end of your pintxos pilgrimage – a true global culinary capital. Chances are you won't even notice its sublime coastal setting, huddled around the crescent Bahía de la Concha, instead making a beeline straight for the *pintxos* bars of the Parte Vieja (Old Town). On-trend bars come and go, however a few favourites endure, such as octopus dishes from Borda Berri and veal cheeks in red wine from La Cuchara de San Telmo.

🛏 **Hotel tip: Arima Hotel**

✈ Day trip

Biarritz

It may be just over the border in France, but in many ways Biarritz is a sister city to San Sebastián, with a windswept seafront setting, grand 19th-century hotels crowding the promenade and its own (resoundingly Gallic) gastronomic scene. It's also a surfing town – lessons and board rentals are readily available should you need to burn off the food indulgences.

🚌 **Buses connect with San Sebastián (1h).**

❸ Logroño

The leafy town of Logroño is set just over the border from the Basque Country in La Rioja. *Pintxos* here are taken every bit as seriously as north of the frontier, but the real draw is Spain's most illustrious wines, produced on the banks of the Rio Ebro, and finding their way into the boisterous bars on Calle Laurel and Calle de San Juan.

🚆 **There's one daily train service connecting Logroño to Vitoria-Gasteiz, changing at Miranda de Ebro (1h). www.renfe.com**

❹ Vitoria-Gasteiz

Centred around a handsome square, Vitoria-Gasteiz is the capital of the Basque Country. Unassuming though it may initially seem, the art scene gives neighbouring Bilbao a run for its money, with the Artium Museum staging audacious modern art exhibitions. Similarly, the best *pintxos* here compete with San Sebastián – mercifully accommodation in Vitoria-Gasteiz is far cheaper than in its coastal cousin.

🚆 **From Vitoria-Gasteiz, seven daily trains depart for San Sebastián (1h30).**

Returning home

Slow local trains with connections trundle west from San Sebastián to Bilbao Abando and onward ferries (3h30). Bearing east, trains take 30 minutes to the border at Hendaye: from here you can catch TGV services to Paris and other French cities.

Above, cutting-edge cuisine; right, Biarritz

Go west: exploring Cork and Kerry

Cork · Kinsale · Killarney · Tralee
Lively Cork is the start of an Irish itinerary that takes in forts, pubs, festivals, two doomed ships and dramatic west coast scenery.

Departure points

London is the most convenient European gateway for Cork. Trains run from London Euston to Holyhead for the ferry to Dublin, where you can catch a direct train to Cork. The quickest crossing (2h15, up to six sailings daily) is with Irish Ferries, making the total journey time around 11 hours. That's very feasible in a day, although Dublin is a great place to stay overnight. Eurostar trains also connect London St Pancras with Amsterdam (4h). From Paris Montparnasse, TGVs run to Morlaix (3h30), from where it's a 40-minute bus to Roscoff, the departure point for the twice-weekly overnight ferry to Cork — the port is a 30-minute bus or taxi ride from the city centre.

❶ Cork

Ireland's second city is enormous fun to explore, and you can stroll its tangled central streets and waterways without an end in mind. The English Market is the heart of an increasingly impressive food scene that majors in local produce, and the striking Glucksman gallery harnesses a cultural energy that also bubbles out in pub singalongs and countless festivals. Battlements, churches and a quirky

The covered English Market in Cork

Fact box

Carbon (kg per person) 18
Distance (km) 200km
Nights 7
Transport budget (€) 60

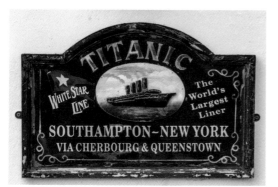

Titanic plates on a pub wall in Cobh

butter museum are among Cork's historic highlights. It's a good base for day trips.
🚌 **Buses to Kinsale (0h50) with buseireann. ie run hourly.**

🔄 Day trip

Cobh

Just southeast of Cork, Cobh looks out to the sea and back to the past. This was the last port of call for the doomed Titanic, which hit an iceberg three days after leaving its harbour. It was also the departure point for three million Irish men, women and children who left here for North America, changing the USA and Ireland irrevocably. You can explore the history of the world's most famous shipwreck at Titanic Experience Cobh, follow the stories of Irish emigrants at the Queenstown Story, or get a ferry to the former prison of Spike Island.
🚆 **Trains between Cork and Cobh (0h30) run at least hourly. www.irishrail.ie.**

❷ Kinsale

Kinsale is a lovely seaside town, home to pubs, restaurants and art galleries, with a

gorgeous curving harbour where yachts bob in the breeze. Its history – which takes in pirates, invasions and the *Lusitania*, an ocean liner sunk off Kinsale in 1915 by a German U-boat – can be appreciated on a tour in the town itself, or by taking a walk out to Charles Fort. The 30-minute stroll to this star-shaped fortress passes two great pubs and offers fine sea views.

Left, the fields of Tralee; below, the River Lee in Cork; right, Ross Castle in County Kerry

🚌 **To reach Killarney, get a bus back to Cork (0h50), then a train to Killarney (1h30). www.irishrail.ie**

❸ Killarney

Justifiably popular – it does get busy in summer – Killarney is a destination in itself, thanks to some good pubs, trad-music sessions and restaurants. As a base for County Kerry, it's hard to beat: there's the idyllic Killarney National Park and wild Gap of Dunloe on its doorstep, and the castles, beaches and viewpoints of the famous Ring of Kerry to the west. To dodge the coach-party crowds, consider renting a bike or lacing up your hiking boots.

🚆 **Around eight trains a day link Killarney and Tralee (0h40). www.irishrail.ie**

❹ Tralee

The farmland of Northern Kerry may not be as dramatic as Killarney, but it can feel like a dose of the real Ireland after the tourist bustle. There are some appealing sights here too, including excellent beaches, the enjoyable county museum, a birdwatching reserve and a 4km-long cave. The Rose of Tralee, celebrated in many a song, is a beauty contest and accompanying five-day festival in August.

Returning home

Trains run from Tralee back to Cork (2h15), while those returning the Holyhead and London route can head straight to Dublin (4h direct, or 3h30 with a change at Mallow).

Hiking into the wild heart of Scotland

London · Glasgow · Corrour & Loch Ericht · Dalwhinnie · Edinburgh
Spectacular railways are the springboard for a hike through Scotland, tasting illustrious whiskies en route and resting weary limbs in Edinburgh at the end of the trip.

Departure points

This itinerary makes the most of the Caledonian Sleeper, the train service that trundles overnight from London to the glens of the Scottish Highlands. It's also possible to start on mainland Europe, with trains to London from Paris Gare du Nord (2h30), Brussels Midi/Zuid (2h) or Amsterdam Centraal (4h). International

Fact box

Carbon (kg per person) 26
Distance (km) 1300
Nights 5
Transport budget (£) 400

Loch Lomond and
Ben Lomond

sleeper and start at Glasgow. Be aware you'll be carrying a backpack full of hiking gear.

❶ London

London's central Euston station is the starting point for northbound Caledonian Sleeper services. Steel yourself for the adventure with a punctual, pre-departure dinner from one of the vegetarian Indian restaurants on Drummond Street, located just behind the station.

🚆 **Nightly sleeper trains depart at 11.50pm (weekdays, earlier at weeekends) arriving in Glasgow at 7.22am (10h). www.sleeper.scot**

🛏 **Hotel tip: Zetter Townhouse Clerkenwell**

services arrive at St Pancras – from here it's a 15-minute walk to Scotland-bound services at Euston. You could also skip the

Left, a red deer stag in the Highlands; below, Glengoyne Distillery in Killearn

Highlands – one that's perfectly accessible from Glasgow is Glengoyne, set in rolling hills close to the bonnie banks of Loch Lomond.

🚌 **The number 10 bus connects the distillery with Glasgow's Buchanan bus station in 40 minutes. www.glengoyne.com**

❸ Corrour & Loch Ericht

One of the movie *Trainspotting*'s most famous scenes was filmed at the desolate Corrour station – the highest in the UK. There's no time for re-enactments as you strike eastwards towards Loch Ericht on a two-day hike through the wild heart of Scotland, taking time to scale the monolith of Ben Alder, overnighting in a bothy or camping by the shores of the lake. You'll need to be a confident, prepared hiker, with maps, food and clothing for the worst of the

❷ Glasgow

Scotland's biggest city may live somewhat in the shadow of the capital, but it's a place for world-class culture in its own right. There's plenty to occupy you for a day or two: admire the aesthetics of Charles Rennie Macintosh in the Kelvingrove Museum or board Glasgow-built ships on the redeveloped Clyde. It's also the last point to get supplies for your hike before boarding the beautiful West Highland Line.

🚆 **From Glasgow Queen Street Station, take West Highland Line northbound towards Corrour (3h). www.scotrail.co.uk**

⏱ Day trip

Glengoyne Distillery

Scottish whisky distilleries are often hidden away in the remote quarters of the

© Anna Kucherova / Shutterstock

Edinburgh Castle overlooks the city centre

Scottish weather. The rewards are vistas of wind-tousled heather, scrambles up granite summits and a precious sense of remoteness in a crowded isle.

🔵 **OS Map OL50 covers the route. Depending on detours, the walk to Dalwhinnie is around 40km.**

❹ Dalwhinnie

The small village of Dalwhinnie marks the end of your hike, with a few b&bs where you can spend the night. Celebrate by dropping by (another) fine distillery, which takes the same name as the village. Dalwhinnie is set on the Highland Main Line – another scenic railway where you catch a southbound service through the glens to Scotland's Central Belt.

🚆 **Six daily trains depart Dalwhinnie for Edinburgh Waverley (2h30). It's also** possible to board the return sleeper straight to London Euston from Dalwhinnie. www.scotrail.co.uk

❺ Edinburgh

Edinburgh is the perfect place to come in from the cold after a big adventure. Hole up in the nooks of Old Town pubs, explore the rejuvenated galleries of the National Museum or climb Arthur's Seat for a prospect towards the Highlands, whose summits you have just conquered.

Returning home

From Edinburgh, catch the sleeper service south to London Euston, or a daytime service to London King's Cross.

Lisbon to the Algarve

Lisbon · Faro · Tavira
Spend a couple of days exploring the hills of Lisbon by tram, Sintra on foot and Setúbal by boat or bike, then whizz south to lounge on the beaches of the Algarve.

Departure points
The easiest city to reach Lisbon from by train is Seville (3h20); Madrid (9-10h) and Paris (21h) can reach Lisbon by overnight sleeper train. Tickets from Spain can be bought through Renfe (www.renfe.com), from France through SNCF (www.oui.sncf).

❶ Lisbon
Lisbon's trademark seven hills are spread across the cityscape like lofty guardians of colour and history. Capped by a collection of terraces known as *miradouros* (viewpoints), the city is criss-crossed by yellow-and-white *eléctricos* (vintage trams), which having been shaking, rattling and rolling since 1901 (they were horse-pulled before that).

The pick of the five lines is tram 28E, which crosses the city centre between the Campo de Ourique and Martim Moniz, passing many must-see sights and neighbourhoods along the way. Don't miss the steep, cobblestoned streets of the Alfama neighbourhood for traditional Lisbon life – or a custard tart from Antiga Confeitaria de Belém, the city's top patisserie.

🚆 **There are five direct trains (www.cp.pt) from Lisbon to Faro daily (4h).**

Fact box
Carbon (kg per person) 9.5
Distance (km) 472
Nights 5
Transport budget (€) 70

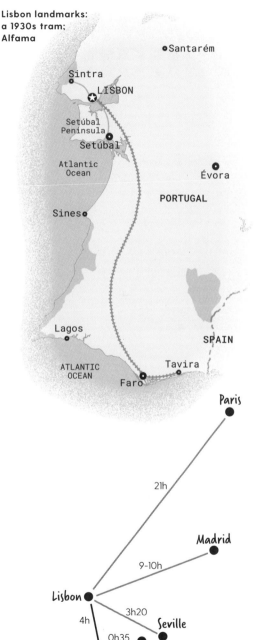

Lisbon landmarks: a 1930s tram; Alfama

Santarém

Sintra

LISBON

Setúbal Peninsula

Setúbal

Atlantic Ocean

Évora

PORTUGAL

Sines

Lagos

SPAIN

Tavira

ATLANTIC OCEAN

Faro

Paris

21h

Madrid

9-10h

Lisbon

3h20

4h

Seville

0h35

Faro Tavira

✈ Day trip

Sintra

With its mountains, forests, gardens and palaces, Sintra is the must-do side trip from Lisbon. The area is littered with extravagant villas, such as Quinta da Regaleira, dreamed up by an Italian opera-set designer; the Moorish-Manueline Palácio Nacional de Sintra, graced by twin conical chimneys; and Palácio Nacional da Pena, a wacky confection of onion domes, Moorish keyhole gates, stone snakes and towers. If you'd like to see some of the attractions beyond Sintra-Vila, Sight Sintra (www. facebook.com/SightSintra) rents out tiny two-person buggies that guide you by GPS along one of three different routes.

Comboios de Portugal (www.cp.pt) runs trains to Sintra (0h40) half-hourly from Lisbon's Rossio station (hourly on weekends), and every 20 minutes from Lisbon's less-convenient Oriente station (half-hourly on weekends). Get off at the last stop, Sintra, from where it's a pleasant 1km walk into the village.

medieval walls. Many of Faro's buildings were rebuilt following two big earthquakes and now house museums, churches, al fresco cafes and a macabre bone chapel. On Faro's doorstep are the lagoons of the Parque Natural da Ria Formosa and nearby beaches, including the islands of Ilha de Faro to the southwest and Ilha da Barreta (aka Ilha Deserta) to the south.

🚆 Trains run to Tavira (0h35) 12 times daily.

❸ Tavira

Set either side of the Rio Gilão, Tavira is arguably the Algarve's most charming town – you'll see the ruins of a hilltop castle, an old Roman bridge and a warren of stone streets concealing gardens and shady squares. Only 3km from the coast, Tavira is also the launchpad for reaching the unspoilt beaches of Ilha de Tavira via ferry or water-taxi.

Returning home

Return to Faro, then Seville lies 2h40 east by train, with Madrid another 3h north. From the Spanish capital, it's easy to reach France and Paris by high-speed train.

✈ Day trip

Setúbal peninsula

The port town of Setúbal (shtoo-bahl) makes a terrific base for exploring the natural assets of the Setúbal Peninsula. The highlight here is a cruise to the marshy wetlands of the Sado estuary, home to bottlenose dolphins, white storks and wintering flamingos. You can also hike or bike along the pine-brushed coastline of Parque Natural da Arrábida.

🚆 From Lisbon's Sete Rios station at least six Intercidades trains run daily to Setúbal (1h), with a change at Pinhal Novo.

❷ Faro

The Algarve's capital has a more Portuguese feel than most resort towns, with a *cidade velha* (Old Town) ringed by

Canoeing the Welsh Marches

Cheltenham · Gloucester · Ross-on-Wye · Monmouth · Tintern
Combine one of the UK's most beautiful canoeing routes with some of its most handsome small towns on this short route, which straddles the England-Wales border.

Departure points

Both Cheltenham and Gloucester are served by regular direct train services from Bristol and London Paddington. From London St Pancras you can then connect with international services to Paris (2h30), Brussels (2h) and Amsterdam (4h). It's also very easy to access this itinerary with trains from Cardiff, Hereford and Worcester. Pack light, as your luggage will need to fit aboard a canoe.

❶ Cheltenham

Renowned as a fashionable spa resort in the 18th century, the dapper town of Cheltenham is these days much better known for its festivals – time your trip to coincide with one of its illustrious jazz,

science, music or literature festivals (www. cheltenhamfestivals.com).
🚆 **It's a 10-minute train ride from Cheltenham Spa to neighbouring Gloucester, with about two trains every hour. www.gwr.com**

❷ Gloucester

Though not as attractive as its neighbour, Gloucester's trump card and defining landmark is its Norman cathedral, one of the most sublime in England, with a spire that looms over the Severn Estuary. The

Fact box

Carbon (kg per person) 6
Distance (km) 130
Nights 4+
Transport budget (€) 200

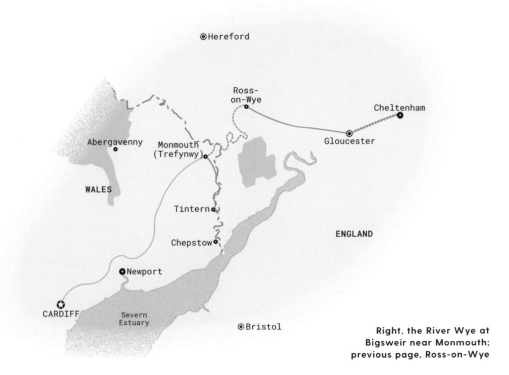

Hereford

Ross-
on-Wye

Cheltenham

Abergavenny   Monmouth   Gloucester
               (Trefynwy)

WALES

Tintern   ENGLAND

Chepstow

Newport

CARDIFF   Severn   Bristol
           Estuary

Severn
Estuary

**Right, the River Wye at
Bigsweir near Monmouth;
previous page, Ross-on-Wye**

city's sensitively regenerated quays are
also well worth a visit.

🚌 **From Gloucester Bus Station, catch the
33 bus to Ross-on-Wye – there are hourly
departures (1h).**

⊕ Day trip
Cardiff
If the sleepy market towns of the Welsh
Marches don't float your canoe, then
make a detour to the Welsh capital –
served by direct trains from Cheltenham,
Gloucester and Chepstow. Recent times
have seen Cardiff reinvigorated, with
new developments popping up around
Cardiff Bay and the transformation of
the excellent St Fagans National Museum.

It's also home to some of the UK's best
nightlife, especially if you time your visit
to coincide with a victorious international
rugby fixture.

❸ Ross-on-Wye
The unassuming English market town
of Ross-on-Wye sits on a hillock by a
languorous bend in the river. It's the ideal
spot to launch off on an adventure along
the Wye – plenty of companies offer
self-guided canoe hire and will pick up
your canoes in Monmouth or other drop-
off points downstream. After four hours'
easy paddling from Ross you'll reach the
hamlet of Symonds Yat, where wooded

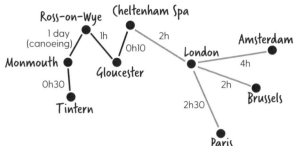

slopes rise up from the riverbank and a waterside pub miraculously materialises in time for lunch. From here it's another three hours paddling before you arrive in Monmouth.

Ross-on-Wye Canoe Hire are among the companies that can provide canoes for the 28km journey. www.thecanoehire.co.uk

❹ Monmouth (Trefynwy)

A town that has see-sawed between England and Wales, Monmouth announces its presence to paddlers with a small castle, a fortified bridge and a museum dedicated to a fellow seafarer, Lord Nelson, who came here to meet his mistress. It's easy to lose a day ambling its genteel and otherwise scandal-free streets.

🚌 **From Monmouth, catch the 69 bus southbound to Tintern (0h30), with a dozen daily departures. www.monmouthshire. gov.uk**

❺ Tintern

Poet William Wordsworth waxed lyrical about the 'sylvan Wye... wanderer thro' the woods' in his famous poem composed at Tintern Abbey. Today, the riverside ruins of the 12th-century monastery are just as stirring. Cross the bridge to England and follow signs for Devil's Pulpit, an outcrop commanding a poetic view of the ruins and the forests marking the Welsh frontier.

Returning home

From Tintern, hop aboard bus 69 again to Chepstow, where there are direct trains to Cheltenham, Gloucester, Cardiff, Birmingham and Nottingham – all have direct onwards train options to London.

Tintern Abbey was founded by monks

Rome, Puglia & Basilicata by train

Rome · Bari · Lecce · Rome
From the capital, travel along Italy's boot: first the heel (Puglia), then the instep (Basilicata), sampling the region's delicious cucina povera dishes along the way.

Departure points

Trains serve Rome's main station, Stazione Termini, from many European destinations including Paris as well as cities across Italy. You can also get to Rome by boat: ferries serve Civitavecchia, 80km northwest of the city, from Mediterranean ports including Barcelona, Tunis, Cagliari and Palermo. Check www.traghettiweb.it for route details, prices and bookings.

❶ Rome

A trip to Rome is as much about lapping up the dolce vita lifestyle as gorging on art and culture. Idling around picturesque streets, whiling away hours at streetside cafes, people watching on pretty piazzas – these are all central to the Roman experience. With limited time, it's best to pick one or two districts: go for the Centro Storico and the Vatican if you enjoy history and museums, head for Trastevere for nightlife and dining, and don't miss a bike ride along the Appia Antica, ancient Rome's superhighway to Brindisi, and the 80-hectare Villa Borghese, the city's most beautiful park.

🚆 **Four trains a day depart from Stazione Termini for Bari (4h).**

Fact box

Carbon (kg per person) 22
Distance (km) 1100
Nights 7+
Transport budget (€) 145

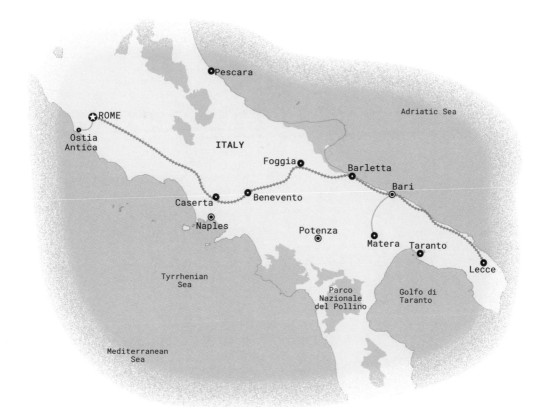

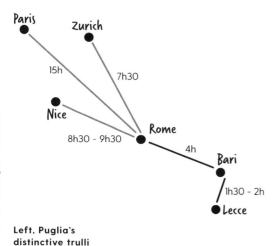

Paris

Zurich

15h

7h30

Nice

8h30 – 9h30

Rome

4h

Bari

1h30 – 2h

Lecce

Left, Puglia's distinctive trulli

✈ Day trip

Ostia Antica

An easy trip by train, Ostia Antica was ancient Rome's seaport. The ruins are wonderfully complete, like a smaller Pompeii. Highlights include the Terme di Nettuno (Baths of Neptune), an amphitheatre, exquisite mosaics and an ancient cafe, complete with traces of its original menu.

🚇 **From Rome, take the Roma–Lido train from Stazione Porta San Paolo (next to Piramide metro station) to Ostia Antica (every 15 minutes). The 25-minute trip is covered by a Rome transport ticket.**

❷ Bari

Most travellers skip Bari on their way to Lecce (the towns have a long-standing rivalry, especially over football), but Bari doesn't lack history or culture. The old town contains the bones of St Nicholas (aka Santa Claus) in its Basilica di San Nicola, and an excellent archaeological museum is concealed in Bari's historic bastions. One of the best things about the city is its trattorias and the simple, delightful *cucina barese* they serve – dishes like *orecchiette con cime di rapa* (broccoli pasta), *fave e cicoria* (fava bean purée with wild chicory) and *spaghetti ai ricci di mare* (spaghetti with sea urchins). You can also sample the freshest raw fish at Bari's seafood market.

🚆 **From the main train station, Bari Centrale, frequent trains travel to Lecce (1h30 to 2h, at least hourly).**

⊕ Day trip

Matera

Matera may be the world's third-longest continuously inhabited human settlement. Natural caves in the tufa limestone, exposed as the Gravina river cut its gorge, attracted the first inhabitants perhaps 7000 years ago. More elaborate structures were built atop them. Today, looking across the gorge to Matera's huddled *sassi* (cave dwellings) it seems you've been transported back to the ancient Holy Land. Old Matera is split into two sections – the Sasso Barisano and the Sasso Caveoso – separated by a ridge upon which sits Matera's gracious *duomo* (cathedral).

🚆 **Ferrovie Appulo-Lucane (www. ferrovieappulolucane.it) trains travel from Bari (1h45, four to six daily).**

❸ Lecce

Lecce has Puglia's most distinctive skyline – it even has its own architectural style, *barocco leccese* (Lecce baroque), characterised by gargoyles, asparagus columns and cavorting gremlins. The Basilica di Santa Croce is the crowning glory: it looks like it's been crafted by hallucinating stonemasons, with sheep, dodos, cherubs and beasties writhing across the facade. For more history, head for the Museo Faggiano, where sewerage excavations uncovered an archaeological treasure trove: Roman crypts, medieval walls, Jewish insignia and Knights Templar symbols.

🚆 **Lecce's main train station, 1km southwest of the historic centre, runs regular services back to Rome (5h30 to 9h).**

Left, Matera, European Capital of Culture 2019; below, it's about 13km to the sea from Lecce

Venice to Lake Bled

Venice · Trieste · Ljubljana · Lake Bled · Lake Bohinj and Triglav
Travel from the shallows of the Venetian Lagoon to the Alpine waters of Lake Bohinj, passing mighty mountain ranges and engaging cities along the way.

Departure points

Venice Santa Lucia can be reached on high speed Frecciarossa trains from Rome stations (3h30). Alternatively, arrive from the north on Austrian Nightjet sleeper trains from Munich Hauptbahnhof (9h) and Vienna Hauptbahnhof (11h).

❶ Venice

No superlatives can do justice to Venice, and though it continues to suffer from overtourism issues there are still ways to catch some serenity in La Serenissima. Be sure to stay the night in the city itself – the streets become far emptier after day-trippers and cruise ship crowds disperse in the early evening. Also consider visiting some of the other islands in the lagoon, such as Burano, Torcello, Murano and the Lido.

🚆 **Over 20 trains a day run from Venice Santa Lucia to Trieste Centrale (2h). www.trenitalia.com**

Venice's Santa Maria della Salute

Fact box

Carbon (kg per person) 7
Distance (km) 350
Nights 7
Transport budget (€) 200

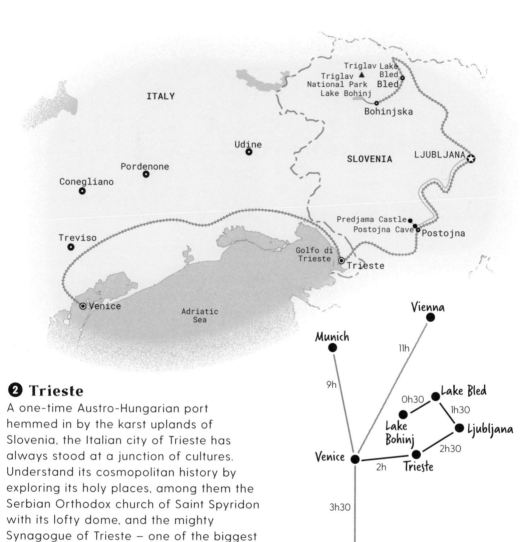

❷ Trieste

A one-time Austro-Hungarian port hemmed in by the karst uplands of Slovenia, the Italian city of Trieste has always stood at a junction of cultures. Understand its cosmopolitan history by exploring its holy places, among them the Serbian Orthodox church of Saint Spyridon with its lofty dome, and the mighty Synagogue of Trieste – one of the biggest on the continent.

🚊 **Irregular trains run from Trieste Centrale to Ljubljana station – check timetables in advance (2h30). www.trenitalia.com**

❸ Ljubljana

The Slovenian capital is one of Europe's most eco-friendly cities – evident in its car-free centre and abundant green spaces. Admire it from on high by catching the funicular up to the battlements of Ljubljana Castle, or idle away an afternoon at the city's excellent Botanical Garden, dating to 1810.

🚊 **Up to 20 trains a day travel from Ljubljana to Lesce-Bled station (1h). From here it's a**

Below, Predjama Castle; right, canalside Venice

further 4km into Bled town, a route served by regular local buses. www.slo-zeleznice.si

 Day trip

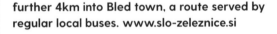

Postojna Cave & Predjama Castle

Slovenia's karst geology is at its most impressive in Postojna Cave – a vast system explored on guided tours featuring subterranean electric trains. Close by you'll also find Predjama Castle, a Renaissance fortress spectacularly built into the mouth of a cave, perched high up on a cliff.
🚊 **Postojna town is 1hr from Ljubljana by rail but to visit both sites, it's easier to join one of many guided day tours from Ljubljana. www.slo-zeleznice.si**

④ Lake Bled

An emerald lake crowned by a tiny island and watched over by a clifftop castle, Lake Bled could almost have been purpose-built for postcards – and consequently there's no shortage of visitors wandering its shores. For a different perspective, strong swimmers can swim across to the church on Bled Island, a feat that's easiest attempted

from the western shore (pack a dry bag with clothing so you can enter the church).
🚊 **From Bled Jezero station, seven daily trains travel to Bohinjska Bistrica station (0h30). www.slo-zeleznice.si**

⑤ Lake Bohinj

Quieter and less developed than Lake Bled, Lake Bohinj sits on the southern fringes of Triglav National Park, with wooded hills and limestone mountains towering above, and the little Church of St John the Baptist on its eastern shore. It's also a trailhead for the ascent of Slovenia's highest mountain, Triglav (2863m), which is accessible from May to October. Enlist the services of an experienced guide and begin your climb from the Savica Waterfall.
🏨 **Hotel tip: Bohinj Eco Hotel**

Returning home

Retrace your steps to Venice via Ljubljana and Trieste. Alternatively if you fancy a detour to Austria, travel from Bohinjska Bistrica north to the Austrian rail hub at Villach via Jesenice. Direct services to Venice depart from Villach.

Norwegian rail odyssey

Oslo · Geilo · Flåm · Aurlandsfjord & Nærøyfjord · Voss · Bergen
The Bergen Railway and the Flåm Railway are an unbeatable double-act: a coast-to-coast mainline linking lively cities, and a highland railway trundling down to the fjords.

Departure points

Oslo is the starting point for this journey. Reach the Norwegian capital on direct trains from Gothenburg (4h), Stockholm (5h) and from Copenhagen changing at Gothenburg (7h30) or on direct ferries from Copenhagen (17h). It's also possible to get to Oslo on trains from Hamburg in less than 24 hours, travelling via Copenhagen.

❶ Oslo

Huddled around a fjord and ringed by dense forests, Oslo's setting gives a small hint of the glorious landscapes awaiting Bergen-bound passengers. But being a cosmopolitan capital, this is very much a place to plunge headlong into art and culture. Start at the Oslo Opera House and the Astrup Fearnley Museum of contemporary art – bold architectural additions to the city's waterfront. From Oslo, board a westbound train on the Bergen Railway, trundling along green valleys to Geilo.

🚃 **Around four trains daily depart Oslo for Bergen, stopping at Geilo midway (3h30).**
www.vy.no
🛏 **Hotel tip: The Thief**

The Bergen train passes Lake Ustevatn

Fact box
Carbon (kg per person) 9
Distance (km) 450
Nights 7+
Transport budget (€) 400

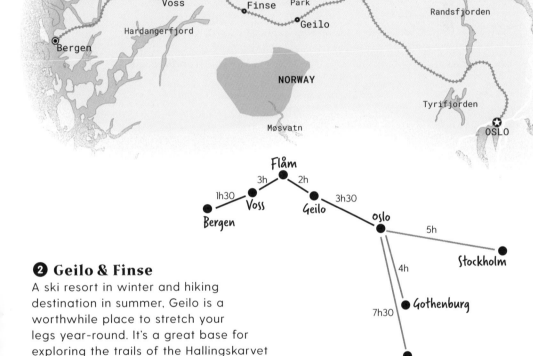

❷ Geilo & Finse

A ski resort in winter and hiking destination in summer, Geilo is a worthwhile place to stretch your legs year-round. It's a great base for exploring the trails of the Hallingskarvet National Park – a barren, glacier-topped plateau northwest of the town. From Geilo, the Bergen Railway climbs uphill towards Finse: the highest station on the Norwegian rail network, it starred as the planet Hoth in Star Wars: Episode V – The Empire Strikes Back.

🚆 **From Geilo, it's a 30-minute trip up the line to Finse, and a further 30 minutes onward to Myrdal where passengers change for the Flåm Railway. www.vy.no**

❸ Flåm Railway

It may only be 20km long, but the Flåm line packs in the drama of a trans-continental railway. It slaloms through 20 tunnels as it descends 850km downhill, from windswept highlands at the top to where meadows meet the mouth of the Aurlandsfjord. Grab a seat on the left as you head downhill, and be sure to look out for freewheeling

The Stegastein viewing platform above Aurlandsfjord

Left and below, Bergen

cyclists on the Rallarvegen – a bike track that runs parallel to the railway.

🚃 It takes roughly one hour to travel from the start of the railway in Myrdal to the terminus in Flåm. www.vy.no

❹ Aurlandsfjord & Nærøyfjord

One of the world's greatest rail journeys segues into one of the world's greatest sea journeys, with hybrid and electric ferries departing Flåm's quays to traverse two parallel fjords. Cliffs rise sheer from the water, with crashing waterfalls, mountaintop farmsteads and snow-dusted peaks looming into view at every turn.

🚢🚌 There are four daily electric ferry departures from Flåm on the Aurlandsfjord for Gudvangen on the Nærøyfjord (2h one-way). From Gudvangen, local buses connect to Voss (1h). www.visitflam.com

❺ Voss

Norway's self-professed outdoor adventure capital, Voss is a staging post for canyoning, rafting and skydiving adventures. It's also where passengers reconnect with the Bergen Railway after returning from the fjords.

🚃 From Voss, regular trains run to Bergen (1h30). www.vy.no

❻ Bergen

Bergen's grand stone station marks the terminus of the line. Make time for one last set of rails in the form of the Fløibanen funicular, which scales a 320m-high hill on the edge of town. From the summit there's a stirring view of the historic timber warehouses of Bergen, and distant ships departing the fjords for the open sea.

Returning home

It's possible to return to Oslo from Bergen in under seven hours non-stop on the Bergen Railway. Alternatively, continue your adventure from Bergen, taking a cruise north along the Norwegian coast.

Swiss Alps and Italian Lakes by rail

Zürich · Chur · St Moritz · Varenna · Milan · Lugano

Lofty Alpine passes and balmy lakeside retreats, plus swanky Swiss resorts and a major Italian metropolis – all connected by some of the world's most spectacular railway lines.

Departure points

This itinerary crosses the Alps using a combination of slow, scenic trains and high-speed intercity services. The starting point is Zürich Hauptbahnhof, an easily accessible European rail hub. Direct TGV-Lyria services depart from Paris Gare de Lyon (4h). Direct ICE services connect from Hamburg Hauptbahnhof (8h) and Frankfurt (Main) Hauptbahnhof (4h), while slower Nightjet sleeper trains link Zürich with Berlin and Vienna.

❶ Zürich

Switzerland's biggest city commands a magnificent setting on the shores of Lake Zürich. Take a day or two to potter the winding streets of the Old Town, or acquaint yourself with Old Masters in the excellent Kunsthaus. Arrive early for your train so you have time to admire Zürich Hauptbahnhof, an appropriately ornate station from which to embark on a railway odyssey.

🚆 **From Zürich, catch a train to Chur (1h). There are departures roughly every hour. www.sbb.ch**

Right, crossing the Landwasser Viaduct

Fact box

Carbon (kg per person) 14
Distance (km) 700
Nights 6+
Transport budget (€) 500

Lake Constance GERMANY

Zürich
Lake Zürich

LIECHTENSTEIN
VADUZ
AUSTRIA

Lake Lucerne

Chur

SWITZERLAND

St Moritz

Lake Lugano

Tirano

Lugano
Varenna

Lake Maggiore
Lake Como

ITALY

Bergamo

Milan

❷ Chur – St Moritz

With cobbled streets and spindly spires hemmed in by steep mountains, Chur is a picturesque place to stretch your legs. It's also a gateway for the magnificent Albula Railway – board a train to St Moritz and you'll soon find yourself soaring high above onion-domed churches and wildflower-strewn meadows. The highlight is the Landwasser Viaduct, where the train rattles over a ravine before plunging into a mountainside tunnel.

🚉 **About 15 trains a day travel from Chur to St Moritz (2h). www.rhb.ch**

❸ St Moritz – Tirano

St Moritz is the original Alpine resort, with

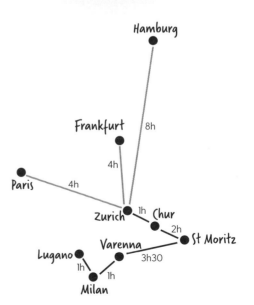

Hamburg

Frankfurt

8h

Paris
4h

4h

Zurich
1h Chur

2h
St Moritz

Varenna
3h30

Lugano
1h

1h

Milan

powdery slopes in winter and shimmering lakes in summer. It's also the starting point for the Bernina Line – perhaps the only railway ride that can make the Albula line seem pedestrian. Leaving St Moritz behind, the line climbs high among glaciers and serrated peaks, barging through tunnels and navigating tight switchbacks, before coming back down to earth just over the Italian border in Tirano for your onward journey.

🚆 **Two daily 'Bernina Express'-branded trains depart St Moritz for Tirano (2h). At Tirano change for southbound services to Varenna-Esino (1h30). www.rhb.ch, www.trenitalia.com**

❹ Varenna

Varenna embodies what's best about the Italian Lakes: pebbly coves and mustard-yellow villas, swaying palms and yacht-lined quays. There's nowhere better to disembark the train for an evening's *passeggiata* by Lake Como with a gelato in hand – realising you have crossed from the Teutonic to the Romance-speaking world.

🚆 **Hourly departures ply the rails from Varenna-Esino to Milan Centrale (1h). www.trenitalia.com**

❺ Milan

Architecturally part station and part Roman temple, Milan railway station might be the most triumphant in Europe. It's an indication of the grandeur of the city that lies beyond – spend a night here and admire the marble majesty of the Duomo and the quintessential shopping mall, the 19th-century Galleria Vittorio Emanuele II.

🚆 **Express trains depart Milan Centrale for Lugano (1h). www.trenitalia.com**
🛏 **Hotel tip: Eco-Hotel La Residenza**

⊕ Day trip

Bergamo

An hour's train journey from Milan is the city of Bergamo, its upper town ringed by stout Venetian walls. Spend a few hours exploring its palaces and churches – ascend to the top of the 12th-century tower, Torre del Campanone, from which on a clear day you might spot the skyscrapers of Milan.

🚆 Around 20 direct services a day depart from Milan Centrale station for Bergamo.

❻ Lugano

Back to Switzerland: set on the eponymous lake, Lugano is the largest Italian-speaking city in the country. To admire the city from its best angle, ascend the funicular to the summit of Monte Bre – a 900m mountain that's the starting point for alpine hikes. Take in the panorama north to snow-capped peaks and south to the Po Valley.

Returning home

There are 11 direct trains daily from Lugano to Zürich (3h) for connections to Northern and Western Europe.

Left, shopping in Milan; below,
fishing in St Moritz

A Danube loop

Prague · Bratislava · Vienna · Prague
Three European capitals full of imperial pomp and splendour are the highlights of this trip – alongside a river cruise down the Danube, Europe's second-longest river.

Departure points

The Czech national railway, České dráhy (ČD; www.cd.cz) has swift connections to neighbouring countries. Fast trains connect Prague with Berlin (4h30) and Dresden (2h11), plus Vienna (4h), Bratislava (4h) and Budapest (6h30). In the Czech Republic and Slovakia, in addition to ČD trains, look out for faster, privately run RegioJet (www.regiojet.cz) trains, identified as 'RJ' on timetables.

❶ Prague

After braving the crowds at Prague's big-ticket sites – Prague Castle, Charles Bridge, St Vitus Cathedral, Wenceslas Square and Old Town Square – you might feel in need of some peace and green space. A hike up the 318m hill of Petřín offers some of the best views over the 'City of a Hundred Spires'. Lovely Letná Gardens occupies a bluff over the Vltava River, north of the Old Town, and also has postcard-perfect views out over the city, river and bridges – with the advantage of a beer garden at the east end of the park. 🚆 **ČD trains travel hourly across the Slovakian border from Prague's central station to Bratislava (4h).**

Fact box

Carbon (kg per person) 10
Distance (km) 600
Nights 8+
Transport budget (€) 100

Cycling beside the River Danube

✪ Day trip

Kutná Hora

Enriched by the silver ore that veined the surrounding hills, the medieval city of Kutná Hora became the seat of Wenceslas II's royal mint in 1308, producing silver *groschen* that were then the hard currency of Central Europe. The town became a Unesco World Heritage Site in 1996, thanks to historic sites like the Gothic Cathedral of St Barbara and the bizarre Sedlec Ossuary, where garlands of bones are strung around like Addams Family Christmas decorations.

🚆 **Trains run from Prague's main station to Kutná Hora about every two hours (0h55). It's a 10-minute walk from the station to Sedlec Ossuary; to get to the Old Town, take the yellow-and-green rail car from platform 1 to Kutná Hora Město station (six minutes).**

❷ Bratislava

Slovakia's capital since independence in 1993, Bratislava is a mosaic of history: a medieval and Gothic Old Town, baroque palaces commissioned by Hungarian nobles and the crowning castle, rebuilt in Renaissance finery. But it's hard to ignore the city's communist past, thanks to a futurist bridge and numerous vast apartment blocks: Bratislava Bike Point (www.bratislavabikepoint.com) runs a three-hour 'Iron Curtain' cycling tour of communist-era sights, including a concrete bunker. For a break, Bratislava Forest Park spreads north of the city and is laced with walking and biking trails; you can huff your way up, or catch a cable car.

🚢 **From April to October, cruises float down**

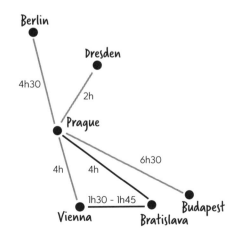

St Vitus Cathedral dominates Prague's skyline

the Danube to Vienna. LOD (www.lod.sk, 1h45) runs daily hydrofoils from Bratislava's hydrofoil dock, while Twin City Liner Boats (www.twincityliner.com, 1h30) leave from the HUMA 6 terminal.

⊕ Day trip

Devín Castle

Perched between Slovakia and Austria, Devín Castle makes a popular day trip from Bratislava. From the ramparts there are admirable views of rivers and goat-speckled hills beyond. Inside, the museum hosts an archaeological exhibition with Neolithic grave finds and bronze-age sculptures.

🚌 Bus 29 (at least hourly) links Devín with Bratislava's Nový Most (stop 6); get a 30-minute ticket.

❸ Vienna

One of the best places to appreciate Vienna's storied skyline is Schloss Belvedere, with two exquisite palaces dedicated to a who's who of Austrian art (Gustav Klimt's painting *The Kiss* is a highlight). Green spots around the city include Prater, central Vienna's biggest park, and the delightful, home to the city's oldest baroque garden. It's also worth wandering around the Zentralfriedhof cemetery, where luminaries including Beethoven, Brahms, Strauss and Schubert are buried.

🚆 You can return to Prague by fast RailJet (4h) trains, which also serve cities including Munich (4h) and Zürich (7h50). The service is jointly run by national rail operators ČD & ÖBB; book online at www.oebb.at. Regiojet also offers its own Prague-Vienna service, often with cheaper fares.

Gastronomic tour of Northern Italy

Bologna · Modena · Parma · Milan · Turin · Genoa
This route plunders the larder of Italy – travelling through the spellbinding cities that have given kitchens of the world parmesan, pesto, ragù and balsamic vinegar.

Departure points

Bologna is set at a crossroads of the Italian rail network. Arrive from the north via Milan Centrale (1h), which in turn has direct services to Paris Gare de Lyon (7h) and Vienna (10h). Arrive from the south on direct Frecciarossa services from Rome (2h) and Naples (3h30).

❶ Bologna

The capital of Emilia-Romagna, Bologna is nicknamed 'La Grassa', or 'the fat one', for its gastronomic credentials. Start a food pilgrimage at the Quadrilatero – a district of alleyways based on a Roman street plan, dotted with delis and market stalls. Try the city's signature dish *tagliatelle al ragu* at the no-frills Osteria dell'Orsa.

🚆 Over 50 trains a day connect Bologna to Modena (0h30). www.trenitalia.com

❷ Modena

The birthplace of Pavarotti and Enzo Ferrari is also the spiritual home of A-list Italian flavours, among them balsamic vinegar and tortellini. Work up an appetite exploring the town's spectacular Romanesque cathedral, before heading to the no-menu Trattoria Aldina for a

Fact box

Carbon (kg per person) 12
Distance (km) 600
Nights 7
Transport budget (€) 150

Via Pescherie Vecchie in Bologna's Quadrilatero

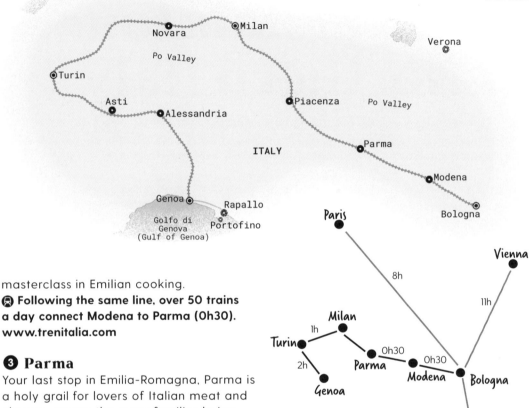

Bologna's characteristic red roof tiles

masterclass in Emilian cooking.
🚄 **Following the same line, over 50 trains a day connect Modena to Parma (0h30).** www.trenitalia.com

❸ Parma

Your last stop in Emilia-Romagna, Parma is a holy grail for lovers of Italian meat and cheese, among the more familiar being prosciutto and parmigiano reggiano, best partnered with Sangiovese red wine in local osterias and trattorias. The city's 12th-century Duomo and pink-marble Battistero count among the architectural feasts of northern Italy.
🚄 **Over 20 a day trains run from Parma to Milan Centrale (1h30).** www.trenitalia.com

❹ Milan

Italy's economic hub, Milan's ever-evolving restaurant scene boasts a smattering of Michelin stars. But it's not hard to dig

down to the city's culinary roots — find Mitteleuropa-accented breaded veal at Trattoria del Nuovo Macello, or try saffron-infused risotto at Trattoria Milanese dal 1933. Afterwards, head to the canalside Navigli district to sip Aperol Spritz until the morning sun catches the Alps beyond.
🚄 **Over 30 trains a day run from Milan Centrale to Turin Porta Nuova (1h).** www. trenitalia.com

© Matt Munro / Lonely Planet

Below, Portofino near Genoa;
right, Italian antipasti

❺ Turin

Surrounded by rolling vineyards and the farmland of Piedmont, Turin is well placed to assert its claim as one of Italy's gastronomic epicentres. One of the main vices here is coffee – served in some of the grandest cafes on the continent. Try sipping espresso in the art nouveau Caffè Mulassano, or ordering cappuccino amid the gilded majesty of Caffè San Carlo.

🚆 **Around 20 trains a day travel from Turin stations to Genoa stations (2h; www. trenitalia.com)**

🛏 **Hotel tip: Bamboo Eco Hostel**

❻ Genoa

With a raffish charm redolent of Marseille or Tangier, the port of Genoa lies sprawled along steep hills beside the Mediterranean. It's the hometown of pesto – you'll find it in the signature *trofie al pesto* (pesto pasta) at Trattoria della Raibetta close to the city's black and white cathedral, or in pesto lasagna on the handwritten menu at Trattoria Da Maria.

❸ Day trip

Portofino

A world away from the clamour and traffic of neighbouring Genoa, the former fishing village of Portofino occupies a small peninsula, with wooded hills dropping down to a little bay where expensive yachts lay anchor. It's a favoured retreat of jetsetters – but anyone can visit by catching a train from Genoa to Rapallo, before boarding a seasonal ferry along the Ligurian coast.

🚆🛳 **Local trains shuttle from Genoa stations to Rapallo (0h30), with nine sailings on to Portofino from May to September (0h30). www.traghettiportofino.it**

Returning home

It's easy to return by train from Genoa to Bologna changing at Milan, taking roughly three hours.

A sojourn in the Scilly Isles

London · Bristol · Exeter · Penzance · Scilly Isles
Follow Isambard Kingdom Brunel's Great Western Railway from London to the tip of Cornwall, then skip over to the Isles of Scilly. Don't forget your bike!

Departure points
London is connected by the speedy Eurostar to Paris (for links to France, Italy and Spain) and Brussels (for connections to the Netherlands and Germany).

❶ London
Brunel's pioneering railway to the Southwest was one of the great feats of Victorian engineering. Find out more about its construction at the Science Museum and London Transport Museum, then take a trip downriver to Greenwich and the National Maritime Museum, where Brunel's other passion - shipbuilding – is exhaustively explored.
🚆 **Hourly GWR (Great Western Railway, www.gwr.com, 1h45) trains to the Southwest leave from London Paddington.**

Fact box
Carbon (kg per person) 14.5
Distance (km) 585
Nights 8+
Transport budget (£) 220

Most trains have bike space, but it's wise to reserve a space when you book your ticket.

❷ Bristol
The Southwest's biggest city has two Brunel-built must-sees: the Clifton Suspension Bridge over the Avon Gorge (opened in 1864), and the SS Great Britain (launched 1846), a huge passenger steamship powered by a groundbreaking screw propeller. It was rescued from dereliction, and you can wander round the cabins, ship's mess and captain's quarters.

Bristol's Clifton Suspension Bridge

Bristol's a very bike-friendly city – have lunch at the Mud Dock (www.mud-dock.co.uk) near the harbour: it's half bike workshop, half cafe.

🚇 **Board another GWR train to Exeter St Davids (up to 1h50).**

🔄 Day trip

Bristol-Bath Railway Path

A cycling trail (www.bristolbathrailwaypath.org.uk) connects Bristol and the stately Georgian city of Bath, travelling for 20km through lovely Somerset countryside along a disused railway track.

🚲🚇 **If you don't have your own, bikes can be hired at both ends, or you can train it if you're feeling lazy (GWR, 0h10).**

❸ Exeter

Exeter's showpiece is its vast Gothic cathedral, dating from the 12th and 13th centuries, renowned for its decorative west front and Gothic vaulting. Elsewhere, you can wander the old Roman walls, explore underground tunnels and enjoy a peaceful pedal or paddle along the canal.

🚆 **Trains from Exeter St Davids to Penzance (3h to 3h30) run through Plymouth, where you'll cross the 1854 Royal Albert Bridge, another Brunel masterpiece.**

❹ Penzance

End of the line Penzance is perched on Cornwall's far western edge. It's an attractive town, with some fine Georgian and Edwardian buildings, best seen along Chapel St. Also worth a look is the Penlee Art Gallery, where you can view work by

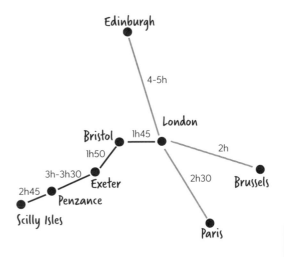

Porthminster beach at St Ives

artists of the Newlyn School.

🚢 **The Scillonian III ferry sails once daily from Penzance's harbour to St Mary's on the Isles of Scilly between March and October. The crossing (2h45) can be rough: pop sea sickness pills just in case. Book in advance to bring your bike.**

⊕ **Day trip**

St Ives

A cluster of slate roofs, fishermen's cottages and church towers spread out around turquoise bays, St Ives is a dazzling sight. It's been a magnet for artists since sculptor Barbara Hepworth moved here in the 1930s: the marvellous Tate St Ives and Barbara Hepworth Sculpture Garden explore the town's artistic connections.

🚆 **Catch a train to St Erth from Penzance (half-hourly, 0h10), then connect onto the pretty branch line to St Ives (hourly, 0h12).**

❺ Isles of Scilly

Twenty-eight miles west of the mainland, the Isles of Scilly feel like a different world. Life on this little archipelago seems hardly to have changed in decades. There are more than a hundred islands in all, but only five are inhabited. You'll arrive on the main island of St Mary's, perfect for exploring by bike with very cars and beautiful beaches. You can also hire electric-powered golf carts on St Mary's. The other four main islands (Tresco, Bryher, St Agnes, St Martin's) and the remote outer islands can be reached via boat with the St Mary's Boatmen's Association (www.scillyboating.co.uk).

Returning home

Backtrack to London for cross-Europe connections via Eurostar or ferries.

Left, Pulteney Bridge in
Bath; below right, the
Tower of London

English & Scottish castles & cathedrals

London · York · Durham · Edinburgh

This trip plunges deep into the annals of British history: from the parks and palaces of London to the castles and crags of Edinburgh, with a few historic towns in between.

Departure points

This route makes the most of the East Coast Mainline (ECML) – a backbone of British railways that shuttles from London King's Cross direct to Edinburgh in around four hours, with stops at York, Durham, and other engaging cities like Peterborough and Newcastle. It's also possible to start this journey at other points on mainland Europe, with Eurostar services to London St Pancras (across the road from King's Cross) from Lille Europe station (1h30), Brussels Midi/Zuid (2h) and Amsterdam (4h).

❶ London

London has landmarks from every chapter in its history – the upheaval of the Norman Conquest echoes in

Fact box

Carbon (kg per person) 12

Distance (km) 600

Nights 5+

Transport budget (£) 450

© BG Photographer / Shutterstock, © Justin Black / Shutterstock

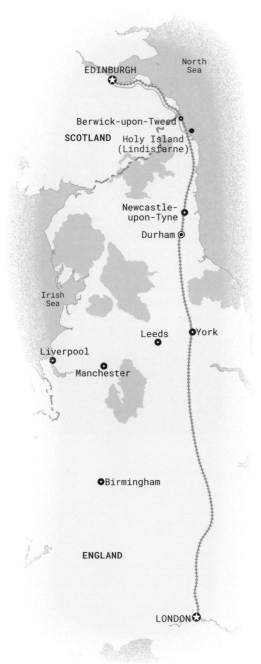

the Tower of London, the rebirth from the Great Fire is writ large in St Paul's Cathedral, the might of the Victorian age shows in stations like King's Cross and St Pancras. London is also a green city: head to Regent's Park, then climb Primrose Hill for a view of the capital's spires and towers, ancient and modern.

🚆 Head to London King's Cross to board one of around 40 daily departures to York (2hr). www.lner.co.uk

❷ York

A capital of northern England for the Romans and later the Vikings, York is a small city with mighty structures from the Gothic nave of York Minster to the longest network of medieval city walls in the UK. It's also rumoured to have once had a pub for every day of the year: if you only have 24 hours, head to the oldest, Ye Olde Starre, with a rabbits' warren of rooms and a courtyard for sunny days.

🚆 From York, daily services to Durham (1hr) run several times an hour. www.lner.co.uk

❸ Durham

Durham has three claims to fame: a venerable university, a Norman castle and, most impressive of all, its Anglo-Romanesque cathedral, presiding proudly over a bend in the River Wear. It's a worthwhile place to hop off for an afternoon's exploration. Bearing north from Durham, the most dramatic stretch of the train journey begins. You'll come within sight of the Angel of the North, swoop high over the River Tyne at Newcastle and traverse windswept cliffs beyond Berwick-upon-Tweed within touching distance of the North Sea.

All roads lead to York Minster

attests to its days as an monastic retreat prone to Viking raids, while its 16th-century castle was converted to a private holiday home by Sir Edward Lutyens. 🚍🚆 **To get there, disembark the East Coast Mainline at Berwick-upon-Tweed (around 0h30 from Edinburgh) and catch the 477 bus southbound (the timetable corresponds with the tides).**

Returning home
From Edinburgh, take one of 30 south-bound trains to London King's Cross. It's a five-minute walk to London St Pancras International for onward trains to Paris, Lille, Brussels, Rotterdam and Amsterdam.

🚆 **About 60 daily trains link Durham and Edinburgh Waverley (1hr30). www.lner.co.uk**

❹ Edinburgh
On the final approach into Waverley Station, many of Edinburgh's defining sights swing into view: the urban mountain of Arthur's Seat reigns over the skyline, competing with the city's castle perched atop vertical cliffs. Wander the higgledy-piggledy closes and courts of the Old Town, or stop by the pubs and restaurants of the New Town, and you'll find Edinburgh is even more beguiling up close.

✪ Day trip

Lindisfarne
Lindisfarne (aka Holy Island) is a tiny pilgrimage island only accessible at low tide via a causeway. Its ruined priory

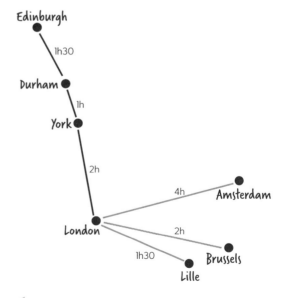

© David Ionut / Shutterstock

A Baltic adventure

Rīga · Pärnu · Tallinn · St Petersburg

Explore some key Eastern European highlights via an adventurous combination of ferries, buses and trains.

Departure points

Tallink (www.tallink.lv) ferries connect Rīga's ferry terminal, 1km downstream (north) of Akmens Bridge, with Stockholm. Buses run from Vilnius, Warsaw, Kaunas, St Petersburg and Moscow.

❶ Rīga

The flamboyance of *jugendstil* (art nouveau) characterises this vibrant cosmopolitan city. Like many northern places, it is quiet and reserved on the outside, but there is some powerful chemistry going on inside its hip bars, modern art centres and experimental restaurants. The Unesco-protected old town is the obvious place to begin,

followed by the city's cathedral, central museum and the Art Museum Rīga Bourse. 🚌 **Buses depart from Rīga's international bus station, behind the railway embankment just beyond the southeastern edge of Old Rīga. Ecolines (www.ecolines. net) and Eurolines Lux Express (www. luxexpress.eu) shuttle across the Estonian border to Pärnu (2h45, hourly).**

Looking over Rīga's Old Town

Fact box

Carbon (kg per person) 32

Distance (km) 870

Nights 8+

Transport budget (€) 55, or 120-200 if you take the Tallinn–St Petersburg ferry

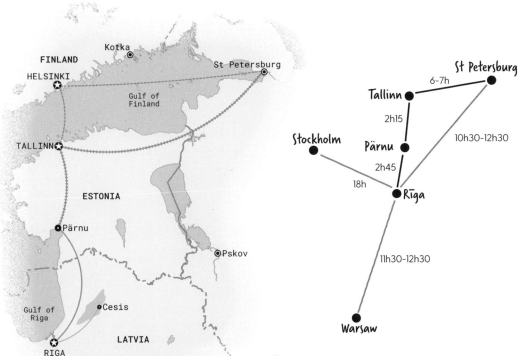

⊙ Day trip

Cēsis Castle

Cēsis Castle is two castles in one. The first is Wenden Castle: founded by Livonian knights in 1214, it was sacked by Russian tsar Ivan the Terrible in 1577, but only after its 300 defenders blew themselves up with gunpowder. The other is the more cheerful, 18th-century manor house once inhabited by the dynasty of German counts von Sievers.

🚆 **Up to five trains per day link Cēsis and Rīga (2h).**

❷ Pärnu

In these parts, the name Pärnu (pair-nu) is synonymous with fun in the sun: it's known as Estonia's 'summer capital' thanks to its beaches, leafy streets and expansive parks. Turn-of-the-20th-century villas reflect the town's fashionable, more decorous past: older visitors from Finland and the former Soviet Union still come frequently, seeking rest, rejuvenation and Pärnu's vaunted mud treatments.

🚆🚌 **Three daily trains run between Pärnu and Tallinn (2h15), but the station is inconveniently located 5km east of the town centre; the only way to get there is a taxi. The other option to Tallinn is to take a bus (2h, hourly): the ticket office is 100m away from the corner of Pikk and Ringi, (look for the red bussijaam sign).**

The turrets and spires of
Tallinn's Old Town

❸ Tallinn

Estonia's cobbled, olde-worlde heart is
made for a leisurely day of wandering.
All roads lead to Raekoja Plats, the city's
pulsing heart since markets began setting
up here in the 11th century. One side is
dominated by the Gothic town hall, while
the rest is ringed by pretty pastel-coloured
buildings dating from the 15th to 17th
centuries. City Bike (www.citybike.ee)
offers 'Welcome to Tallinn' tours exploring
various other areas of the city and also
rents bikes.

**There are several ways to get to
St Petersburg: ferry (about 3 days, www.
stpeterline.com), often via Stockholm and
Helsinki; bus (www.luxexpress.eu, 6-7h);
or train via Russian Railways (www.rzd.ru,
7h). The good thing about the ferry is that
you qualify for 72-hour visa-free travel;
otherwise, you need a pre-arranged visa to
enter Russia.**

❹ St Petersburg

The sheer grandeur of St Petersburg is
hard to get your head around: it's a city
that fairly glitters with imperial buildings,
elegant canals and public parks. The truly
enormous Hermitage Museum is most
people's first stop, with everything from
Egyptian mummies to Picassos, but don't
overlook the Russian Museum, which
holds the best collection of Russian art
in the world, and the Fabergé Museum,
where you get to see those incredible
bejewelled imperial eggs. A canal cruise
is a must: Astro Marine (www.boattrip.ru)

offers hop-on, hop-off circuits, departing
from the Fabergé Museum on the
Fontanka River or next to Dvortsovy Most
(Palace Bridge).

Returning home

High-speed Sapsan Trains whizz to
Moscow in four hours (www.rzd.ru);
express trains to Helsinki take just 3h30
(www.vr.fi). For a more laid-back trip,
take the slow boat to Stockholm.

A Tuscan tour

Milan · Florence · Pisa · Lucca · Florence
Indulge in the heady flavours, world-class wines and hilltop towns of la bella Toscana on this bewitching Italian tour.

Departure points

Milan's monumental Stazione Centrale receives international, high-speed trains from France, Switzerland, Austria and Germany.

❶ Milan

Flashy Milan is Italy's city of the future, a fast-paced metropolis where money talks, creativity is big business and looking good is an art form. It's rich with history, with landmarks including the 14th-century Duomo and the imposing Castello Sforzesco (home of the Sforza dynasty, who ruled Renaissance Milan). But it's Leonardo da Vinci's *Last Supper* that steals the Milanese show: hidden on a wall of the refectory adjoining the Basilica di Santa Maria delle Grazie, it's one of the world's most recognisable images.

🚆 **Trenitalia trains to Florence run at least hourly (1h45 to 2h, www.trenitalia.com).**
🛏 **Hotel tip: Built with ethically-sourced materials, Starhotels E.C.Ho (www. starhotels.com) is the city's most eco-conscious hotel.**

❷ Florence

Few cities are as masterpiece-packed as Florence. The fabric of this pocket-

Fact box

Carbon (kg per person) 16
Distance (km) 505
Nights 9+
Transport budget (€) 90

sized city has hardly changed since the Renaissance, and its cobbled streets are a cinematic feast of chapels and palazzi (palaces), frescoed churches, basilicas and art museums. Foremost among them is the Galleria dell'Accademia (www.galleriaaccademiafirenze.beniculturali.it), home of Michelangelo's David, and the Galleria degli Uffizi (www.uffizi.it), brimming with works by Giotto, Botticelli, Michelangelo, Da Vinci, Raphael, Titian and Caravaggio. Unsurprisingly, the entire city centre's been designated a Unesco World Heritage Site.

Florence is easily navigated on foot. City bikes can be rented in front of Stazione di Santa Maria Novella and other locations; the city also has an efficient network of buses and trams. Trenitalia trains run every 15 minutes to Pisa (0h45 to 1h).
Hotel tip: Overnight at Eco Urban B&B (www.ecourbanbb.com), where the six stylish rooms are decorated with reclaimed materials and organic fabrics.

◆ Day trip

San Gimignano
The 14 towers of the walled town of San Gimignano rise like a medieval Manhattan. One of Tuscany's most picturesque (and popular) hilltop towns, it makes a perfect day trip from Florence – avoid July and August unless you're a glutton for crowds.
Buses depart from Florence (1h15 to 2h, 14 daily) for Poggibonsi, from where you'll need to change to another bus for San Gimignano (0h50); repeat the process on the return trip.

---

❸ Pisa
When's it going to topple? That's the

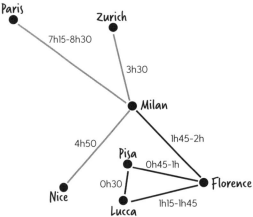

This page, Florence, its Boboli Gardens,
Giotto's Campanile; previous page,
Milan's Piazza del Duomo

Below, the Leaning Tower of Pisa; right, San Martino Cathedral in Lucca

question. The answer is no time soon: the Torre Pendente (Leaning Tower) was already listing when it was unveiled in 1372, and the tilt got progressively worse before a major stabilisation project in the 1990s ensured it'll stay at its current 5.5-degree tilt for good. Officially the Duomo's campanile (bell tower), the tower took almost 200 years to build. It forms the centrepiece of one of Italy's great public squares, Piazza dei Miracoli.
🚆 **Hop on a regional train from Pisa Centrale to Lucca (0h30, every half hour).**

❹ Lucca

Italy has no shortage of hilltop towns, but not many can truly hold a candle to Lucca – a storybook combo of alleyways, piazzas and promenades, all wrapped up behind imposing Renaissance walls. At the day's end, the town's cafes and trattorias will tempt you in for a glass or two of Lucchesi wine and a slow, stomach-busting progression of rustic dishes from the Garfagnana region. Buon appetito.
🚆 **Return to Florence by train (1h15 to 1h45, hourly).**

❺ Florence

You could easily while away another two or three days in Florence, getting your teeth into Tuscan cuisine, exploring the city's glittering Duomo and climbing to the summit of the 85m campanile.

Returning home

Florence has direct trains to Turin and Milan, which have onward connections to various cities in France, Austria and Switzerland.

The Glacier Express

Zermatt · Brigg · Andermatt · Chur · St Moritz
Ride Switzerland's rollercoaster railway through the Alps, starting in Zermatt with a unparalleled view of the Matterhorn and ending in the glitzy ski resort of St Moritz.

Departure points

High-speed trains travel to Zermatt from destinations including Geneva (3h45), Bern (2h) and Zürich (3h15), with their connections to elsewhere in Europe. The Glacier Express (www.glacierexpress.ch) route covers 290km and can be done in a day (7h45). Tickets are valid for 15 days, meaning you can break the journey at any point along the way, then continue onwards (but note that reservations are compulsory between Zermatt and Chur). It's also expensive: consider using regional express SBB trains (www.sbb.ch) instead: they follow the same route, are cheaper, more frequent, and no reservations are required, making it easy to break the journey.

❶ Zermatt

Since the mid-19th century, Zermatt has starred among Switzerland's glitziest alpine resorts. Its most famous asset is the mighty Matterhorn, the fang-shaped 4478m mountain first conquered by British climber Edward Whymper in 1865. Discover the mountain's history at the state-of-the-art Matterhorn Museum, then climb

Fact box

Carbon (kg per person) 6
Distance (km) 290
Nights 5
Transport budget (€) 120

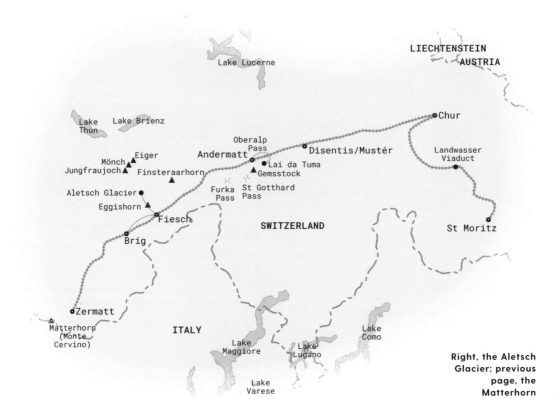

LIECHTENSTEIN
AUSTRIA

Lake Lucerne

Chur

Lake Thun   Lake Brienz

Oberalp Pass

Eiger   Andermatt   Disentis/Mustér

Landwasser Viaduct

Mönch
Jungfraujoch   Finsteraarhorn   Lai da Tuma
Gemsstock

Aletsch Glacier   Furka   St Gotthard
Pass   Pass

Eggishorn

Fiesch   SWITZERLAND

St Moritz

Brig

Zermatt

Matterhorn
(Monte
Cervino)   ITALY   Lake
Maggiore   Lake
Lugano   Lake
Como

Lake
Varese

Right, the Aletsch
Glacier; previous
page, the
Matterhorn

aboard the Matterhorn Glacier Paradise (the world's highest cable car at 3883m) to see the real thing – along with 14 glaciers and 38 peaks over 4000m.
🚆 **There are three daily Glacier Express trains direct from Zermatt to St Moritz; one extra train a day travels as far as Chur. All stop at stations in between including Brig. Hourly SBB trains leave for Brig (1h30).**

❷ Brig

Close to the Italian border, Brig has been a crossroads since Roman times. Admire the cobbled Stadtplatz, framed by al fresco cafes and candy-hued townhouses, and the impressive Stockalper Palace,

built by 17th-century merchant Kaspar von Stockalper.
🚆 **Hourly SBB trains and four daily Glacier Express trains shuttle along to Andermatt (1h30 to 2h).**

🔄 Day trip

Fiesch

Fiesch's most famous feature is the spectacular 23km-long Aletsch Glacier, ringed by the summits of Jungfrau (4158m), Mönch (4107m), Eiger (3970m) and Finsteraarhorn (4274m). It's reached via two funiculars, which climb to Eggishorn at 2927m (www.aletscharena. ch/cableways).

Hourly trains link Fiesch with Brig (0h40) and Andermatt (1h30).

❸ Andermatt

Andermatt contrasts low-key village charm with big wilderness. Several major mountain passes converge nearby, including the St Gotthard Pass (2106m), Furka Pass (2431m) and Oberalp Pass (2044m). Take a cable car up to 2691m Gemsstock (www.skiarena.ch) for toboggan runs, walking trails and sleigh rides.

SBB trains from Andermatt to Chur require a change at Disentis/Mustér; Glacier

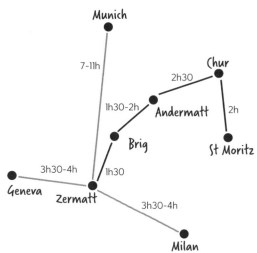

© Pete Seaward / Lonely Planet

Wear crampons to walk on
the Aletsch Glacier

Express trains travel direct. The travel time
is similar (2h20 to 2h30, half-hourly).

⊕ Day trip

Hike to Lai da Tuma

This popular hike leads from Oberalp Pass
(2044m) to sparkly Lai da Tuma (2344m;
Tomasee), the source of the Rhine. The
11km return trip takes three to four hours.
⊛ Catch a train (20 minutes, hourly) up to
the pass.

❹ Chur

The biggest city in Switzerland's biggest
canton, Chur is well worth a wander,
especially the attractive Altstadt (Old
Town). The city itself is like a vibrant
gallery, with arty boutiques, cosy
Swiss restaurants and relaxed bars.
Martinskirche, built in the late-Gothic style
in 1491, is Chur's most notable landmark,
particularly renowned for its spire and
clock face. As you travel on to St Moritz,
you'll cross the famous six-arch, 65m-high
Landwasser Viaduct, which frequently
features on promotional material plugging
the Glacier Express.
⊛ **Hourly express SBB trains and three daily
Glacier Express trains travel to St Moritz
(2h).**

❺ St Moritz

The cradle of Alpine tourism, St Moritz
has been luring royals, celebrities and
moneyed wannabes since 1864 with its
aquamarine lake, emerald forests and
distant mountains. Outdoor activities are
superb: skiing in winter, hiking in summer
and plenty more besides. Funiculars and
rental bikes make it easy to get around;
buses and postal buses shuttle between St
Moritz-Bad and St Moritz-Dorf. Look out
for the Norman Foster-designed Chesa
Futura ('House of the Future'), an eco-
friendly apartment building built between
2000 and 2004. The Clean Energy Tour
(www.clean-energy.ch) visits local
renewable energy projects in sublime
Alpine settings.

Returning home

Trains run at least hourly from St Moritz to
Zürich (3 to 4h), for onward connections to
Munich, Innsbruck and other international
destinations.

Behind the Iron Curtain

Berlin · Warsaw · Moscow
A historical journey by train into the former Eastern Bloc, exploring places once behind the Iron Curtain.

Departure points
Berlin is easily reached by high-speed train from most major European cities, including Paris, Amsterdam, Vienna, Prague and Zürich.

❶ Berlin
No city symbolises the tragedy of the Cold War more than Berlin – a place divided in two between 1961 and 1990 by the watchtower-lined Berlin Wall. Brought down in 1989, it exists now only in fragments: to see the longest remaining stretch, head to the mural-festooned East Side Gallery, followed by the Gedenkstätte Berliner Mauer, which stretches 1.4km along Bernauer Strasse and incorporates an original section of Wall, border installations and escape tunnels, a chapel and a monument. Also essential are Checkpoint Charlie, the gateway for foreigners and diplomats between the two Berlins, and the grim Stasi Prison, where enemies of the state were incarcerated. For a lighter take, don't miss the DDR Museum, which entertainingly illustrates daily life in socialist East Germany – from potty-training to nudist holidays.

🚆 **Three direct daily trains link Berlin**

Fact box
Carbon (kg per person) 36.5
Distance (km) 1830
Nights 8+
Transport budget (€) 190

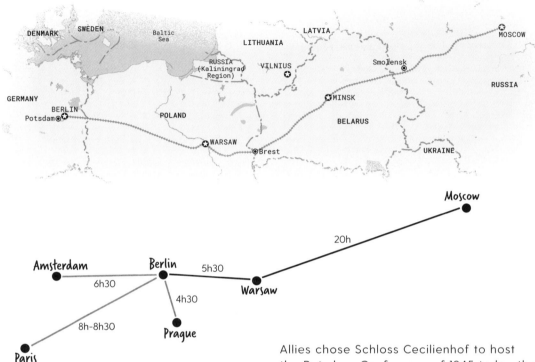

**Ostbahnhof to Warsaw Centralna (5h30).
Check http://rozklad-pkp.pl for times and
fares.**

✈ Day trip

Potsdam

Potsdam, 25km southwest of central
Berlin, lures visitors with its splendid
gardens and palaces, which garnered
Unesco World Heritage status in 1990.
Headlining the sights is Schloss Sanssouci,
the private retreat of King Friedrich II
(Frederick the Great), the mastermind
behind many of Potsdam's other fabulous
parks and palaces. Miraculously, most
survived WWII with nary a shrapnel
wound. When the shooting stopped, the

Allies chose Schloss Cecilienhof to host
the Potsdam Conference of 1945 to lay the
groundwork for Germany's post-war fate.
🚆 Regional trains leaving from Berlin
Hauptbahnhof and Zoologischer Garten
take 25 minutes to reach Potsdam
Hauptbahnhof; some continue to Potsdam
Charlottenhof and Potsdam Sanssouci,
which are closer to Park Sanssouci. The S7
from central Berlin makes the trip in about
40 minutes.

---

❷ Warsaw

Warsaw has endured the worst history
could throw at it, including near
destruction at the end of WWII. Much
has been rebuilt and the fragments
that survived are now preserved in
a superb selection of museums and

Left, the Brandenburg Gate; below, Moscow's Red Square; previous page, Berlin's Alexanderplatz

cultural storehouses. The exhibitions at the Warsaw Rising Museum and POLIN Museum of the History of Polish Jews leave practically no stone unturned on the city's experiences during WWII and the ensuing Cold War, while the Neon Museum gathers together some of Warsaw's most dazzling pieces of signage, many dating from the communist era. The museum is the passion project of photographer Ilona Karwińska and her partner David Hill.

 Warsaw Centralna is connected with Moscow Belorusskaja by overnight train (20h, three times weekly). Moscow-bound trains enter Belarus near Brest, so you'll need a Belarus visa or transit visa. Border crossings can be slow, but do not normally mean leaving the train – customs personnel work their way through the carriages checking passports and visas. Polrail (www. polrail.com/en) **is a really useful planning and ticket-buying tool.**

❸ Moscow

The remains of the former Soviet state are scattered around the Russian capital. Monuments remember fallen heroes and victorious battles, and museums attempt to analyse and synthesise the past. See Lenin and Stalin – off their pedestals – at the whimsical Art Muzeon. Step into the socialist-realist fantasy at VDNKh amusement park. Descend into the depths of the Soviet system at Bunker-42 Cold War Museum. Ride the museum-like metro and remember the millions who suffered at the Gulag History Museum. Nowadays, retro clubs and cafes give their guests a taste of the Soviet experience. You can try your hand at Soviet-era arcade games.

Returning home

Extend your trip with a visit to St Petersburg, which can be reached by train in 8h30 to 9h30. From St Petersburg there are trains and ferries to Scandinavian cities including Stockholm and Helsinki. Alternatively, simply retrace your journey.

© Jonathan Stokes / Lonely Planet, © Mordolff / Getty Images

Stockholm to the Arctic Circle

Stockholm · Uppsala · Mora · Östersund · Jokkmokk · Gällivare
This summertime escape ventures north to the Arctic Circle, with little trains rattling beside icy lakes and forests, stopping at remote communities under the midnight sun.

Departure points

Stockholm Central is the starting point for this adventure – it's easy to reach by train from Copenhagen Central (5h30) Gothenburg Central (5h), or else board a 17-hour ferry from Helsinki to the Swedish capital.

❶ Stockholm

Stockholm may count as one of the more easy-going European capitals, but it's a pulsating metropolis compared with other points on this itinerary. There are islands for every mood in this city: delve into the past among the 18th-century townhouses of Gamla Stan, sink artisanal beers in Södermalm, or take a stroll among the venerable museums and rolling parkland of Djurgården.

🚇 **From Stockholm, up to six trains an hour depart for Uppsala (1h). www.sj.se**

✈ Day trip

Stockholm Archipelago

East of the capital lie the myriad islets and skerries of the Stockholm archipelago – a paradise for sailors and a summer retreat of city-bound Swedes. The island of Vaxholm is the gateway,

Gamla Stan, Stockholm's Old Town

Fact box

Carbon (kg per person) 44
Distance (km) 2200
Nights 8+
Transport budget (€) 400

Gällivare
1h30
Jokkmokk
12h30
Östersund
6h
Mora
3h
Uppsala
1h
17h
Helsinki
Stockholm
5h
Gothenburg
5h
Copenhagen

NORWAY

Gällivare

Jokkmokk

SWEDEN

Östersund

Gulf of
Bothnia

Mora

Borlänge

Uppsala

Stockholm
Archipelago

STOCKHOLM

Baltic
Sea

and a worthwhile place to amble amid boutiques, timber cottages and a 16th-century fortress that once defended the capital from seaborne invasion.

🚢 **Waxholmsbolaget operate ferries from central Stockholm (1h). www. waxholmsbolaget.se**

❷ Uppsala

As Oxford is to England and Heidelberg is to Germany, so Uppsala is to Sweden: the country's foremost university town, huddled around the lofty spire of the Domkyrka – Scandinavia's largest cathedral. Catch a scent of sunnier climes inside the Tropical Greenhouse at the Linnaean Gardens of Uppsala, before commencing your journey north to the Arctic Circle.

🚆 **From Uppsala, board a train to Borlänge and change for the service to Mora (3h). www.sj.se**

❸ Mora

Unassuming Mora sits on the northern shore of Lake Siljan. It was the home of early 20th-century painter Anders Zorn, whose extraordinary home, Zorngården, is open to the public along with a gallery of his works. Its other claim to fame is being the starting point of the Inlandsbanan

Left, the Inlandsbanan; right,
icy lakes around Jokkmokk

a mountain bike to hit the trails around town and visit Jamtli – a living museum of Swedish life through the centuries. Heading north from here, the scenery becomes more dramatic as the railway enters the ancestral lands of the Sami – the indigenous inhabitants of the Arctic. Look out for reindeer from the train window.

🚆 **From Östersund, the 7.35am Inlandsbanan service departs on the long day journey to Gällivare – dismount before the end, at Jokkmokk (12h30).**

❺ Jokkmokk

Jokkmokk is the capital of Sámi culture in Swedish Lapland – get to grips with their reindeer herding lifestyle and their shamanic beliefs at the excellent Ájtte Museum. It's also a convenient staging post for hiking and camping excursions in the mountains to the west. Buses 47 and 94 connect from Jokkmokk to the Kungsleden (King's Trail) – Sweden's most famous long-distance walking path.

🚆 **Catch the 7.50pm Inlandsbanan service for Gallivare (1h30).**

❻ Gällivare

Industrial Gällivare marks the northerly terminus of the Inlandsbanan. For one month a year it welcomes the midnight sun – climb Dundret hill on the edge of town to see rays crowning the horizon in June and early July.

Returning home

From Gällivare, board direct sleeper services back to Stockholm (14h).

(Inland Railway) – a single-track line that trundles through remote pine forests in the summer, with drivers who have been known to slam the brakes on so everyone can get out and pick berries. Board the afternoon service to Östersund – rather peculiarly, the train halts for passengers to have dinner at a lineside restaurant.

🚆 **Inlandsbanan services depart Mora at 2.45pm for Östersund (6h). www. inlandsbanan.se**

❹ Östersund

Set among the dappled forests of the Swedish interior, the small town of Östersund marks the midpoint of the Inlandsbanan. You'll need to stay the night to continue north, but there's plenty to occupy you while you change trains: check out the resurgent food scene, hire

Paris to Glasgow

Paris · London · Birmingham · Manchester · Windermere · Glasgow
This route travels up the spine of the UK, calling at world-changing industrial cities with serious cultural clout and terminating at the foothills of the Scottish Highlands.

Departure points

This trip focuses on the UK's West Coast Mainline (WCML) – a major rail corridor stretching northward from London Euston along the western edge of the Pennines. Close to Euston, London St Pancras International is easily accessed from Paris Gare du Nord (2h30). Otherwise travel to London with Paris train connections from Barcelona Sants (6h30), Marseille Saint-Charles (3h) or Hamburg (8h).

❶ Paris

Paris makes for an easy starting point for this itinerary – if you've time to kill waiting at Gare du Nord, make for Brasserie Terminus Nord – an art deco brasserie with leather banquettes and linen-clad tables, just across the road from the train station.

🚆 **14 trains per day travel from Paris to London (2h30). www.eurostar.com**

❷ London

Once upon a time, passengers disembarking at St Pancras would have made a beeline into central London: not so today. The regeneration of the King's Cross neighbourhood has seen new

Regent's Canal passes through London's Little Venice

Fact box

Carbon (kg per person) 23
Distance (km) 1150
Nights 9+
Transport budget (€) 450

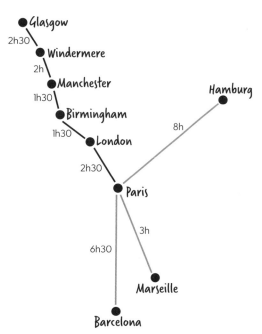

restaurants, pubs and street food outfits setting up among once derelict Victorian warehouses. Following the Regent's Canal towpath to Camden Market makes for a fine afternoon stroll.

🚆 **Daily trains to Birmingham stations leave several times an hour from London's Euston and Marylebone stations – fast WCML services depart from Euston (1h30). www. virgintrains.co.uk**

❸ Birmingham

Many visitors to England bypass its second city, but to do so would be to ignore a town that set the blueprint for

the industrial age. Amble the regenerated canals of Gas Street Basin for a glimpse of the city's industrial past, or catch a screening at the Electric – the UK's oldest working cinema, an art deco masterpiece in operation since 1909. It's directly over the road from Birmingham New Street Station, which is now looking sprightly after a recent overhaul.

🚆 **From Birmingham New Street there are upwards of 30 daily departures to Manchester Piccadilly (1h30). www. virgintrains.co.uk**

❹ Manchester

Manchester thrived in the 19th century as a global cotton hub: in recent times its better-known exports have been football clubs – United and City – and bands such

© Will Rodrigues / Shutterstock

Left, Windermere; right,
Glasgow's Riverside Museum

as The Smiths, Joy Division and Oasis. Get back to the city's roots at the excellent Science and Industry Museum, set on the site of the world's first passenger station, dating back to 1830. Otherwise make for the Lowry, a complex that pays tribute to the British artist LS Lowry, whose distinctive works immortalised Northern England's urban landscapes.

🚆 **Around five daily direct trains serve Windermere from Manchester Piccadilly (2h). www.northernrailway.co.uk**

❺ Windermere

Transition from grey to green by boarding a direct train to the Lake District. Windermere is England's largest natural lake, with a resort town on its eastern shore and heathery fells to the west whose reflections quiver in its waters. It's a hub for hiking, kayaking and other excursions into the surrounding national park.

🚆 **From Windermere, change at Oxenholme Lake District for services to Glasgow Central (2h30). www.virgintrains.co.uk**

❻ Glasgow

Glasgow is a handsome city from any angle, whether you're admiring the civic grandeur of George Square or pacing the museums of the West End. One corner that's undergone serious upheaval is the Clyde, the river that built and dispatched ships to far corners of the globe. Visit the Zaha Hadid-designed Riverside Museum, or board the museum ship *Glenlee* – a sometime Spanish Navy vessel that circumnavigated the world, welded into existence in Glasgow.

❂ Day trip

Loch Lomond

Glasgow has quick access to the southern parts of the Highlands. The picturesque village of Balmaha sits on the southern shore of Loch Lomond – grab a pub lunch before scaling Connick Hill behind the village for a sublime view over the forested banks of the loch.

🚆🚌 **To get there, catch a train from Glasgow Queen Street to Balloch and change for the 309 bus to Balmaha. www. scotrail.co.uk**

Returning home

Direct trains run from Glasgow Central to London stations (4h30) for connections across the continent.

© Daniel Kay / Shutterstock. © Jeremy Sutton - Hibbert / Alamy Stock Photo

Cities & castles of the Czech Republic

Prague · Brno · Olomouc · Prague
Starting in Prague, take a tour through the Czech countryside into Moravia, visiting vineyards, medieval towns and hilltop strongholds en route.

Departure points

Prague is well integrated into European rail networks. Trains travel to/from Berlin and Dresden to the north or Vienna, Kraków, Bratislava and Budapest to the east and south. All international trains arrive at Praha hlavní nádraží, Prague's main station. Most services are operated by the Czech state rail operator, České dráhy (www.cd.cz).

❶ Prague

If any city rivals Paris for style, it's Prague. The cobbled lanes and hidden courtyards are a paradise for the aimless wanderer, always beckoning you to explore further. Just a few blocks away from the Old Town Square and sights like Charles Bridge you can stumble across chapels, unexpected gardens, cute cafes and old-fashioned bars with hardly a tourist in sight. One of the most fun ways to explore is Nostalgic Tram No 91, with vintage cars dating from 1908 to 1924 trundling along between the Public Transport Museum via Prague Castle, Wenceslas Square and náměstí Republiky and finishing at Výstaviště. You can get on or off at any stop and buy tickets on board.

🚆 **Express trains to Brno depart from Praha hlavní nádraží (3h, every two hours).**

Fact box

Carbon (kg per person) 20
Distance (km) 595
Nights 8+
Transport budget (€) 35

Prague's 14th-century Charles Bridge

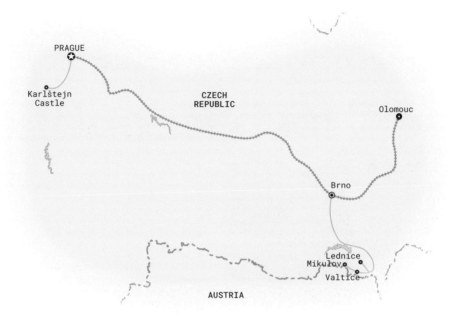

PRAGUE

Karlštejn
Castle

CZECH
REPUBLIC

Olomouc

Brno

Lednice
Mikulov
Valtice

AUSTRIA

⊕ Day trip

Karlštejn Castle

Karlštejn Castle, 30km southwest of Prague, started life in 1348 as a hideaway for the crown jewels of Holy Roman Emperor Charles IV. After falling into disrepair, it's been restored to fairy-tale perfection. Even if you don't go inside, the exterior is worth the trip alone.

🚆 **Trains from Prague's main train station to Beroun (via Praha-Smíchov) stop at Karlštejn station (45 minutes, half-hourly).**
⊕ **From here, it's a 20-30 minute uphill walk to the castle.**

❷ Brno

East of Prague lies the eastern province of Moravia, home to the Czech Republic's most renowned vineyards. The region's capital is Brno, whose cafes, cocktail

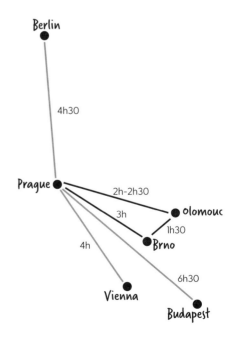

Berlin

4h30

Prague

2h-2h30

Olomouc

3h

1h30

Brno

4h

Vienna

6h30

Budapest

Left, Karlštejn Castle; right,
Prague's St Nicholas Church

Trail connects small vineyards and offers wonderful views of the countryside. Mikulov's tourist information office (www. mikulov.cz) can suggest day trips if you don't want to do the whole route, including to the nearby castles at Valtice and Lednice. RentBike (www.rentbike.cz) will kit you out for getting around.

🚌 **The bus is generally the best way to access Mikulov from Brno (1h30), with coaches leaving hourly.**

❸ Olomouc

Practically unknown outside the Czech Republic, Olomouc is a seriously handsome city, with a main square surrounded by historic buildings and a Unesco-protected trinity column. Explore the foundations of ancient Olomouc Castle at the must-see Archdiocesan Museum, then head for one of the city's many pubs or microbreweries, fuelled by the thousands of students who attend university here. Don't forget to try the cheese, Olomoucký sýr or tvarůžky, reputedly the smelliest in the Czech Republic.

🚆 **To get back to the capital, you can take normal ČD trains (2h20, two per hour) or high-end private trains run by RegioJet (2h20, every two hours, www.regiojet.cz) or LEO Express (2h, every two hours, www. le.cz).**

bars, restaurants and student population have made it the nation's next liveliest city after Prague. The medieval Old Town Hall is packed with architectural quirks, but it pales in comparison to the Bauhaus-style Vila Tugendhat, designed by Modernist master Mies van der Rohe for Greta and Fritz Tugendhat in 1930. Take the tram from Moravské náměstí up Milady Horákové to the Dětská nemocnice stop, then walk 300m north.

🚆 **There are around two trains an hour from Brno to Olomouc (1h30). The train station is 2km east of the centre and accessible via several tram lines.**

❖ Day trip

Mikulov Wine Trail

Mikulov is the heart of the Czech wine country. The 82km-long Mikulov Wine

Bavaria to Berlin

Munich · Nuremberg · Weimar · Leipzig · Dresden · Berlin
This captivating itinerary shuttles between the cultural titans of Germany, taking in palaces and parks, poets and painters – and serene landscapes on the urban fringe.

Departure points

Munich Hauptbahnhof is readily accessible from points in Western and Eastern Europe – trains run direct from Paris Gare de L'Est (6h), Vienna stations (4h) and Budapest Keleti (7h).

❶ Munich

Don't tell Berliners, but Munich has the swagger of a capital city: all opulent palaces, lofty churches and world-class museums, with snow-dusted Alps as a backdrop. Start a Teutonic odyssey with a performance at the Nationaltheater, where some of Wagner's greatest works were first performed. Witness another pillar of Bavarian culture with a tour or a ticket for a game at the Allianz Arena – home ground of serial European football champions FC Bayern Munich.

🚆 **Around 50 services a day connect Munich Hauptbahnhof to Nuremberg Hauptbahnhof (1h). www.bahn.de**

❷ Nuremberg

The city of Holy Roman Emperors and later a hub for Nazi rallies, Nuremberg has weathered the storms of German history and is today stronger for it. It was the

Nuremberg lies on the River Pegnitz

Fact box

Carbon (kg per person) 16
Distance (km) 800
Nights 10+
Transport budget (€) 250

Goethe's House
in Weimar

hometown of Old Master Albrecht Dürer
– visit his house, set in the shadow of
the town's medieval castle. Alternatively,
get acquainted with a familiar fixation at
the Deutsche Bahn Museum, chronicling
the story of railways across the
Bundesrepublik.

**To reach Weimar from Nuremberg
Hauptbahnhof (1h30), change at Erfurt.
www.bahn.de**

❸ Weimar

Weimar may look like an modest small
town of cobbled squares and red roofed
houses, but this is Germany's cultural
Goliath, the sometime haunt of poets
Goethe and Schiller, composers Bach
and Liszt, artists Kandinsky and Klee.
Visit Weimar's new Bauhaus museum to
understand how this town shaped global
design and architecture.

🚆 **Around 40 trains a day connect Weimar
to Leipzig Hauptbahnhof (1h). www.bahn.de**

© Jonathan Stokes / Lonely Planet

Opposite, the green waterways of Spreewald; left, Dresden

total collapse and reconsecrated in 2005, crowned by an altar pieced together from some 2000 fragments.

🚄 **Around 30 trains a day run from Dresden Hauptbahnhof to Berlin Hauptbahnhof (2h). www.bahn.de**

❻ Berlin

The city that defined 20th-century history remains a cultural epicentre in the 21st. You could easily lose a week exploring its museums and Cold War monuments, ambling the shady lawns of the Tiergarten and plunging into some of the best nightlife on the continent.

🛏 **Hotel tip: Landmark Eco Hotel**

✈ Day trip

Spreewald

A Unesco Biosphere reserve on the edge of the city, the Spreewald is a favoured escape for Berliners. It has dense forests criss-crossed by trails, and meandering waterways that could be purpose-made for kayaking expeditions.

🚄 **The town of Lübben is one of the Spreewald's easiest access points – you can get there in under an hour from Berlin Hauptbahnhof, with about 50 trains each day. www.bahn.de**

❹ Leipzig

The capital of Saxony, Leipzig earned the moniker 'City of Heroes' for its role in bringing about the fall of the Berlin Wall. Learn about life under surveillance in the former GDR at the town's Stasi Museum, set inside the former headquarters of the infamous secret police.

🚄 **Over 30 trains a day run between Leipzig Hauptbahnhof and Dresden Hauptbahnhof (1h). www.bahn.de**

❺ Dresden

Few cities have risen phoenix-like as Dresden has: once known as Florence on the Elbe, it was all but reduced to ashes by Allied bombing raids in World War II. The past decades have seen its former glory reinstated, not least the 18th-century Frauenkirche, rebuilt from

Returning home

Direct ICE trains run to Munich Hauptbahnhof from Berlin Hauptbahnhof (4h). Alternatively return south via a detour to the Czech Republic, catching a train from Berlin to Prague, followed by another service to Munich.

Grand Tour of Switzerland

Zürich · Lucerne · Bern · Neuchâtel · Lausanne · Geneva
*Presenting Switzerland in a nutshell, this road trip takes in glaciers, mountain passes,
castles and lakes — all connected by a network of charging points for electric vehicles.*

Departure points

Switzerland's 'E-Grand Tour' is a 1600km there-and-back route connected by the world's first long-distance network of charging points for electric vehicles. This itinerary follows the 783km Zürich to Geneva leg, which gives a great taster. High-speed trains run to Zürich, where you can rent an e-car, from Paris Gare de Lyon (4h), Frankfurt (4h) and Milan (3h40). Visit https://grandtour.myswitzerland.com for information on the 300 charging stations en route, as well as detailed maps.

❶ Zürich

Before getting behind the wheel, spend a day or two in Zürich roaming the alley-woven Altstadt (Old Town). This culturally wired city endears with outstanding art (see Old Masters at the Kunsthaus), post-industrial cool (check out the indie bars and boutiques in Züri-West), and outdoor living in lakeside parks, open-air cafes and bathing pavilions. Don't miss the mountain viewpoints, including top-of-the-city Uetliberg (871m), which can be reached by a 30-minute train ride from Zürich's main station.

🚗 **Drive south via Lake Lucerne (2h).**
Pit stops: This is Switzerland's historic

Fact box

Carbon (kg per journey) 39
Distance (km) 863
Nights 7
Transport budget (€) 1400

Sunset over Zürich

© Travelerpix / Shutterstock

heartland: stop in Schwyz, birthplace of the federation in 1291; Brunnen, a Turner favourite for its views of fjordlike Lake Uri; and Sisikon, steeped in William Tell legend.

❷ Lucerne

Ringed by mountains of myth, lakeside Lucerne is a Swiss dream of a city. Post-drive, cross the covered wooden Kapellbrücke bridge to the medieval Old Town. Or see what's happening exhibition-wise at the post-modern KKL cultural centre and Sammlung Rosengart, with its prized stash of Picassos. The promenade is perfect for picnics, bike rides and strolls.

🚘 **The tour takes the circuitous, scenic route west to Bern (3h30).**

Pit stop: Get out and walk for a while in Entlebuch Biosphere Reserve, a wonderland of karst formations, moorlands and wild mountain streams.

❸ Bern

The chilled Swiss capital's pride and joy is its Unesco-listed Altstadt, a warren of flag-festooned lanes, arcades, ornate clock towers and cellar shops and bars. The other big-hitter is the Renzo Piano-designed, wave-shaped Zentrum Paul Klee, showcasing the colour-charged works of the Swiss-born Expressionist. Beyond this, Bern appeals with its riverside swimming spots and upbeat nightlife.

🚘 **Don't hurry the spectacular 252km drive from Bern to Neuchâtel.**

Left, the Swiss Alps; below, Geneva; right, a train in Lavaux's vineyards

Switzerland's largest archaeology museum, Laténium. A funicular rises to 1160m Mt Chaumont for wonderful lake and mountain views.

🚗 It's a 170km drive through Switzerland's watchmaking heartland to Lausanne.

🚶 Day trip

Cycling

Hike or cycle in off-the-radar Val-de-Travers, exploring peaceful forests, streams and the vast Creux du Van abyss.

🚗 Val-de-Travers is around a 40-minute drive from Neuchâtel.

🚶 Day trip

Hiking

Nature works on an epic scale in the Bernese Oberland, where the glacier-encrusted Eiger, Mönch and Jungfrau lord it above jewel-coloured lakes Thun and Brienz. Trains (0h30) run half-hourly from Interlaken to Grindelwald, the starting point for epic half- and full-day hikes.

🚗 Drive to Interlaken (1h), which makes a good springboard for exploring.

❹ Neuchâtel

Stirring Alpine views give way to rolling dairy country on the drive to French-speaking Neuchâtel, spread at the foot of the Jura Mountains. Spilling down to the lake of the same name, this château-topped town has fairy-tale looks and

❺ Lausanne

Backed by terraced vineyards and gazing out across the lake to the Alps, Lausanne is an instant heart-stealer. Sight-wise, you'll want to see the impressive Gothic cathedral, the Olympic Museum, and cultural hub Plateforme10, which brings together fine and contemporary arts, design and photography. Students drive the party scene in this town.

🚗 The onward road to Geneva hugs the lakeshore (1h).

© Roman Babakin / Shutterstock

🕙 Day trip

Wine-tasting

Tack on a day to hike a section of the 30km Swiss Wine Trail, dipping into the breathtakingly sheer vineyards of the Unesco-listed Lavaux region. The trail runs between Saint-Saphorin and Lutry.

🚗 **Lutry is a 10-minute drive from Lausanne.**

---

⑥ Geneva

Round out your trip in lakeside Geneva, where sights, alpine views and fine bistros and bars will amuse for a day or two. The Vieille Ville, threaded with alleys, is topped off by the Gothic Cathédrale Saint Pierre and rainbow-kissed Jet d'Eau fountain. There are also museums galore devoted to art, history, the Reformation, ethnography, watchmaking and the Red Cross – you name it!

Returning home

At the time of writing, it was not possible to drop the e-cars off in Geneva; you'll need to return to Zurich (3h30).

Exploring Cornwall

Truro · Falmouth · St Ives

Britain runs into the sea in a riot of foaming waves, maritime history and Celtic connections. This short break takes in a few highlights.

Departure points

To get to Cornwall you must get to England and take the Great Western Railway from London to Truro. Coming from northern Europe this will mean Eurostar from Amsterdam, Brussels or Paris to London, a quick jaunt on the Underground and then an onward train from Paddington. Day services take around 4h30 to reach Penzance. The Cornish Riviera sleeper serves the same route six nights a week. Alternatively the Brittany Ferries service from Roscoff in Brittany to Plymouth, Devon is an alternative if coming from Spain or southwest France.

❶ Truro

At Truro, county town of Cornwall, you'll find a towering cathedral and the Royal Cornwall Museum, a fine place to begin explorations of the county's past with some notable collections of art and antiquities to browse.

🚆 **From here a branch line of the Great Western Railway runs half-hourly to Falmouth (0h25).**

⚓ **Two miles downriver of Truro ferries float down to Falmouth offering an alternative to the train (1h15, six daily, check www.falriver.co.uk/ferries for timetables).**

Fact box

Carbon (kg per person) 5.5kg

Distance (km) 280

Nights 7+

Transport budget (£) 118

Trebarwith Strand beach near Tintagel

❷ Falmouth

This fishing town, home to the third-deepest natural harbour in Europe, is an appealing place to settle in, with a branch of the National Maritime Museum, good shops and restaurants, and sweetly puttering ferries crossing the Fal estuary to the pretty village of Flushing and fashionable St Mawes on the Roseland Peninsula. Ferries run half-hourly between Falmouth and Flushing (0h10) and every 20 minutes to St Mawes (0h20).

🚆 **Trains from Falmouth to St Ives depart at least hourly from 6.30am to 7.30pm, involving changes in Truro and St Erth, and taking 90 minutes.**

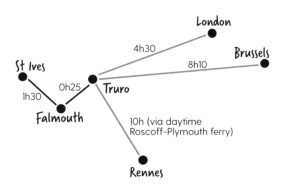

Below, fresh seafood in Falmouth; right, Pendower beach

⊕ Day trip

Bodmin Moor & Tintagel

To dive into the mysterious side of Cornwall hire a car (electric vehicles and plenty of charging stations are available) from nearby Penryn (www.enterprise.co.uk) and head north across Bodmin Moor. This ancient landscape is dotted with mysterious rock formations, standing stones and neolithic tombs. Travel on to Tintagel, a world-famous ruined castle now connected to a neighbouring headland via a spectacular bridge. Be warned, you may leave with an obsession with King Arthur.

🚂 **Penryn is less than 10 minutes from Falmouth by half-hourly train or more-frequent bus, or grab a taxi. It's around 100km, or an hour and half's drive, from Penryn to Tintagel via Bodmin Moor, but make time for stops on the way.**

❸ St Ives

Taking the train from Falmouth to St Ives allows you to travel on two of Cornwall's famed branch line services and deposits you right in the heart of Cornwall's art scene. There's a Tate outpost here as well as the Barbara Hepworth Museum and the Leach Pottery, honouring influential local artists. Kids will be more interested in the boat trips and picture-perfect beaches. Overnight in St Ives.

Returning home

If you took a day train from London, consider taking the sleeper on the way home to experience one of the world's most up-to-date rolling hotels. Otherwise head back the way you came.

On an Austrian high

Innsbruck · Kitzbühel · Zell am See · Salzburg · Linz · Vienna
Whisking you from the ravishing Tyrolean Alps to regal Vienna, this train ride through Austria's heartland will have you glued to the window all the way.

Departure points

This itinerary taps into Austria's excellent, hyper-efficient ÖBB rail network. The departure point is Innsbruck, easily reachable by high-speed train from Munich (1h45), Milan (6h) and Venice (5h20). By TGV from Gare de Lyon in Paris, the journey time is 8h15.

❶ Innsbruck

Kick off in Innsbruck, Tyrol's cultured and charismatic capital, where the Nordkette Alps rise like a theatre curtain. Breeze up to the highest point, Hafelekar (2334m), in the space-age funicular designed by Zaha Hadid, or linger in the medieval, arcaded lanes of the Altstadt (Old Town). It's well stocked with opulent Hapsburg palaces,

Gothic churches, and cafes, bars and restaurants.

🚆 **Fast trains with Eurocity and Railjet depart at least twice hourly for Kitzbühel, taking 1h10 with a change at Wörgl.**

⟳ Day trip

Zillertal

Head to the nearby Zillertal for high-level hiking trails, mountain biking and rafting adventures on the foaming Ziller River.

Fact box

Carbon (kg per person) 11
Distance (km) 552
Nights 8+
Transport budget (€) 115

Innsbruck and the Nordkette Alps

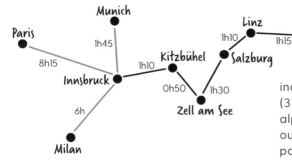

Winter in Salzburg

🚆 **There are three hourly trains between Innsbruck and Jenbach (0h20) at Zillertal's entrance. Eurocity services are quickest.**

❷ Kitzbühel

Its ski pistes are the stuff of Olympic legend, but there's more to the ritzy town of Kitzbühel than downhill thrills. In summer, the slopes hum with hikers and a cable car swings up to the alpine flower garden at Kitzbüheler Horn. Paragliding, and mountain- and electric-bike tours ramp up the action.

🚆 **Direct trains to Zell am See (0h50) depart hourly, involving a highly scenic journey through the Alps.**

❸ Zell am See

Sitting astride a petrol-blue lake and backdropped by glacier-encrusted peaks,

including Austria's highest, Grossglockner (3798m), Zell am See is every inch the alpine dream. The major draw here is the outdoors: bike around the lake, windsurf, paraglide, raft, climb, or take the cable car to Schmittenhöhe, the trailhead for the Pinzgauer Spaziergang – a challenging day hike with uplifting views of Hohe Tauern National Park.

🚆 **Trains depart hourly for Salzburg (1h30).**

❂ Day trip

Hiking

Ski or hike at 3000m on a glacier at Kitzsteinhorn mountain, a half-hour bus ride from central Zell am See.

🚌 **Buses depart twice hourly and are free with a guest 'summer card' from May to October (www.zellamsee-kaprun.com).**

❹ Salzburg

With its cake-topper of a medieval fortress, alpine backdrop and Unesco-listed baroque centre straddling the Salzach River, Salzburg is an instant heart-stealer. As the home town of Mozart

© Candastock / Shutterstock

Left, torte at Aida Cafe, Vienna; below, Belvedere Palace in Vienna

the future, with its clutch of on-the-pulse museums. Highlights include glass-and-steel Lentos – with modern art from Warhol, Schiele and Klimt – and the interactive Ars Electronica Center, spotlighting technology, science and digital media.

🚆 **Fast trains to Vienna run twice hourly (1h15).**

❻ Vienna

Oh, Vienna! There's nowhere like it for imperial pomp, rococo palaces, cake-filled coffeehouses, concert halls and more art than you could ever hope to gawp at in a lifetime. Marvel at Klimt masterpieces at Schloss Belvedere, treasures amassed by the Hapsburgs at the Hofburg and edgy creations at MuseumsQuartier. Afterwards, detour to the cooler, more offbeat 2nd, 7th and 9th districts.

Returning home

From Vienna, there are fast trains to Munich (4h), where you can connect to regular services going north, including trains to Paris (5h40).

and the place where Maria taught the world to sing in *The Sound of Music*, this city has music in its DNA. Try to catch a performance in one of its palaces, churches or concert halls.

🚆 **There are twice hourly fast trains to Linz (1h10).**

🔄 Day trip

Hiking

Go to Werfen for a frosty walk at Narnia-like Eisriesenwelt, the world's largest accessible ice caves.

🚆 **Hourly fast trains link Salzburg to Werfen (0h40).**

❺ Linz

This refreshingly dynamic city on the Danube makes an exciting leap towards

North and west Sicily

Palermo · Trapani · Egadi Islands · Selinunte · Palermo
Venture around Sicily's capital and into the island's west for near-deserted ancient sights, mosaic-covered cathedrals and wild, sandy beaches.

Departure points

Palermo can be reached by rail from mainland Italy by day or night trains, with direct services from Rome being shunted on to the ferry to cross the Straits of Messina. There are also ferries from Genoa, Civitavecchia and Naples direct to Palermo. From Paris, take the Thello sleeper to Milan and travel on to Rome.

❶ Palermo

Devote at least a day to Palermo. The city's street markets, Norman cathedral and spectacular Palatine Chapel are must-sees. A taxi from the centre will take you on an excursion to the hillside town of Monreal (0h30), whose cathedral church has a Technicolor riot of mosaics. In the evening, grab dinner and drinks in the

Cefalù's beach, east of Palermo

Fact box

Carbon (kg per person) 51.5

Distance (km) 461

Nights 9+

Transport budget (€) 400

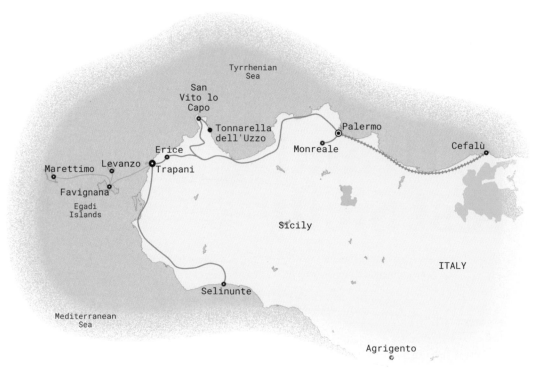

Vucciria neighbourhood.

🚗 **Hire a car for the trip west. Keep your carbon count low by choosing an electric vehicle – readily available from rental agencies in Palermo, and well-catered for by charging stations along the route. Allow a day to make the 160km journey along the coast including stops. Some driving is on slower roads.**

⟳ Day trip

Cefalù

An hour's train ride from Palermo is the iconic cathedral city of Cefalu. It's a pedestrian paradise, with a sandy beach, picturesque port and cobbled old town perfect for slow exploration.

🚆 **Twelve trains per day run from Palermo to Cefalu and back (1h10).**

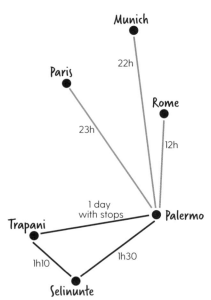

Nightlife in Palermo

Palermo's Piazza Bellini

❷ Trapani

The traffic thins out heading west out of Palermo towards the lovely small beach at Tonnarella dell'Uzzo, from where it's half an hour further on to the rugged coastal scenery of San Vito Lo Capo. An hour's drive from here is hilltop Erice, reached via a thrilling cable-car ride with terrific views of the city of Trapani and the west coast. Overnight in Erice or Trapani.

🚗 **Selinunte is 95km by road from Trapani.**

✚ Day trip

Egadi Islands

The Egadi Islands, just off the west coast of Sicily, offer a slow-travel day trip – or longer – themed around doing not a lot. The appeal of Favignana, Levanzo and Marettimo lies in their laid-back pace and simple activities. Favignana is the largest

and a logical starting point. Most people come for a leisurely lunch, swim or hike.

⛴ **Hydrofoils (0h20 to Favignana and Levanzo, up to 15 a day) and ferries (1h, three per day) connect Trapani with the islands.**

Selinunte

It's a dramatic drive along the coast and through Sicily's hilly interior to the archaeological site of Selinunte. This complex of fields and ruined temples makes for wonderful wandering. Some superb beaches by the modern town of the same name offer temple sunsets.

🚗 **It's 103km back to Palermo.**

Returning home

Reverse your steps from Palermo or switch from ferry to train, or vice versa.

Northern Europe tri-country tour

Strasbourg · Colmar · Basel · Freiburg

Tick off three countries by train on this journey from canal-woven Strasbourg in France to art-mad Basel on the Rhine and Germany's storybook Black Forest.

Departure points

This tri-country tour kicks off in Strasbourg, easily accessible by Eurostar from Paris Gare du Nord (2h15) and London St Pancras (5h, one change). Strasbourg is also well connected to major European cities by high-speed train, including Zürich (2h20, by TGV).

❶ Strasbourg

Devote at least a day or two to the Alsatian capital, with its split Franco-German personality. The Unesco-listed heart, Grande Île, is a medieval warren of cobbles and half-timbered houses. Its centrepiece is a hefty Gothic cathedral, complete with flying buttresses, jewel-like rose window and astronomical clock.

Fact box

Carbon (kg per person) 3.5

Distance (km) 175

Nights 7

Transport budget (€) 60

Strasbourg swings between quaint and cool, with a melange of canals, cutting-edge contemporary art and student-driven nightlife.

🚆 **Direct trains depart half hourly for Colmar (0h30).**

⊙ Day trip

Wine-tasting

Use local buses or hire a bike or e-bike to spin along a section of the Route des

The slow way to see Strasbourg

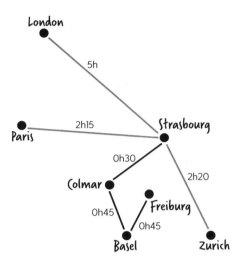

Vins d'Alsace (Alsace Wine Route, www.vinsalsace.com), where family-run *caves* open their doors for tastings of their pinots and Rieslings. **The gateway is Marlenheim, about 20 minutes west of Strasbourg.**

❷ Colmar

Try to snag a window seat for the short train ride south to Colmar, which unzips rolling, wooded hills and vineyards. Birthplace of sculptor Bartholdi (of Statue of Liberty Fame), Colmar looks as though it has leapt straight out of the pages of a Grimm fairy tale, with its ludicrously pretty ensemble of half-timbered houses in chalk-box colours and bridge-laced canals. Stay overnight to experience the full-on romance of its lantern-lit lanes and cosy *winstubs* (wine taverns).
🚆 **There are hourly regional TER trains from Colmar to Basel SBB (0h45).**

⊕ Day trip

Neuf-Brisach
Shaped like an eight-pointed star, fortified Neuf-Brisach is a Unesco-listed citadel 17km southeast of Colmar. It was laid out by famous French military engineer Vauban in 1697, and is well worth a detour.
🚌 **Hop on a 1076 bus (0h40) from Colmar.**

Below, Freiburg; right, Neuf-
Brisach; opposite, Colmar

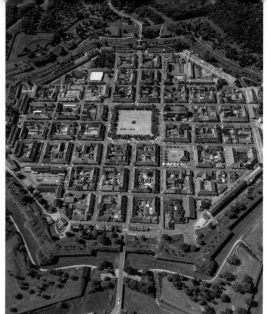

❸ Basel

Clipping the French and German borders, this Swiss city on the River Rhine excels in art and architecture, with no fewer than 40 museums and galleries to dip into, including Kunstmuseum Basel and its phenomenal fine arts collection. Spiralling around the Marktplatz, the medieval old town contrasts strikingly with the city's avant-garde architecture, which bears the imprint of Pritzker Prize winners like Frank Gehry, Pierre de Meuron and Zaha Hadid.
🚆 Direct ICE trains depart roughly twice hourly from Basel's SBB train station for Freiburg im Breisgau over the border in Germany (0h45).

❹ Freiburg

Surrounded by the deep, dark fir-clad hills of Germany's Black Forest, Freiburg is a vivacious little city, with a well-preserved medieval centre for strolling, an impressive 11th-century minster sprouting a riot of lacy spires and leering gargoyles, and a healthy student population propping up the bar scene. Officially Germany's sunniest city, Freiburg is a beacon of green energy, too.

⚙ Day trip

Titisee

Go for a splash in or a hike around Titisee, a blue-green glacial lake rimmed by forest. The lakefront promenade is ideal for picnicking, renting a boat or swimming.
🚆 Trains run from Freiburg to Titisee twice hourly (0h38).

Returning home

From Freiburg, there are regular trains to Strasbourg (1h10, change at Offenburg), where you can easily connect to Eurostar services heading back north, such as Paris and London.

© Richard Fairless / Getty Images. © Hans Blossey / Alamy Stock Photo © Art Kowalsky / Alamy Stock Photo

Scotland's Outer Hebrides

Barra · Berneray · Harris · Lewis
This archipelago of golden beaches backing on to wind-swept lochs and remote villages is connected by ferry, causeway and surprisingly good local bus transport.

Departure points

A flight-free visit to the Western Isles (Na h-Eileanan Siar in Scottish Gaelic) will usually start on the Scottish mainland with a Caledonian Macbrayne (www.calmac.co.uk) ferry from Oban to Castlebay on Barra (4h45) or from Ullapool to Stornoway on Lewis. Oban is three hours by train from Glasgow – a wonderful journey in itself – which is a further four hours from London. Easy Eurostar connections from Paris, Brussels and Amsterdam to London mean you can leave mainland Europe in the morning and be in Barra the following day via a stop in Glasgow or Oban. Note bus services on most islands do not run on Sundays, and most services are reduced in winter. For details and timetables see www.cne-siar.gov.uk/roads-travel-and-parking/public-transport.

❶ Barra

There are good reasons to linger in small but perfectly formed Barra. The island's high point of Heaval offers wonderful views, while one of the best sea-bound activities is taking a boat trip to Kismuil Castle, standing sentinel and giving

The Mangersta sea stacks off the Isle of Lewis

Fact box

Carbon (kg per person) 9
Distance (km) 288
Nights 7+
Transport budget (€) 35

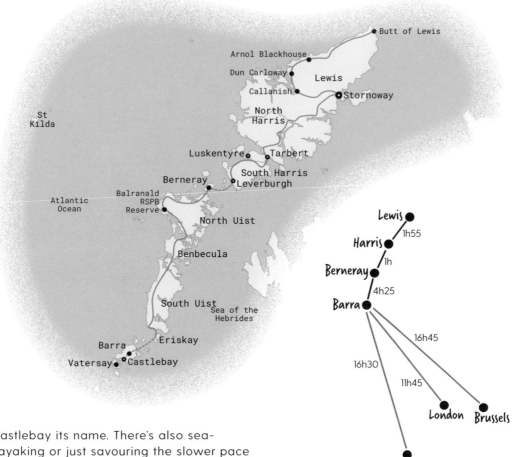

Castlebay its name. There's also sea-kayaking or just savouring the slower pace of island life. The journey on to Berneray involves crossing South Uist, Benbecula and North Uist – each one watery, wild and worth detouring on.

🚌🚢 **In summer, five daily buses (0h20) connect Castlebay with ferry departures to neighbouring Eriskay (0h40, five daily). From there, two twice-daily buses (with a 1h transfer at Balivanich) will get you to Berenay (3h30). The whole trip from Barra to Berneray can be done in a day if you leave Castlebay by 10.25am, otherwise connections become less convenient.**

⏱ Day trip

Vatersay

Vatersay has especially lovely beaches. Bring a picnic and spend the day as a – possibly slightly chilly – castaway on this most pristine slice of Scottish coastline. Or combine a visit here with a whale-shark spotting outing by local launch. These gentle giants can be seen offshore during summer months.

Vatersay is reached by a causeway from Barra. Buses run twice daily (0h30), or bike hire is available in Castlebay.

❷ Berneray

Tiny Berneray, where otters and sea eagles may be seen, makes a good overnighting spot. The Gatliff hostel or small B&Bs offer accommodation.

Three or four ferries run daily from Berneray to Leverburgh on Harris (1h) – check tidal restrictions at www.calmac. co.uk.

❸ Harris

An island of two parts, connected to a third, Harris may be best known for its eponymous tweed woollen products but it is also home to some of Europe's most wonderful beaches and wild mountains. The bus from Leverburgh will provide views of Luskentyre and other bays stretching off towards St Kilda while crossing South Harris. After a change of bus in Tarbert you'll climb into North Harris and through a breathtaking green, highland landscape before descending to Lewis.

Buses to Tarbert (0h45) connect with ferries from Leverburgh (three to four daily). From Tarbert, direct services go to Stornoway (1h) at the same frequency.

❹ Lewis

Lewis' scenery is more like the islands to the south than Harris, with some of the archipelago's must-sees. This ancient landscape is dotted with reminders of the distant past – don't miss Callanish stone circle, Carloway Iron Age broch and the Arnol Blackhouse. The Butt of Lewis, the northern tip of the Hebrides, is one for extremity fans and is also served by buses (1h, eight daily). Stornoway, the largest settlement in the islands, is the last stop in the Hebrides for many visitors and offers a gentle reintroduction from island life to the rest of the world.

Buses serve the west side of the island (Callanish) from Stornoway (two daily). Two daily ferries to Ullapool leave from Stornoway (2h45).

Returning home

Scottish Citylink (www.citylink.co.uk) buses serve Inverness from Ullapool and connect with ferry services. From Inverness trains head south to Edinburgh, Glasgow and London.

A ride along the Rhine

Mainz · Bingen · Koblenz · Bonn · Cologne
Head downstream from Mainz to Cologne to explore one of Europe's great highways by bicycle. Charming villages, castles you can sleep in and fine food and drink await.

Departure points

Frankfurt's transport connections make it the most convenient major city to jump off from. It's only 35 minutes by train to the start of the ride at Mainz. This route can easily be joined coming from Brussels and Amsterdam in the west and Strasbourg or Basel to the south. BYOB (bring your own bike) to be master of your touring destiny. While high-speed ICE trains aren't much help in carrying unboxed bikes, slower regional trains of the sort that make up much of the useful rail traffic along this section of Rhine are better suited to flexible plans.

❶ Mainz

Mainz is where the Rhine meets the Main and is a great place to get into the

swing of what's found in this region – fantastic wine, half-timbered old towns and a relaxed, riverside vibe. Don't expect, therefore, to travel quickly through this wonderful landscape of vineyards, castles and small villages and towns.

🚲 **From Mainz it's easy to get on the EuroVelo 15 bike path along the Rhine. It's 28km to Bingen.**

❷ Bingen

After a stretch of the quintessential Rhine,

Fact box

Carbon (kg per person) 0 if only cycling

Distance (km) 180

Nights 8+

Transport budget (€) 30

© Instamatics / Getty Images. © Dennis Cox / Alamy Stock Photo

Left, Stolzenfels Castle; opposite, vineyards on the River Mosel

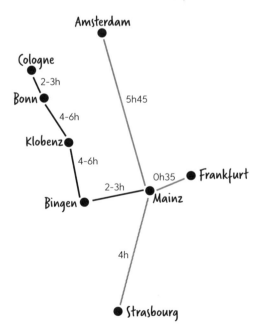

Bingen can seem more of a working town than neighbouring villages that are given over completely to tourism. It still has strong visitor appeal though, with Klopp Castle looming overhead and connections with Hildegard, one of medieval Europe's great visionaries. Pop over the river to Rudesheim from Bingen on the ferry to visit a pretty town on the Rhine's right bank.
🚲 **It's 62km on to Koblenz.**

✛ Pit stop

Boppard
Take a breather en route to Koblenz in beautiful Boppard, one of a succession of gorgeous riverside towns.
🚲 **Boppard is 43km into the ride from Bingen.**

❸ **Koblenz**
On this section you'll pass the Loreley, a rocky outcrop rich in myths and legends. Stately Koblenz is where the Rhine meets the Mosel, marked by a colossal statue. It's a good place to overnight and refuel.
🚌 **After Koblenz you will leave the Unesco-listed Upper Middle Rhine Valley, so if the bike is becoming a drag, put it on one of**

Right, Mainz Christmas market; below, Cologne's cathedral on Domplatte

the regional trains that have been whizzing past you so far (1h30, hourly or better), or ride on to Bonn (63km).

⊕ Day trip

Mosel Cruise

A day spent cruising up the Mosel from Koblenz allows you to explore this quieter and more beautiful tributary.

🕑 Cruises are high-season only and not daily, so book in advance where possible.

❹ Bonn

The laid-back former capital of West Germany is a celebration of its most famous son, the composer Beethoven, with some terrific museums and the nostalgic old government quarter for 20th-century architecture buffs to explore.

🚲🚆 **Ride on through slightly more urban landscapes to Cologne (28km), or take an intercity train (0h20 or 0h30, two per hour).**

Right, Mainz Christmas market; below, Cologne's cathedral on Domplatte

❺ Cologne

Cologne is the perfect full stop to a Rhine tour and a reintroduction to big-city life. You can bid farewell to the Rhine with a ride over it in a trans-river cable car. The beer halls of the Altstadt are the perfect place to toast the completion of your journey. Cologne's Hauptbahnhof (central train station) is adjacent to the city's unmissable cathedral.

Returning home

From Cologne let the train take the strain either back upstream for a northern or easterly destination, or south and west towards Belgium and Paris.

Lake Maggiore to Lake Geneva

Milan · Stresa · Borromean Islands · Brig · Geneva
Take a leisurely train trip between two great lakes of Europe – one Italian, the other Swiss – crossing over the Alps en route.

Departure points

Milan is a major Italian rail hub, with links to many other European cities, particularly in Switzerland, Austria and Germany. International tickets can be booked online through www.sncf.com, www.sbb.ch and www.bahn.de.

❶ Milan

Milan is renowned for its design culture and as the centre of Italy's fashion industry. The city's most famous sight is, of course, Da Vinci's Last Supper, but at the science and technology museum, Museo Nazionale della Scienza e della Tecnologia Leonardo da Vinci, you'll see another side to his genius: it's filled with models of his outlandish inventions. Other halls are devoted to astronomy, aeronautics, printing, acoustics and horology, while outdoor pavilions house steam trains, planes, ships and even a decommissioned submarine.

🚉 **Stresa, on the west bank of Lake Maggiore, is 1h15 from Milan on the Domodossola–Milan train line. Trains run every 30 to 90 minutes.**

Fact box

Carbon (kg per person) 6
Distance (km) 290
Nights 8+
Transport budget (€) 105

Leonardo da Vinci's flying contraption

The Borromean
Islands on Lake
Maggiore

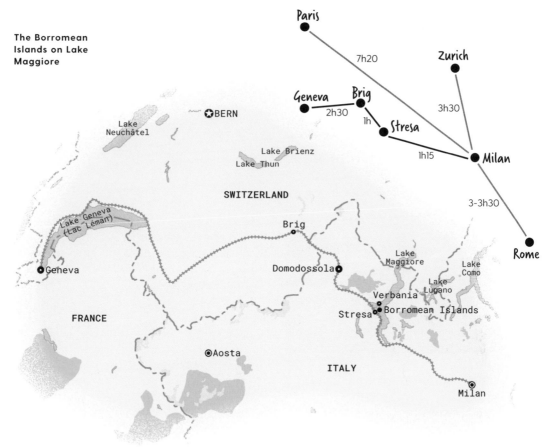

Paris

Zurich

7h20

Geneva · Brig
2h30   1h   3h30
Stresa

BERN
Lake
Neuchâtel

Lake Brienz
Lake Thun

1h15   Milan

SWITZERLAND

Lake Geneva
(Lac Léman)   Brig

3-3h30

Geneva   Domodossola

Lake
Maggiore   Rome

Lake
Como

Lake
Lugano

FRANCE   Verbania
Stresa   Borromean Islands

Aosta

ITALY

Milan

❷ Lake Maggiore & Stresa

Free of Como's overt glamour or Garda's
Disney-esque theme parks, Lake Maggiore
is the most peaceful of northern Italy's
great bodies of water, its shores a little
less crowded and its hinterland intriguingly
wilder. The town of Stresa, with a ringside
view of sunrise, captures the lake's
prevailing air of elegance and bygone
decadence. Meander along its promenade
(the lungolago) and explore the hive of
cobbled streets in its old centre.

🚆 **Catch a local train northwest to
Domodossola (0h30), on the Swiss border,**
from where seven trains daily head to Brig
(0h30).

✈ Day trip

Borromean Islands & Verbania

Maggiore's star attractions are the
Borromean Islands, anchored at the
entrance to the Borromean Gulf (Golfo
Borromeo). The noble Milanese Borromeo
family has owned these islands since the
17th century. Three of the four islands –
Bella, Madre and Superiore (aka Isola
dei Pescatori) – can be visited (tiny San
Giovanni is off limits). The highlight is the

Left, Lake Geneva; right, the Basilica of St Sernin, Toulouse

lavish Palazzo Borromeo on Isola Bella and its ten-tiered terraced gardens.

🚢 **Half-hourly ferries chug from Stresa: day tickets cover all three islands and include a stop in Verbania. For a quick trip, private taxi boats can zip you straight to your island of choice.**

❸ Brig

There's a cross-border feel to Brig, which sits hard against the Swiss-Italian frontier. Traditionally, the main route across the mountains was over the Simplon Pass (2005m): a road was built around 1800, then a 19km railway tunnel, the longest in the world at that time, opened in 1906. The town itself deserves a look: cobbled Stadtplatz is framed by al fresco cafes and candy-hued townhouses. Local merchant Kaspar von Stockalper (1609–91) became rich trading salt over the Simplon Pass, and built the grandiose Stockalper Palace on the proceeds: explore the main court and baroque gardens for free.

🚆 **Brig is on the main train line to Geneva (2h30, hourly).**

❹ Geneva

Overlooking its eponymous alpine lake (Europe's largest), Switzerland's second-largest city is cosmopolitan and cultured. It's split in two by the Rhône: on the *rive gauche* (left bank), the highlight is the picturesque Vieille Ville (Old Town), while the *rive droite* (right bank) holds grungy Pâquis, where neighbourhood bars hum with attitude and energy. This is the Geneva of the 'real' Genevois – or as close as you'll get to it. Don't miss the 140m Jet d'Eau, which sprays seven tonnes of water into the sky, followed by a cruise on the lake with CGN (www.cgn.ch) aboard one of its handsome belle époque steamers.

Returning home

Options include crossing into France by ferry or a zippy TGV to Paris' Gare de Lyon. Alternatively take a train to Zürich for onward connections to Stuttgart, Munich, Innsbruck and Vienna.

Southwest France

Toulouse · Carcassonne · Narbonne · Perpignan

Venture into France's sultry southwestern corner, with stops in the pink city of Toulouse, fairy-tale Carcassonne and Roman Narbonne, linked by the stately Canal du Midi.

Departure points

Toulouse is served by superfast TGVs from Bordeaux (2h10), Montpellier (2h to 2h15) and Marseille (3h40); there are also direct services every two hours to Paris Montparnasse (4h30), plus a daily direct service to Barcelona (3h15).

❶ Toulouse

Named 'La Ville Rose' thanks to the dusky pink stone used in its buildings, Toulouse is an essential southwestern stop. Home to the region's largest university as well as the huge Airbus factory, it's blessed with several Michelin-starred restaurants and a fabulous covered market, Marché Victor Hugo, where you can sample classic southwest dishes like duck confit and *saucisse* (sausage) *de Toulouse*. It's also an excellent place to begin a jaunt down the Canal du Midi.

🚉 **Toulouse's main station, Gare Matabiau, is 1km northeast of the city centre. Trains zip to Carcassonne (1h) a couple of times per hour.**

Fact box

Carbon (kg per person) 4

Distance (km) 200

Nights 9+

Transport budget (€) 50 by train, more if you hire a boat

Vineyards of
Carcassonne

Toulouse — Cité de l'Espace
Garonne
Ariège
Canal du Midi
Bram
Carcassonne
Canal du
Midi
Béziers
Colombiers
Narbonne
FRANCE
Pyrenees
Perpignan

Paris

Geneva

4h30

8h

Toulouse
Carcassonne
Narbonne
1h
0h30
1h
3h15
Perpignan

Barcelona

✈ Day trip

Cité de l'Espace

This space museum presents Toulouse's aeronautical history, with a moon-running simulator, a rotating pod to test your tolerance for space travel, a planetarium and an observatory. The highlights are the full-scale replicas of the Mir space station and a 52m-high Ariane 5 space rocket.
🚌✈ **Catch bus 15 from allée Jean Jaurès to the last stop, from where it's a 500m walk.**

❷ Carcassonne

Perched on a hilltop and bristling with zigzag battlements, stout walls and spiky turrets, the fortified city of Carcassonne looks like something out of a children's storybook when seen from afar. A Unesco World Heritage Site since 1997, it's most people's idea of the perfect medieval castle. Dating back more than two millennia, the fortified town is encircled by two sets of battlements and 52 stone towers, topped by distinctive 'witch's hat' roofs (added by architect Viollet-le-Duc during 19th-century restorations).
🚆 **Trains run to Narbonne hourly (0h30).**

Left, the Canal du Midi; below, laidback life in Perpignan

❸ Narbonne

Two millennia ago, Narbonne was a major Roman city – the capital of the province of Gallia Narbonensis. Exceptional sights include its cathedral and former archbishops' palace, and the town is now a popular stop-off for boaters. The Canal de la Robine runs right through the centre, and connects the Étang de Bages-Sigean with the Canal du Midi.

🚆 **Trains serve Perpignan (1h, about hourly).**

❹ Perpignan

Framed by the Pyrenees, Perpignan radiates out from the tight knot of the old town's warren of alleys, palm-shaded squares and shabby tenements, painted in shades of lemon, peach and tangerine. Historically, Perpignan (Perpinyà in Catalan) was capital of the kingdom of Mallorca: the Mallorcan kings' palace still guards the southern end of the old town.

Returning home

Perpignan is 13km west of the coast and 38km north of the Spanish border. By train, you can be in Barcelona in 1h30, Bordeaux in 2h, or at Paris Gare de Lyon in 5h30.

❂ Day trip

Canal du Midi

The 241km Canal du Midi was constructed under Louis XIV to link the Atlantic to the Mediterranean. Inscribed by Unesco since 1996, it's one of Europe's great waterways. Many companies offer canal cruises from Toulouse and Carcassonne, or you can hire your own boat. Bram is a popular weekend trip from Carcassonne (48km, 9h); Colombiers (95km, 17h) and Agde (126km, 25h) are good for longer trips. If you don't fancy boating, you can still enjoy the canal by cycling along its banks.

🚤🚲 **For boat hire try Locaboat (www. locaboat.com), Minervois Cruisers (www. minervoiscruisers.com) or Les Canalous (www.canalous-canaldumidi.com). Evadeo Cycles (www.evadeocycles.com) rents bikes and runs cycle tours from Carcassonne.**

Minsk mini-break

Minsk · Mir · Nyasvizh · Dudutki · Stalin Line · Minsk

Discover the intriguing capital of Europe's least touristy country and time-travel to medieval castles and open-air folk and WWII museums on easy day trips from Minsk.

Departure points

This itinerary takes advantage of the train connections between the capital of Belarus and nearby European countries as well as the proximity of some heavyweight historic sights to Minsk, making them easily accessible by car or public transport. The journey starts in Minsk, which can be reached by train from other European capitals including Berlin, Warsaw and Vilnius.

❶ Minsk

Still largely undiscovered by tourist crowds, these days Belarus' lively capital makes for an enjoyable short break. Razed to the ground in WWII, the city was rebuilt in bombastic Stalinist Empire style, which is embodied in the architecture of Pr Nezalezhnostsi, Minsk's main thoroughfare. Several worthwhile museums are a must for art and history lovers, including the Russian masters and Soviet social realism at the Belarusian State Art Museum and the moving displays honouring WWII suffering at the Museum of the Great Patriotic War.

In a curious contrast to its Soviet time-warp side, Minsk today is also a city of

Fact box

Carbon (kg per person) 46

Distance (km) 388

Nights 7

Transport budget (€) 85

Minsk's National Library of Belarus

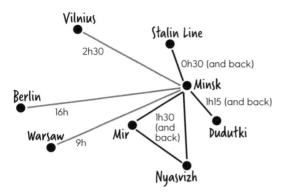

cosmopolitan wine and cocktail bars, heaving craft-beer joints and excellent bistros and food halls. Before saying goodbye to Belarus' capital, spend some time exploring Vul Kastrychnitskaya, the city's flourishing arts district, where giant spray-painted murals vie for attention alongside food trucks, hipster cafes and art galleries such as the cavernous Gallery of Contemporary Art which showcases the best local visual and multimedia artists.

🛏 **Hotel tip: Hotel Manastyrski (https://monastyrski.by/)**

🔄 Day trip

Mir & Nyasvizh Castles

Both under Unesco protection, these two 16th-century castles were once properties of the powerful Radziwills, a Lithuanian noble family. The gorgeous Mir, perfectly reflected in an adjacent pond, has a thoroughly restored interior with period furniture, armour, hunting trophies and other displays on the life of its medieval owners. The enormous castle and park complex of Nyasvizh also boasts refurbished, opulent state rooms and an impressive inner courtyard.

🚗 **The best way to visit Mir and Nyasvizh castles is by car (1h30); they are only 35km** from each other and easily combined into a day trip. Rental cars are widely available: there are Avis and Europcar outlets at the airport and Hotel Minsk.

🔄 Day trip

Dudutki Open-Air Museum

For an enjoyable experience of rural Belarusian life, visit this interactive folk museum, 40km south of Minsk. More than a typical museum, it's a self-sufficient farm where fun activities on offer range from horse riding and sleigh rides to hands-on pottery-making and blacksmithing demonstrations. Foodie

Minsk at dusk beyond the River Svislach

highlights include delicious farm-made sausages, cheese and bread, as well as fresh *salo* (cured pork fat), honey-dipped pickles and homemade *samahon* (moonshine). For souvenirs to take home, choose from wool and leather goods crafted at the farm.

🚌 **Catch bus 323 from Minsk's Central Bus Station to Dudutki (1h15). Departures are at 9.45am and 12.55pm, with two afternoon buses back to Minsk departing at 2.20pm and 5.40pm.**

🧭 Day trip

Stalin Line Museum

This fascinating collection of Soviet war paraphernalia – including tanks, missiles and helicopters – scattered in an open field about 25km northwest of Minsk is a must for military buffs. You can also explore the site's original bunkers, now restored, which formed part of a defence line that stretched through the steppe for more than 1000km along the Soviet Union's western border. The grounds include a movie set and you can even take a ride in a Soviet tank.

🚐 **Take the Maladzechna-bound marshrutka (minivan) 700-TK from the Druzhnaya stop behind Minsk's train station (0h30). There are frequent services to and from the capital throughout the day.**

Returning home

From Minsk, trains run west and north to Berlin, Warsaw or Vilnius. Alternatively, Ecolines (www.ecolines.net) has international bus services to Kyiv, Lviv and Rīga.

Rails to Europe's roof

Basel · Bern · Lauterbrunnen · Wengen · Kleine Scheidegg · Jungfraujoch · Grindelwald

Discover the wonders of Switzerland's high mountains, including an impressive feat of railway engineering – all that's needed is a rail pass and a pair of hiking boots.

Departure points

Basel is one of Europe's crossroads. Served by regular and very popular TGVs from Paris, its main station (Basel SBB) has platforms in Swiss and French territory. From the French platforms regional trains arrive from and depart for Strasbourg. Some regional German services terminate at Basel Badischer, a tram ride from the main Swiss railways-operated station, but long-distance services continue through. From Milan and points to the south, trains may pass through Bern en route to Basel making the first stop optional.

❶ Basel

Fine art and modern architecture vie for attention alongside Basel's picture-perfect medieval Old Town and Switzerland's largest Roman remains. Venture outside

The Jungfrau Railway

Fact box

Carbon (kg per person) 6

Distance (km) 312

Nights 4-6

Transport budget (€) 392 (4 day Swiss Travel System Pass (€257) plus Good Morning Jungfraujoch ticket (€135)

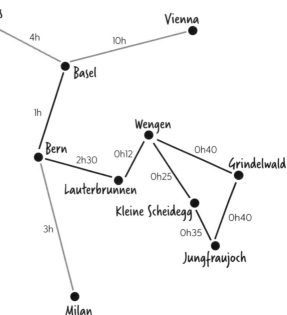

the historic core to stroll the Fondation Beyeler, a fine gallery in a Renzo Piano–designed building. Don't miss a ride on the city's (emissions-free) passenger ferries, which use the fast flow of the water and the skills of river pilots to cross the Rhine. **It takes under an hour by train from Basel to Bern with at least one direct train an hour.**

❷ Bern

Switzerland's clean, green capital is compact enough to be explored on foot, with a funicular heading down to the Aare riverside. In summer find a sunbathing spot on the grass at the Marzili swimming complex and join the locals strolling upstream in their bathers to enjoy a high-speed float back down again. From the benches of Europapromenade there is a fabulous

panorama of your next destination, the high peaks of the Berner Oberland.

🚋 **Take the train from Bern to Interlaken Ost (2h, half-hourly), changing here for the narrow-gauge rack railway to Lauterbrunnen (0h30, also half-hourly from 6am to 10pm).**

❸ Lauterbrunnen

One of the Europe's most spectacular valleys, Lauterbrunnen is home to cascading waterfalls and a good place to spot paragliders and base-jumpers. The village of Lauterbrunnen also offers the best coffee fix for miles around at Airtime Cafe. A busy bus – or gorgeous and much quieter walk – takes you to the pounding water of the Trümmelbach Falls.

🚋 **Services run to Wengen every half-hour from Lauterbrunnen and take 12 minutes.**

❹ Wengen

This beautiful car-free village makes a great place to overnight.

✪ Day trip

Jungfraujoch

From Wengen, you can make a round trip by cog railway to the top of the Jungfrau Railway. Be sure to stop off at the beautiful mountain pass of Kleine Scheidegg (25 minutes from Wengen, two trains per hour). Build in some time to hike around here for views of the jaw-dropping high Alpine scenery. From here you will join the Jungfrau Railway – a true once-in-a-lifetime journey with a price to match. Reaching 3500m, this engineering miracle travels as high as a train can take you in Europe and offers utterly spectacular views of

The glacial Lauterbrunnen valley

giant peaks like the Mönch, Jungfrau and Eiger. At the Jungfraujoch stop you can visit the Top of Europe complex, with an observation deck, restaurants and access to high Alpine hiking.

When you do come back down to earth, toast a busy day with an Aperol-with-a-view in the village of Grindelwald (30 mins from Kleine Scheidegg) before heading back to Wengen via a change of trains at Zweilutschinen.

🚋 **The Jungfrau Railway operates from 8am till mid-afternoon, every day, all year round. Cheapest tickets are for early morning services. See www.jungfrau.ch for more information.**

✪ Day trip

Murren

From Wengen you can take the Allmendhubel cable car and then a train to tiny Murren, perched on the edge of the Lauterbrunnen valley. The even smaller village of Gimmelwald is a cable car ride or hike away.

🚋 **Murren is 20 minutes from Lauterbrunnen by cable car and narrow-gauge railway, with services departing half-hourly.**

Returning home

Reverse your outbound journey to well-connected Basel to head north and west, or continue on to Zürich to head for Austria and further into central Europe. There are myriad train connections for southern Europe too – see www.sbb.ch for tickets and advice.

In Flanders' fields

Paris · Brussels · Lille
This itinerary takes in the French and Belgian capitals and underrated Lille, paying homage at the Somme battlefields along the way.

Departure points

Paris is linked by high-speed train to Spain, Italy, Germany, Belgium and the Netherlands, plus the UK via the Eurostar.

❶ Paris

There are myriad ways to experience the City of Light. Alongside big-ticket attractions like the Eiffel Tower, the Louvre and the Musée d'Orsay, make time for more leisurely pursuits: wandering the banks of the Canal St-Martin, exploring the wooded paths of the Bois de Boulogne or browsing for bargains at the sprawling Marché aux Puces St-Ouen.

Ⓜ Metro is the quickest way around Paris; RATP (www.ratp.fr) tickets are valid on RER trains, buses, trams and the Montmartre funicular. The Vélib' bike-hire network (www.velib-metropole.fr) has docking stations across the city.

🚆 Super-fast Eurostar and Thalys trains run direct to Brussels (1h20, www.oui.sncf).
Hotel Tip: The wood-clad Eden Lodge (www.edenlodgeparis.net) offers LED lighting, purified air and zero-carbon heating.

Brussels' Grand Place

Fact box

Carbon (kg per person) 13
Distance (km) 657
Nights 5+
Transport budget (€) 160

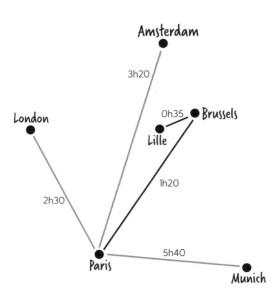

❷ Brussels

Home of the European Union, Brussels is often eclipsed by Europe's glitzier capitals, and that's a shame: it's sprinkled with fabulous medieval and art nouveau buildings, has a wealth of art museums and serves arguably the best frites anywhere on the planet. Begin on the stately Grand Place, and don't miss the old masters on show at the Musées Royaux des Beaux-Arts, with canvases by Rubens, Brueghel, Rembrandt and Magritte.

🚌Ⓜ **Brussels' integrated bus-tram-metro system is operated by STIB/MIVB (www. stib-mivb.be).**

🚆 **TGV trains whizz to Lille at least 12 times a day (0h35, www.oui.sncf).**

✪ Day trip

Planetuin Meise

Belgium's 93-hectare national botanic garden is located in Meise, 12km north of Brussels. Home to 18,000 plant species, the park's most prized orchids, carnivorous plants and giant Amazonian water lilies are housed in the Plantenpaleis (Plant Palace), a series of 13 connecting greenhouses. From May to September, a free tourist 'train' loops the expansive gardens.

🚌 **DeLijn buses 250/251 run every 15 minutes from Bruxelles-Nord (0h35) via Bockstael metro station (0h20).**

🏨 **Hotel tip: Hotel Agora (www.hotelagora. be) is a great green choice, with rainwater toilets and solar heating.**

❸ Lille

Capital of the Hauts-de-France region, Lille may be the country's most underrated metropolis. Once an industrial centre, it's now been transformed into a cultural and commercial hub. The highlight is its enchanting old town, replete with magnificent French and Flemish architecture. For dinner, head for a traditional *estaminet*, which serves Flemish specialities like *carbonade flamande* (braised beef slow-cooked with beer, onions, brown sugar and gingerbread) and *potjevleesch* (cold jellied chicken, pork, veal and rabbit). Lille is also a bastion of beer brewing; local brews are served at cafes and bars all over town.

⊕ Day trip

Somme Battlefields

The Battle of the Somme has become symbolic of the slaughter of WWI, and its killing fields are now sites of pilgrimage. Tourist offices (including in Amiens, Arras, Albert and Péronne) can book organised tours of the key battlefield sites and memorials. Alternatively, you could hire a bike from the Albert Tourist Office (€8/12 per half/full day, www.tourisme-paysducoquelicot.com).

The Somme's cemetery; below, Parisian parks; right, the Pont des Arts, Paris

🚆 **Frequent trains run from Lille-Flandres to Amiens (1h30, six to 12 daily) from where there are onward connections to most of the area's towns, including Arras (0h45, five to 10 daily) and Albert (0h25, up to two per hour).**

Returning home

By TGV, it's just an hour from Lille back to Paris, but get the right station: half the TGVs use Gare Lille-Europe, the other half Gare Lille-Flandres (also the terminus for regional trains). You can catch a fast train from Paris to pretty much every capital in Europe.

© River Thompson / Lonely Planet. © Jon Nicholls Photography / Shutterstock. © Adrienne Pitts / Lonely Planet

Danish design

Copenhagen · Aarhus · Billund · Copenhagen
Discover the highlights of Danish art and design on this easy tour of Denmark, from the Louisiana Museum of Modern Art to the LEGO® House.

Departure points

From Sweden, take a train from Stockholm via Malmö to Copenhagen (from about 5h). From Germany, there's a frequent direct service from Hamburg, including overnight trains (taking about 7h). And from Paris (or London) travellers will need to overnight in Brussels and take an early train to Copenhagen, changing at Cologne and Hamburg, a 12h trip.

❶ Copenhagen

Denmark's capital is regularly rated as one of the most 'liveable' and sustainable cities in the world. Shoals of cyclists flow through the streets, the waterways are clean enough to swim in and post-industrial neighbourhoods are filled with intriguing spaces to explore: cutting-edge restaurants and cafes, craft breweries, galleries and one-off shops. Spend a couple of days meandering around the city, perhaps using the white, battery-powered cycles of the Bycyklen bike share network. The Ørestad district has abundant examples of contemporary architecture. Also check out Copenhagen's opera house, library, theatre and dry-ski slope, Copenhill, on

Fact box

Carbon (kg per person) 16
Distance (km) 800
Nights 8
Transport budget (€) 340

Copenhagen's Nyhavn (new harbour)

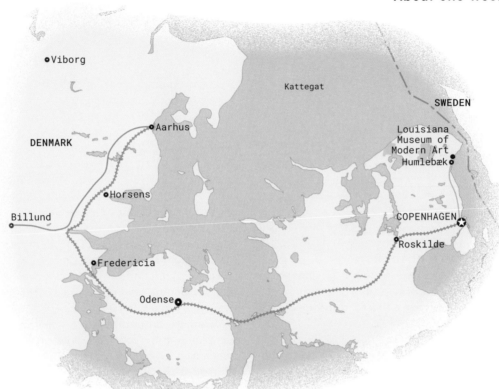

top of a waste-to-energy plant (yes, really) that opened in 2019.

🚆 **From Copenhagen it takes about 3h to reach Aarhus by train, with more than 30 departures daily (www.dsb.dk).**

🕑 **Day trip**

Louisiana Museum of Modern Art
Pedalling along the coast north of Copenhagen, with the sea breeze in your hair (few Danish cyclists wear helmets), it's hard to believe you're on your way to Denmark's most invigorating art gallery. Louisiana Museum of Modern Art is a simple, white building containing intriguing contemporary art installations (a recent exhibition was of Yayoi Kusama's work).

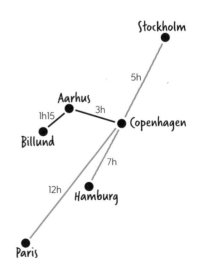

Copenhagen's Royal Danish Playhouse, designed by Danes

a bus ride out of town, is a similarly exciting experience, documenting human history in a modern, partly subterranean building constructed with 5000 tonnes of concrete. An outdoor walk can take in a beach, Stone Age burial sites and restored prehistoric houses. Continuing the architectural tour, don't miss the Isberget (Iceberg) apartment complex in the former docklands. Two or three days in Aarhus allows visitors to eat anything from street food to New Nordic cuisine in fashionable Frederiksbjerg.

⊖ From Aarhus, the most time-efficient way to reach Billund is by hiring a hybrid vehicle from any of the major car-rental companies in the city. They'll come with a full charge, which will get you the 100km to Billund (1h15).

The sculpture garden extends down to the narrow Kattegat (or Cat's Throat), the stretch of water before Sweden.

⊛⊛⊕ Your destination is Humlebœk and it's an easy (flat) pedal of about 35km on cycle paths and thanks to Denmark's joined-up transport policies you can take the train there or back with your bike (depending on the wind direction for the day). There are departures every 20 minutes, taking about 30 minutes.

❷ Aarhus

Denmark's second city rivals the capital for bold contemporary art and design. Check out the ARoS Aarhus art museum and its rainbow-coloured circle of windows on the roof offering panoramic views of the city. The Moesgaard Museum,

❸ Billund

The first buildings that any wannabe architect designed were often constructed from Denmark's most famous national product: LEGO® bricks. In 2017 the 12,000 sq metre LEGO® House opened, delighting families and budding designers. More than 25 million blocks were used and the result is a playful and utterly engaging experience, whatever your age. And you can recharge the EV in the car park while you indulge your creative impulses inside. Elsewhere in Billund, the LEGOLAND® resort awaits but that merits an overnight stay in the city. Start with the house first, and families can add the resort.

⊕ Return the recharged EV to Aarhus and take the direct train back to Copenhagen (3h, more than 30 departures daily).

Sea-kayaking Scotland

London · Fort William · Arisaig · Fort William · London
Learn new skills, gain confidence and fill your lungs with fresh air on an adventure-packed trip to Britain's 'outdoors capital', Fort William.

Departure points
If you can get to London, then Fort William is just an overnight train ride away on the Caledonian Sleeper. Paris, Amsterdam and Brussels are all just a couple of hours from London via high-speed Eurostar trains. Fort William can also be reached from other British cities, such as Manchester, Newcastle and Birmingham, typically with a change or two of trains, often in Glasgow or Edinburgh – but bear in mind that journey times can be slow (8h plus) so it may be more time efficient to take the sleeper from London anyway.

❶ London
If you're travelling from mainland Europe, the British capital is your staging post: you've got all day to get there in readiness for your evening departure. Whet your appetite for adventure with a guided climb across the roof of the O2's dome with Up at the O2. Then practise your paddling skills with a kayaking trip on the River Thames.

🚆 **The Caledonian Sleeper train departs just after 9pm from London Euston six days per week, arriving at 10am the following day (www.sleeper.scot).**

Fact box
Carbon (kg per person) 24.5
Distance (km) 880
Nights 6
Transport budget (€) 180

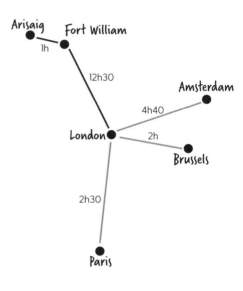

centre has mountain bikes for hire and some of the signposted trails are suitable for beginners – others are assuredly for experts only and what goes up on the mountain gondola must come down somehow.

If you're planning on biking, you may prefer to bring your own kit (though helmets are included in rentals). Take note of the return bus times – taking a taxi back is an option.

🚌🚂 **Take the Mallaig bus from Fort William (route number 500, www.shielbuses.co.uk), which stops at Arisaig after an hour's drive east along Loch Eil to the sea. There are five to six services on weekdays but only one at weekends and not at a useful time. There's also a direct train service that takes a few minutes more (four departures daily).**

❷ Fort William

Britain's adventure capital has the country's tallest mountain, a World Cup mountain-biking venue and refreshing lochs and beaches on its doorstep. All of these can be sampled by bike, kayak and boot over a few days. For the biking, head to Nevis Range, 11km from Fort William on the Shiel bus (route number 41). The trail

Left, Glenfinnan Valley; below, Arisaig sea kayaking; previous page, Ben Nevis

⟳ Day trip

Ben Nevis

Scotland's highest peak has a broad-shouldered bulk to it. The 1345m mountain is no giant by European standards but, depending on the route and the ever-changeable weather, it remains a challenge, whether you're walking up the Mountain Track or scrambling up via the steep and exposed Carn Mor Dearg Arête ridge. The former can take 7 to 9h and begins from the Glen Nevis visitor centre car park, 3km from Fort William's centre.

🚌 **An infrequent daily bus service (route number N42, operating May to October) runs from the centre of Fort William to Glen Nevis but the first service may not get you to the trailhead early enough (or back late enough). Check timings and be prepared to walk for 30 minutes to or from town.**

❸ Arisaig

There are white sandy beaches and turquoise waters but as a glance at a thermometer reveals, this is no tropical bay. Scotland's west coast has been shaped by the retreat of glaciers over the last three million years, leaving a rocky, endlessly indented outline that is perfect for exploring by sea kayak. Arisaig is one of Britain's top sea-kayaking destinations and local operator Arisaig Sea Kayak Centre caters for first-timers and beginners or more advanced paddlers (French and German is spoken). Depending on your experience and the weather, you might head out onto Loch Ailort or Loch Moidart, both formed during the last Ice Age, or paddle along the west discovering 'skerries', beach-fringed islands. Possible wildlife spots include seals, otters and eagles.

🚌 **Catch the bus or train back to Fort William.**

Returning home

From Fort William take the Caledonian Sleeper back to London, departing in the evening and taking 12h.

Oxford and Bath

London · Oxford · Bath · London
Three beautiful cities, London, Oxford and Bath, are launchpads for this literary tour of southern England; be inspired by some of Britain's best writers in these places.

Departure points
The most efficient way of arriving at the start of this itinerary will be by train to London. Amsterdam, Brussels and Paris have high-speed connections to the British capital with Eurostar and those three mainland cities are the best hubs for travellers from the north, east or south.

❶ London
From Charles Dickens to George Orwell, London has been the setting and inspiration for many of Britain's greatest writers. In fact, there's such a wealth of literary talent at work here that you can pick and choose your preferred genre to explore, whether that's detective tales at 221B Baker Street or Romantic poetry

Fact box
Carbon (kg per person) 8
Distance (km) 450
Nights 7
Transport budget (€) 52

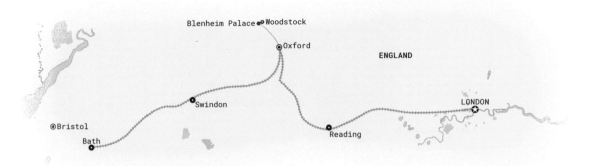

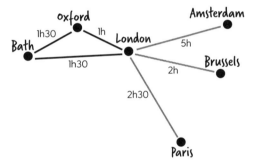

at John Keats' house in Hampstead. Two or three days is barely sufficient if you're also visiting London's museums but try to get to some of the fascinating sites in the capital's suburbs: William Morris' enthralling Arts and Crafts home, Red House, in southeast London is a 15-minute walk from Bexleyheath train station and on numerous bus routes. In the north, Hampstead's literary hangouts are similarly absorbing.

🚆 **There are more than 130 departures daily for Oxford from London's Paddington and Marylebone stations combined. Direct journeys take about an hour. Book tickets in advance for off-peak savings.**

❷ Oxford

Arriving by train at Oxford's central station leads to just a brief 10-minute walk into the heart of Britain's most famous university city. The college quads (there are around 30 university colleges), vast bookshops and hushed libraries are to be expected, but the city is also home to some of Britain's best pubs – allow for

at least two days to do justice to all of this. A shortlist of colleges to visit should include Christ Church, Queen's (opposite the Bodleian Library), Exeter (JRR Tolkien was an undergraduate) and Magdalen (where CS Lewis taught). The two authors would meet at the Eagle and Child pub on St Giles'. A short stroll in Jericho, the neighbourhood behind this pub, reveals plenty more pubs to try, including the Old Bookbinders.

🚆 **Trains to Bath depart Oxford regularly (1h30, about 50 per day) via Didcot Parkway.**

Previous page, Trinity College, Oxford; below, Blenheim Palace; right, Bath's Roman spa; opposite, Christ Church, Oxford

✈ Day trip

Blenheim Palace

Take a break from the books and hop on a bus to Blenheim Palace near the town of Woodstock, north of Oxford. It's the stately home of the Dukes of Marlborough and the birthplace of Sir Winston Churchill. The grounds and gardens – designed by Lancelot 'Capability' Brown – are gradually being restored and provide a beautiful backdrop to the palace.

🚌 **The S3 or number 7 buses from Oxford's Gloucester Green bus station (more than 50 departures daily) will take you to Blenheim's gates. The 500 bus service from Oxford Parkway also stops at Blenheim. Journeys take about 40 minutes.**

❸ Bath

Bath brings together the best characteristics of Britain's 18th-century Georgian period: its symmetrical, classically influenced architecture, the affluence of the Industrial Revolution and the social and artistic whirl of the Regency (from 1811, when King George III was deemed too mad to rule and the Prince Regent took the reins). A stroll along the glorious limestone arc of the Royal Crescent puts you in Jane Austen's world. For five years she lived in Bath, initially on Gay St, and her characters peopled the city, whether taking afternoon tea at the Pump Room or browsing the shops of Milsom St. In Austen's time, taking the waters of Bath Spa was regarded as a cure-all, as it has been since the Romans recuperated here. Relax at Thermae Bath Spa with a good book.

🚆 **Head back to London's Paddington station on a direct service from Bath; there are departures every 30 minutes, taking at least 1h30.**

Returning home

From London take the most convenient train service onward.

Zürich's Planet Trail

Paris · Dijon · Zürich
Stock up on great wine in Dijon before exploring the solar system on a short trip to Zürich.

Departure points
This itinerary follows the route of the TGV-Lyria line from Paris to Zürich. You can reach Paris from numerous European capitals including London (2h30), Amsterdam (3h30) and Berlin (8h15).

❶ Paris
The French capital is famous for its food and art scenes. But this trip is all about wine and the wonders of space so prepare with a visit to the science museum Palais de la Découverte and its planetarium on Ave Franklin Delano Roosevelt (8th arrondissement) before hitting happy hour at a wine bar like Le Baron Rouge in the 12th arrondissement for some rillettes and red wine research.

Fact box
Carbon (kg per person) 14.5
Distance (km) 650
Nights 7
Transport budget (€) 80

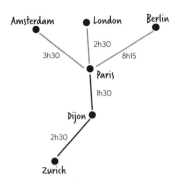

the region's wine, for example at L'Age de Raisin (extra points for the pun).

🚆 **Three daily direct trains depart Dijon-Ville for Zürich with the TGV-Lyria taking 2h30. But there are also other services with one or two changes taking up to 4h.**

⊕ Day trip

Route des Grands Crus

Although Dijon is not short of fantastic places to taste what Burgundy's winemakers can conjure from the pinot noir grape, there's no substitute for exploring vineyards to understand the lie of the land. From Marsannay-la-Côte, just 8km south of the city centre, the Route des Grands Crus heads south through such famed villages as Nuits-Saint-Georges in the Côte des Nuits then the Côte de Beaune. To be carbon-neutral (and allow yourself a little flexibility on the wine-tasting) it's straightforward to rent bicycles (including e-bikes) in Dijon and pedal through the backroads of Burgundy. Several operators offer guided and supported tours or construct your own itinerary. It's about 40km to Beaune

🚆 **Head out of the City of Light on an early train from Gare de Lyon to Dijon-Ville (15 departures daily on a TGV).**

❷ Dijon

The elegant 17th- and 18th-century architecture of Burgundy's capital indicates the wealth of this city. Much of Dijon's affluence was marshalled by Burgundy's powerful dukes, and some of the art and relics from their centuries-long reign are displayed in the Palais des Ducs and the Musée des Beaux-Arts. But you don't have to be aristocratic to have a great time in Dijon: the city is blessed with some brilliant places to eat and drink

Previous page, Paris; below, swimming in the River Limmat; right, cycling the Côte de Beaune; opposite, Zürich

but you will likely want to stay overnight along the way or focus just on the northern section.

3 Zürich

Switzerland's largest city sits at the junction of the River Limmat and Lake Zürich and consequently Zürich is noted for its welcoming green and watery spaces. In the summer there are few better places to hang out than on one of the beaches around the lake or at such swimming spots as Flussbad Au-Höngg on the River Limmat before an *apero* as the sun goes down. Many bathing pavilions, including Seebad Utoquai and Seebad Enge serve drinks into the night. And the Swiss mountains are easily reached by train for hiking: families can try the Walensee waterfalls (1h by train) or the Zwerg-Bartli-Erlebnisweg themed trail in Braunwalk (1h30 by train).

Day trip

The Planet Trail

From the Zürich train station of Uetliberg to the local station of Felsenegg, the Planet Trail spans 6km and the expanse

of our solar system with one metre representing one million kilometres and models of our solar system's eight planets from giant Jupiter to the dwarf Pluto spaced at accurate intervals along the easy-going, surfaced trail suitable for all ages and abilities.

Trains on the S10 line depart Zürich's central station for Uetliberg every 0h30 and take 0h30. To return from the cable-car mountain station at Felsenegg, take the cable car down Adliswil and the direct S4 train back to Zürich (similar frequency and duration).

Returning home

You can return to Paris on the TGV-Lyria by the same route or continue home from Zürich if that's closer.

TWO WEEKS OR MORE

Belgrade to Bar adventure

Belgrade · Užice · Tara National Park · Bar · Virpazar · Lake Skadar National Park
Take a spectacular train journey across the Balkans from Belgrade to the Adriatic for hiking and kayaking adventures in Serbia and Montenegro's scenic national parks.

Departure Points

This itinerary takes advantage of the Belgrade–Bar railway line, which runs both daytime and overnight services and directly links the Serbian capital with Montenegro's Adriatic coast. Belgrade can be reached by bus from Western European cities including Budapest, Vienna and Trieste. Trains also run from many cities, including Venice, but they often take longer.

❶ Belgrade

Spend a day in the Serbian capital before embarking on the morning Bar-bound train. Ramble around the ancient Kalemegdan citadel, time-travel to Belgrade's heyday at the fascinating Museum of Yugoslavia, sample the intriguing New Balkan cuisine and hit the city's ultra-cool nightspots in Dorćol or Savamala neighbourhoods.

🚆 **The daytime train leaves Belgrade's Topčider Station every day at 9am, arriving in Bar at 8pm; you can buy a ticket as far as Užice (3h30). For up-to-date info, check the Serbian Railways website (www.srbvoz.rs/eng).**

Lake Skadar in Montenegro

Fact box

Carbon (kg per person) 26
Distance (km) 774
Nights 11
Transport budget (€) 60

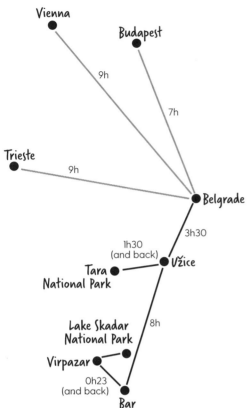

❷ Užice

This historic western Serbian town is located 49km from Tara National Park. Eco Hostel Republik's enthusiastic guides offer a host of adventures and day tours (from €30) around Tara's great outdoors, so you can conveniently base yourself in Užice for a few days. Don't miss the twists and turns of the wonderful heritage railway, stationed in Mokra Gora on Tara's outskirts and chugging through 22 tunnels and stupendous mountain scenery.

🚌 **At least 10 buses throughout the day connect Užice with Bajina Bašta, the gateway to Tara National Park (1h30). It's easy to get around the national park from**

Left, the banks of the Sava river in Belgrade; below, houseboats on Perućac lake; opposite, pelicans on Lake Skadar

Bajina Bašta by local buses or taxis.
🛏 Hotel tip: Eco Hostel Republik (www. republik.rs)

❸ Tara National Park

With forested slopes and emerald waterways, Tara – the westernmost point of the Dinaric Alps – is scenic Serbia at its best. Explore some of its 25 hiking trails (many of which are shared with mountain bikers) for fantastic views from Banjska Stena and Crnjeskovo lookouts. The Drina river canyon offers exhilarating yet not too challenging rafting, while two lakes, Perućac and Zaovine, are ideal for calm-water kayaking. The visitor centres can help organise any outdoor activities; there's a handful of hotels and traditional restaurants within the park.
🚌🚍 If not staying in Užice, catch a bus

back to town on your last morning to continue the train journey to Bar (8h): the daily train from Belgrade to Bar stops in Užice in the middle of the day.

❹ Bar

There's no reason to hang around Montenegro's shabby port apart from the gloriously dilapidated Stari Bar (Old Bar), the town's predecessor that was probably founded by the Illyrians in 800 BC and today lies in ruins amid olive groves at the foot of Mt Rumija. It's only 4km northeast of Bar; catch a taxi or one of hourly local buses from the town centre to explore the enigmatic site.
🚆 Several trains make the short journey to/from Virpazar, the gateway to Lake Skadar National Park, every day (0h23).

❺ Virpazar

The tiny village was once a strategically important trading town, connected to Bar by Montenegro's first narrow-gauge railway. If you're interested in sampling local wines, you'll find family-run vineyards and tasting cellars in the surrounding hills. The region is sprinkled

© Issy Crocker / Lonely Planet. © Alberto Loyo / Shutterstock

with tavernas dishing up hearty fish-based soups and meals.

🚲😋 **Get around Virpazar and the park along walking paths and biking trails (bike rental €10 per day). Small boats are easy to find in summer (€25 per hour).**

🏨 **Hotel tip: Plavnica Eco Resort (www.plavnica.me)**

❻ Lake Skadar National Park

Dolphin-shaped Skadar, shared between Montenegro and Albania, is the Balkans' largest lake and one of Europe's top bird habitats. The blissfully pretty area encompasses steep mountains, island monasteries, timeless villages and floating meadows of water lilies.

Undiscovered Montenegro (www.undiscoveredmontenegro.com) is an excellent agency specialising in lake-based itineraries including kayaking, guided hikes and wine/gastronomy tours; horse riding and birdwatching can also be arranged. Accommodation is also available in its lovely stone cottage near Virpazar.

🚆 **Hop on a train back to Bar before the evening.**

Returning home

From Bar, take the overnight train back to Belgrade (11h, leaving at 7pm and arriving at 6am), to connect with buses north and west to Hungary, Austria and Italy.

A Icelandic saga by sea

Hirtshals · Tórshavn · Seydisfjördur · Egilsstadir · Borgarfjördur Eystri

Follow in the wake of Viking adventurers on an epic voyage that goes from Denmark to Iceland, taking in puffins, waterfalls, remote islands and mythical beasts.

Departure points

Hirtshals is accessible by from Copenhagen (7h) with DSB train services, or from Hamburg Hauptbahnhof (9h) with Deutsche Bahn. It's also five hours from Gothenburg via the Frederikshavn ferry.

❶ Hirtshals

Hirtshals sits near the tip of Northern Jutland, a region famous for its soft light and seafood. This Danish port is the only place in mainland Europe to offer ferries to the Faroe Islands and Iceland. Unsurprisingly its appeal is tied to the sea, with a white-sand beach, great seafood including clam chowder, and the impressive Nordsøen Oceanarium, where the hypnotically vast main tank holds oceanic sunfish, dogfish and turbot.

🐟 **The MS Norröna ferry has one crossing a week (36h; two a week June–Aug) to Tórshavn, the Faroe Islands' capital. Cabins and couchettes are available (www. smyrilline.com).**

❷ Tórshavn

The ferry journey to Tórshavn alone is impressive (and the boat has stabilisers to make the journey as comfy as possible). Look out for the Shetland Islands, oil rigs, bird life and whales en route. Approaching the Faroe Islands, you'll see glorious green

Fact box

Carbon (kg per person) 211
Distance (km) 1900
Nights 14+
Transport budget (€) 500

The boat harbour in Tórshavn

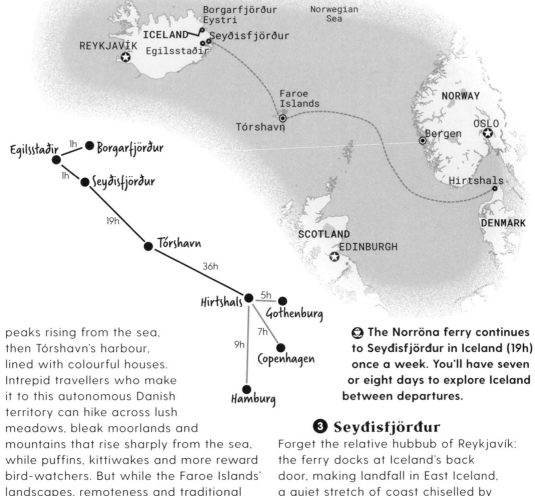

peaks rising from the sea, then Tórshavn's harbour, lined with colourful houses. Intrepid travellers who make it to this autonomous Danish territory can hike across lush meadows, bleak moorlands and mountains that rise sharply from the sea, while puffins, kittiwakes and more reward bird-watchers. But while the Faroe Islands' landscapes, remoteness and traditional music scene give it a richly mythical feel, this is modern Europe, with good transport and comfortable accommodation. Depending on the Norröna's schedule, you can spend anything from a few hours to a long stay on the Faroes – overnighting in Tórshavn will help you get under the salt-lashed skin of this unique place.

🜨 **The Norröna ferry continues to Seyðisfjörður in Iceland (19h) once a week. You'll have seven or eight days to explore Iceland between departures.**

❸ Seyðisfjörður

Forget the relative hubbub of Reykjavík: the ferry docks at Iceland's back door, making landfall in East Iceland, a quiet stretch of coast chiselled by fjords. Seyðisfjörður is the region's most compelling town, its multicoloured houses set against mountains and waterfalls. Several of its lovely timber buildings are home to craft workshops, there's an iconic pastel Blue Church, and it's a popular spot for musicians and artists. Several hikes run straight from town to waterfalls, a 'dwarf

Left, the church at Borgarfjördur Eystri; below, a farm cabin at Borgarfjördur Eystri; right, eastern Iceland's mountainous landscape

tour companies offer activities, including hiking and angling.

🚌 **One bus a day runs to Borgarfjördur Eystri (1h) on weekdays (www.austurfrett. is/svaust).**

⑤ Borgarfjörður Eystri

The coastal village of Borgarfjördur Eystri is a peaceful base for excursions to puffin-packed cliffs (the birds are usually home between April and August). There's also the Musterid spa, the Álfaborg rock (allegedly home to the queen of the elves) and numerous walks. But while you can keep yourself busy with activities, don't forget to stop: half the fun of this entrancing nation comes when you just listen to the sea, gaze at the horizon and let the shifting light wash over you.

Returning home

Travelling back from Borgarfjördur Eystri to Egilsstadir: you should have time to make the connecting bus on the same day, but timings do vary seasonally so check timetables. That aside, you'll be retracing your tracks, heading back to Denmark via the Faroes.

church', sound sculptures and a frozen mountain lake, and there's a ski area too.

🚌 **Buses run to Egilsstadir one to three times daily (1h); no Sunday services in winter.**

④ Egilsstaðir

The road journey to the regional hub of Egilsstadir takes you inland, past waterfalls and through a high pass, with the chance of seeing reindeer. After this lovely taste of the country's charms, functional Egilsstadir can feel underwhelming at first. But there's plenty of appeal on its doorstep, including a lake allegedly inhabited by a giant worm and Iceland's biggest forest (though it's all relative – the Vikings chopped most of the country's trees down). Some excellent restaurants and the Lake Hotel spa make it a good place to kick back, and numerous

The French Riviera

Barcelona · Montpellier · Marseille · Nice · Monaco
Cruise the Mediterranean coast via the fabled Côte d'Azur, with side-trips to Cannes and Monaco en route.

Departure points

Barcelona has fast train links to Paris and Madrid, plus ferry routes around the Mediterranean. If you don't mind missing the Spanish leg, Montpellier is connected to Paris Gare de Lyon in just three hours; you can easily pick up the rail line along the Riviera from there.

❶ Barcelona

Spain's sexiest city kicks this trip off in style. Celebrated for its Modernista architecture and its wildly overdue cathedral, the Sagrada Família (dreamt up by visionary architect Antoni Gaudí), it's a city that begs to be explored on foot (don't miss hilltop Parc Güell) or by bike (the seafront makes for fine cycling).

Fact box

Carbon (kg per person) 14
Distance (km) 690
Nights 10+
Transport budget (€) 160

🚆 Barcelona to Montpellier (3h, four to six daily) is a joint Renfe/SNCF train service, but you can buy tickets easily online from Oui SNCF (www.oui.sncf).
🛏 Hotel tip: Hostal Grau (www.hostalgrau.com) scores high for sustainability.

❷ Montpellier

Graceful and easy-going, Montpellier is characterised by grand *hôtels particuliers* (private mansions), stately boulevards and shady backstreets, and has some gorgeous beaches on its doorstep. It's

La Rambla in Barcelona

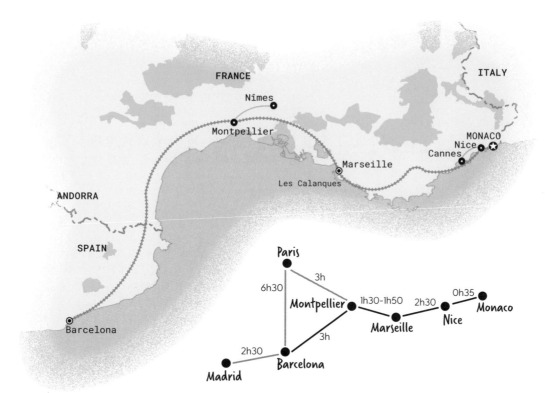

France's fastest-growing city, and one of its most multicultural. The premier sight is the Musée Fabre, home to one of France's richest collections of European art. With more time, catch a bus to the beach: avoid overdeveloped Palavas-les-Flots and La Grande-Motte, and head southeast to Plage de l'Espiguette instead, popular with kitesurfers and kite-buggiers.

🚆 **TER trains (www.oui.sncf) travel along the coast to Marseille at least every hour (1h30 to 1h50).**

➕ Day trip

Nîmes

Fascinating Roman sites including a magnificent amphitheatre, a 2000-year-old temple and a flashy new Roman-themed museum, the Musée de la Romanité, make Nîmes a rewarding side-trip from Montpellier.

🚆 **Trains run half-hourly (0h30).**

---

❸ Marseille

The gritty port city of Marseille gets a bad rap. Admittedly it lacks the glamour of Cannes or St-Tropez, but it's home to a beautiful Old Town (Le Panier), a picturesque port and some swanky new museums including Mucem, devoted to Mediterranean civilisation. It's also the home of bouillabaisse, a rich seafood stew, usually ordered a day ahead.

Left, Marseille's Le Panier district; right, Plage du Midi, Cannes at sunset

des Anglais (on foot, bike, Segway or Rollerblade), head into town to visit the Picasso Museum and MAMAC (Musée d'Art Moderne et d'Art Contemporain).

🚆 **The train-trip from Nice to Monaco hugs the coast, providing dreamy Mediterranean views. Trains run at least half-hourly; the trip only takes 35 minutes.**

✈ Day trip

Cannes
Film festivals don't get glitzier than Cannes, but this Riviera town is best visited outside festival season. The old area around Le Suquet is great for wandering, and the seafront is lined by sandy beaches (although you'll have to pay for the ones around La Croisette). Boat trips also leave for St-Tropez, Monaco and the Corniche d'Or.

🚆 **Cannes is easily reached by train from Nice (0h40, four per hour).**

🚆 Catch another train to Nice (2h30, up to six per day).
🛏 Hotel tip: Green Key-certified Hotel Belle-Vue (www.hotelbellevuemarseille.com)

✈ Day trip

Les Calanques
The coastline around Marseille, slashed by *calanques* (coves), became France's newest national park in 2012. The best way to explore these coves and their sapphire-blue water is by sea kayak. **Destination Calanques Kayak (www.destination-calanques.fr) runs day-trips from Marseille.**

❹ Nice
Synonymous with seaside chic since the 1920s, Nice is the belle of the Riviera's ball. Yes, it's busy and chaotic, the traffic's terrible and the beaches are all pebbles, but it still has a certain je ne sais quoi. Once you've buzzed along the Promenade

❺ Monaco
Half an hour east of Nice you're in another country: specifically the Principality of Monaco, known for its Grand Prix, belle époque casino and notoriously lax tax laws. Highlights include the royal palace and the marine-themed Musée Océanographique.

Returning home
From Nice, TGVs whizz to Paris St Lazare (6h). To connect on to Eurostar services to Brussels and London, you need to take the metro to Gare du Nord. Nice to Madrid by train takes 11h25.

Pilgrimage through Northern Spain

Pamplona · Burgos · León · A Coruña · Santiago de Compostela
Taking in Basque culture, Spain's northern heartland and lush Galicia, this is a tour of hidden corners, exquisite cathedrals and fine food.

Departure points

You can get to Pamplona by train from Barcelona Sants (4h), Madrid Atocha (5h) and Paris Montparnasse (12h30) with a change in Barcelona. This entire itinerary is connected by Renfe trains (https://venta.renfe.com).

❶ Pamplona

The wild Fiesta de San Fermín, with the Running of the Bulls its dramatic centrepiece, brings hordes of visitors to Pamplona in early July. But with a vast citadel, a compact and atmospheric centre and city walls offering views down to the plains and up to the Pyrenees, Navarre's capital is almost as appealing – and a damn sight more tranquil – the rest of the year. Like every city on this tour, it features on the Camino de Santiago pilgrimage routes, and the section between here and Burgos is a popular one, taking in monasteries, vineyards, towns and mountain views. Should you choose to get off the train and strap on your hiking boots, it'll take around 10 days.
🚆 **There are two direct trains a day from Pamplona to Burgos (2h).**

Riders and hikers on the Camino de Santiago

Fact box

Carbon (kg per person) 17
Distance (km) 850
Nights 10+
Transport budget (€) 120

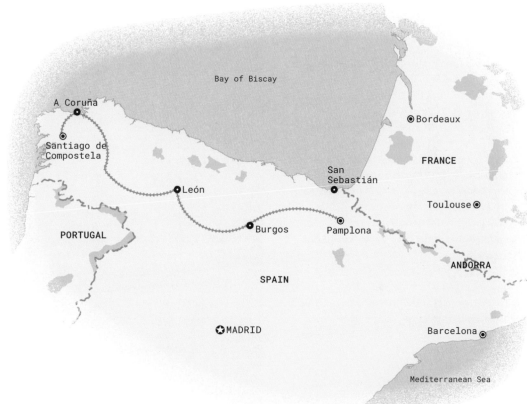

A Coruña

Santiago de
Compostela

Bay of Biscay

Bordeaux

FRANCE

San
Sebastián

León

Toulouse

Burgos   Pamplona

PORTUGAL

ANDORRA

SPAIN

★MADRID

Barcelona

Mediterranean Sea

❷ Burgos

You might visit Burgos for its
cathedral, an imposing, intricate and
extraordinary Gothic marvel that's one
of the finest in Spain – and contains the
body of El Cid, the legendary medieval
hero of Spain's reconquest. Or you might
come for the *morcilla* (blood sausage),
revered as the best in the country and
offered in many tapas bars. Either way,
don't be put off by the rather soulless
modern suburbs where the train station
is located – Burgos' old town is an
underrated jewel in Spain's crown.

🚊 **Around three trains daily connect Burgos
and León directly (2h).**

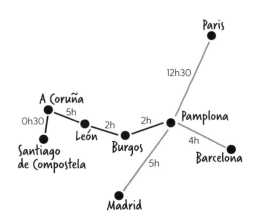

Paris

12h30

A Coruña
              5h
0h30   2h   2h   Pamplona
        León   Burgos
                                            4h
Santiago
de Compostela   Barcelona
                              5h

Madrid

❸ León

Did we mention cathedrals? León's is truly magnificent, built when the city was still one of the driving forces in the reconquest of Spain, and its vast stained glass windows create a magical light within. There's great food and drink here too, with a phenomenal (and meaty) selection of tapas bars and throbbing nightlife. Romanesque frescoes, modern art and one of Spain's most famous Semana Santa (Easter) celebrations complete the picture.

🚆 **One direct train a day runs from León to A Coruña (5h).**

❹ A Coruña

This buzzing port, jutting out from Galicia's northern coast, doesn't appear on too many travel itineraries. Their loss: here you'll find beaches, the cutting-edge Aquarium Finisterrae, and museums and parks, many of them accessible via a walkway that circles the peninsula. The Tower of Hercules is a World Heritage-listed Roman lighthouse offering great views, and back in the old town the alleyways are packed with bars and restaurants.

🚆 **Roughly half-hourly trains connect A Coruña with Santiago de Compostela (0h30).**

❺ Santiago de Compostela

The end point of the Camino de Santiago and your trip, Santiago de Compostela is something else. Its twisting lanes, arcaded streets and – you guessed it – wonderful cathedral astound, whatever the weather. This being Galicia, the rain is a regular

Pilgrims arriving in Santiago De Compostela

visitor. All that water feeds a lush landscape, and if you prise yourself away from the enchanting architecture you can chow down on some of Spain's best food and drink: succulent seafood, punchy green peppers from nearby Padrón and light, fresh white wine.

Returning home

Barcelona, from where you can head back to Pamplona or connect with services to France and beyond, is around nine hours by train from Santiago de Compostela.

Scandinavia calling

Stockholm · Helsinki · Savonlinna · Kuopio · Tampere · Turku · Åland Islands
Explore Sweden, Finland and Estonia by train and ferry, with an invigorating stop-off in the idyllic Åland Archipelago.

Departure points

Stockholm is well-linked to its Scandinavian neighbours by train, with regular services to Copenhagen (5h30) and Oslo (5h30). From Copenhagen, you can connect onwards to German cities including Hamburg and Berlin.

❶ Stockholm

Sweden's stylish capital overflows with iconic buildings and cutting-edge design. Wander round the old town, Gamla Stan, and the imposing royal palace, Kungliga Slottet, then hop over to Moderna Museet for modern art and the folky model village of Skansen for a picture of Sweden's past. ✪ **Viking Line (www.vikingline.com) and Tallink Silja (www.tallinksilja.com) operate** ferries to Helsinki, an overnight journey of around 14 hours.

✪ Day trip

Uppsala
Home to Sweden's oldest university, Uppsala has a youthful buzz and a lovely setting on the river Fyris. The city's centrepiece is Gamla (Old) Uppsala, once a flourishing 6th-century religious centre, now a fascinating archaeological site.

Fact box

Carbon (kg per person) 100

Distance (km) 1790

Nights 12+

Transport budget (€) 380

One of hundreds of islands near Helsinki

Stockholm's Gamla
Stan

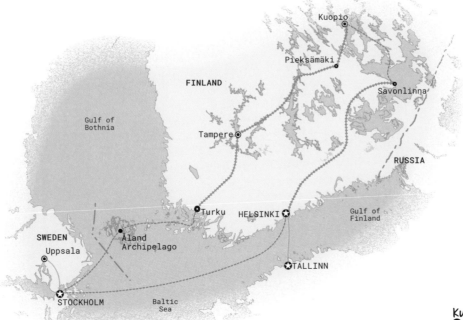

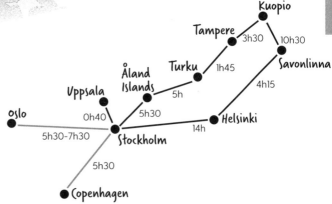

SJ Rail (www.sj.se) operates regular services to/from Stockholm (0h40, four to six per hour).

❷ Helsinki

Finland's capital shares the same sense of understated Scandinavian style as its neighbours, with a particular penchant for innovative architecture. The best way to explore is via the city's trams: check out the Museum of Finnish Architecture, sample Finnish flavours at the central market hall, then get steamy Swedish-style at the waterfront Löyly Sauna.

From Helsinki's main station, VR trains (www.vr.fi) run to Savonlinna (4h15, up to four daily) with a change in Parikkala.

⚙ Day trip

Tallinn

Tallinn's Old Town (vanalinn) feels like strolling back into the 15th century, with Hanseatic merchants' houses, medieval courtyards, and footworn stone stairways and cobbled streets galore.

Tallink (www.tallink.com) runs multiple daily ferries to/from Helsinki (2h).

Kayaking in the Turku archipelago

❸ Savonlinna

Scattered across a lattice of islands between Haukivesi and Pihlajavesi lakes, Savonlinna is one of Finland's prettiest towns. Its Olavinlinna Castle, built in the 15th century, is now home to an opera festival. When the lakes shimmer in the summer sun, it's a magical place.

☻ Lake boats ply the waters of Savonlinna in summer. Check www.oravivillage.com for seasonal boat schedules to Kuopio; the M/S Puijo (www.mspuijo.fi, three per week on Monday, Wednesday and Friday, 10h30) cruises regularly in summer.

❹ Kuopio

Kuopio is a quintessential lakeside town, offering pleasure cruises, hikes in spruce forests, tasty local fish specialities and plenty of terraces and beer gardens.

☻ Hop on a Helsinki-bound train, then change at Pieksämäki for Tampere (3h30, four daily).

❺ Tampere

The lakeside city of Tampere was once an industrial centre, but its old mills have been reimagined as museums, galleries, restaurants and cafes. A block of wooden houses – including a bakery, a shoemaker, a sauna, shops and a cafe – is preserved at the Amuri Museum of Workers' Housing, evoking life from 1882 to 1973.

☻ Trains run from Tampere to Turku (1h45, up to six daily).

❻ Turku

Turku is dominated by two architectural landmarks: Turun Linna (Turku Castle) and Turun Tuomiokirkko (Turku Cathedral), both dating from the 13th century. Through the age-old network of bustling streets and squares, the Aurajoki River meanders picturesquely, heading out to sea.

☻ Turku's harbour is 3km southwest of the centre. Tallink Silja and Viking Line sail to the Åland Archipelago twice daily (5h).

❼ Åland Islands

The sunny Åland Archipelago's white-sand beaches and scenic cycling routes attract holidaymakers during summer, but finding your own remote beach among the 6500 skerries (rocky islets) is surprisingly easy. Ferries dock at Fasta Åland, the largest island; bridges and free cable ferries connects the central islands. Car ferries run to the archipelago's outer reaches.

☻ Ferries travel from Fasta Åland back to Stockholm up to four times daily (5h30).

Route of the Orient Express

Paris · Munich · Budapest · Bucharest · İstanbul

The Orient Express has had many incarnations: capture its original spirit of trans-continental travel with this journey to the cusp of Asia on ordinary sleeper trains.

Departure points

Paris was generally considered the western terminus of the Orient Express in its early 20th-century heyday. Today you can arrive from London St Pancras (2h30) as well as Barcelona Sants (6h30) and Amsterdam (3h30).

❶ Paris

In June 1889 the first 'Orient Express' through-train from Paris to Istanbul departed from Gare de L'Est. Sadly no such regular service exists today, but Gare de L'Est is still a departure point for eastbound trains. Before boarding, take a short walk to the Bassin de la Villette – an artificial lake whose shores are dotted with cafes. Pools here are open to swimmers throughout the summer months.

🚊 **From Paris, catch one of about 20 services a day to Munich Hauptbahnhof (6h). www.sncf.com**

❷ Munich

Another stalwart stop on the original Orient Express, Munich's Hauptbahnhof station sits on the threshold of the Altstadt (Old Town) – a magnificent maze of onion-domed towers and cobbled thoroughfares meriting

Fact box

Carbon (kg per person) 52

Distance (km) 2600

Nights 12+

Transport budget (€) 600

The Golden Horn in Istanbul

at least a full day's exploration. Leave time to sink a *stein* in the Hofbräuhaus – the city's 16th-century beer hall. Explore the palatial corridors of the Residenz or stretch your legs in the sprawling parkland of the Englischer Garten ahead of your first sleeper on this itinerary.

🚆 **The EuroNight Kálmán Imre sleeper train runs from Munich Hauptbahnhof to Budapest Keleti, departing at 11.20pm and arriving shortly after 9am. www.bahn.de**

❸ Budapest

There's no better place in Europe to soothe travel-weary limbs than Budapest, where ornate spas bubble away on both banks of the Danube. A walk north of Keleti station will take you to the art nouveau Széchenyi baths – one of the city's largest, set in

Glimpse the Eiffel Tower across the Seine

Left, the Hungarian Parliament building in Budapest; below, İstanbul's Hagia Sofia

leafy parkland. Alternatively cross the river in the shadow of Castle Hill in search of the Gellért Baths – a cathedral-like structure, whose thermal waters have been put to use since the Ottomans ruled the city.

🚆 **The Ister sleeper train departs Budapest Keleti at 7.10pm and reaches Bucharest Gara de Nord at 12.30pm the following day. www.mavcsoport.hu**

🏨 **Hotel tip: Casati Budapest Hotel**

❹ Bucharest

It may have few landmark sights compared with other European capitals, but Bucharest's appeal is of the slow-burn sort: lingering on cafe-lined thoroughfares, exploring its excellent museums or contemplating the dark relics of dictator Nicolae Ceaușescu. Of the latter, the most visible is the Palace of Parliament –

one of the largest buildings in the world, covering some 330,000 sq m and open to visitors for guided tours.

🚆 **From June to October, direct services run from Bucharest Gara de Nord to Istanbul Halkalı, departing 12.40pm and arriving 7.40am the next day. From Halkalı, complimentary bus services run to Istanbul's Sirkeci railway station. During the rest of the year, connect via Dimitrovgrad in Bulgaria. https://bileteinternationale.cfrcalatori.ro**

❺ İstanbul

İstanbul's grand Sirkeci station was the easterly terminus of the Orient Express, and there could be no better finishing line for an epic rail adventure. You'll find the minarets of the Blue Mosque to the south, labyrinthine bazaars to the west, the fishermen of the Galata bridge to the north and to the east the Bosphorus with the city's Asian shore beyond.

Returning home

The quickest way to return to Paris is to retrace your steps – or consider a more southerly route connecting to Munich via Sofia, Belgrade, Zagreb and Ljubljana.

Land of the Sámi

Helsinki · Oulu · Rovaniemi · Inari
This Arctic adventure travels into the Finnish far north via Lapland, home of Santa Claus and the semi-nomadic Sámi people.

Departure points

Helsinki has sea links to cities including Stockholm, Malmö, Tallinn and St Petersburg. Finland's only international trains are to/from Moscow and St Petersburg in Russia.

❶ Helsinki

The Finnish capital is highly walkable, but trams are fantastic for sightseeing when time is short. Tram 4 passes the architectural highlights; pick it up at the gold onion-dome-topped Uspenskin Katedraali, and see the Lutheran cathedral Tuomiokirkko, the Finnish parliament Eduskunta, the Alvar Aalto–designed Finlandia Talo concert hall and more. Tram 6 takes in design and culinary highlights.

🚆 **Helsinki's central train station is linked to the metro (Rautatientori stop) and is situated 500m east of Kamppi bus station. VR trains (www.vr.fi) run to Oulu (6 to 7h, four daily) via Kajaani.**

❷ Oulu

Prosperous Oulu is one of Finland's most enjoyable cities. The *kauppatori* (central square) is bordered by old wooden storehouses now serving as restaurants,

Fact box

Carbon (kg per person) 49
Distance (km) 1025km
Nights 10+
Transport budget (€) 170

The Old Town pier in Helsinki

176

bars and craft shops. The city centre is spread across several islands, connected by pedestrian bridges and cycleways: Hupisaaret Park, north of the city centre, has bike paths, museums, greenhouses and a summer cafe.

🚆 **From Oulu's railway station, trains continue north to Rovaniemi (2h15, four daily).**

❸ Rovaniemi

Right by the Arctic Circle, Rovaniemi is the 'official' residence of a chap by the name of Santa Claus – and you'll find a host of Yule-themed sites round town, including a Santa Claus Village where you can visit the old fella in his grotto, send a postcard from the post office and take a reindeer-drawn sleigh-ride. But Rovaniemi has some fascinating non-Santa sights too – particularly Arktikum, an informative Arctic museum examining Sámi culture and polar flora and fauna.

🚌 **Two direct daily buses from Rovaniemi travel north to Inari (5h).**

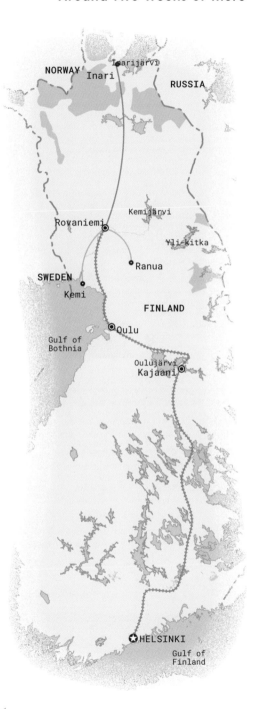

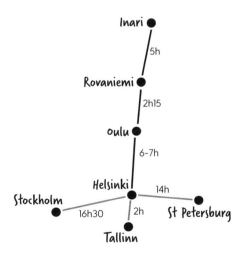

© scanrail / Getty Images

Left, a Sámi man rides a
reindeer in Finnish lapland;
right, a Sámi tent glows at dusk

project and has become a Lapland winter highlight, rebuilt every winter from only snow and ice. Bathed in ethereal light and with a sumptuously decorated interior, the design changes every year but always includes a chapel, a snow hotel, an ice bar and a restaurant.

🚉 It's in the town of Kemi, halfway between Oulu (1h) and Rovaniemi (1h20); trains run several times a day to both towns.

❹ Inari

The tiny village of Inari (Sámi: Anár) is Finland's Sámi capital and the logical place to immerse yourself in Sámi culture. It's home to the wonderful Siida museum, which offers a comprehensive overview of the Sámi and their environment, and Sajos (a cultural centre and the seat of the Finnish Sámi parliament). The village sits on Lapland's largest lake, Inarijärvi, a spectacular body of water with more than 3000 islands in its 1084-sq-km area. From June (as soon as the ice melts) to late September, cruises sail to Ukko Island (Sámi: Äjjih), sacred to the Sámi.

Returning home

You're a long way north by the time you reach Inari. You can retrace your steps or continue your Arctic adventure by taking a bus over the Norwegian border to Nordkapp (5h30), climbing aboard a Hurtigruten ferry (www.hurtigruten.com, 4½ days) from Honningsvåg to Bergen, then a VY train (www.vy.no) to Oslo (6h30-7h).

🚌 Day trip

Ranua Zoo

Ranua's excellent zoo (www.ranuazoo.com) focuses on Finnish animals, although there are also polar bears and musk oxen. A boardwalk runs past the creatures, which include minks and stoats, impressive owls and eagles, wild reindeer, elk, bears (they hibernate from November to March), lynx and wolverines. The zoo is 78km southeast of Rovaniemi on Rd 78.

🚌 Up to six daily buses serve Rovaniemi (1h).

🚌 Day trip

Lumilinna

Few things conjure fairy-tale romance like a snow castle. Lumilinna (www.visitkemi.fi) was first built in 1996 as a Unicef

Balkan Capitals

Vienna · Zagreb · Sarajevo · Belgrade · Budapest
Immerse yourself in the history, culture, gastronomy and nightlife of three characterful Balkan capitals on this memorable overland journey from Vienna to Budapest.

Departure points

This itinerary takes advantage of the proximity of Croatian, Bosnian and Serbian capitals, which are a breeze to explore in a single trip thanks to their relatively small size and good bus connections between the three countries. The starting point for the journey is Vienna, which can be reached by train from other Western European cities including Strasbourg, Frankfurt and Venice.

❶ Vienna

The Austrian capital is the ideal place to kick-start your urban discovery of the Balkans. Its imperial palaces, masterpiece-filled museums and centuries-old coffee culture set the stage perfectly for

what awaits further south. Stay for a couple of days to explore the baroque Schloss Belvedere or the rococo Schloss Schönbrunn, admire the old masters at the Kunsthistorisches Museum Vienna and the avant-garde works at the contemporary MUMOK, and indulge in hearty Wiener schnitzel followed by spectacular Sachertorte at one of Vienna's opulent coffee houses.

🚌 **From Vienna, there are eight buses to Zagreb every day (5h).**

Fisherman's Bastion, Budapest

Fact box

Carbon (kg per person) 158

Distance (km) 1453

Nights 10

Transport budget (€) 115

❷ Zagreb

Croatia's capital is made for strolling: the Upper Town's cobblestone lanes, red roofs and church spires are set against secessionist, neo-baroque and art deco architecture in the Lower Town, while colourful murals by local artists adorn the side streets. Taste some fresh produce at the bustling Dolac Market, then pick one of the many bistros that use the same ingredients. Head to lush Mirogoj cemetery for a quiet walk among its ornate tombstones, contemplate the intriguing Museum of Broken Relationships and discover Croatia's homegrown art genre at the Museum of Naive Art. In the evenings, delve into Zagreb's emerging craft-beer scene.

🚌 **There are five daily services from Zagreb bus station (www.akz.hr) to Sarajevo (7h30).**

❸ Sarajevo

The distinctive East-meets-West

Left, Viennese coffee; right, a bather at Gellért Thermal Bath in Budapest

❹ Belgrade

The gritty exuberance of Serbia's capital makes it one of Europe's most happening cities. Behind socialist-Modernist monoliths and neoclassical masterpieces you'll find an old-world culture beside cutting-edge cosmopolitanism. Soak up the street life along the pedestrian Knez Mihailova, around the ancient Kalemegdan citadel and the quaint Zemun neighbourhood. Visit the Museum of Yugoslavia and Nikola Tesla Museum, then hop on the circular Tram 2 to take in the city's iconic sights. For boho Belgrade, dine in a Skadarlija tavern; come nightfall, join the party on a river barge or in the Dorćol quarter's cool clubs.

🚌 **From Belgrade, there's a morning and an evening bus (www.fudeks.rs) to Budapest every day (7h).**

❺ Budapest

As the grand finale, Hungary's capital offers historic sights, art nouveau buildings, thermal waters and a nightlife that is unrivalled in Central Europe. Ramble around the medieval Royal Palace on Castle Hill, and stroll down the tree-lined Andrássy út for some knock-out architecture. Stay for at least one night to get a taste of Budapest's famous ruin pubs such as the landmark Szimpla Kert, and relax after your whirlwind Balkans tour by 'taking the waters' at the Széchenyi Baths.

atmosphere of the Bosnian capital is hard to resist. Start getting to know Sarajevo in the Baščaršija – a medley of coppersmiths' alleys, mosques and caravanserai (inn) restaurants. Stop for essential Balkan snacks, ćevapi and burek, and sip Turkish coffee accompanied by traditional sweets in a courtyard cafe. For a sobering insight into Sarajevo's recent past, visit the War Childhood Museum and Galerija 11/07/95, then admire the beautifully reconstructed neo-Moorish City Hall. Catch the cable car up Mt Trebević for glorious city views and the graffitied, abandoned Olympic bobsled track. Evenings are best spent in the Old Town's bars and cafes.

🚌 **There are two daily buses from eastern Sarajevo bus station (www.centrotrans-ad.com) to Belgrade (7h30).**

Returning home

Budapest has good train connections to Western European cities such as Munich, Paris or Milan. Or catch one of the frequent daily trains back to Vienna (3h).

© Julian Love / Lonely Planet. © Will Sanders / Lonely Planet

A meander through Moorish Spain

Seville · Córdoba · Ronda · Granada · Málaga
For 800 years Muslim Moors from North Africa ruled the Iberian Peninsula, gifting southern Spain monumental mosques, colourful bathhouses and epic palaces.

Departure points

High-speed AVE trains link Madrid and Seville (2h30), so you're likely to stop in Spain's capital before arriving in Andalucía. The Trenhotel Lusitania sleeper train between Lisbon and Madrid (10h15) makes for a leisurely arrival, and TGV trains from Paris Gare de Lyon (9h45) travel via Barcelona, where you'll switch to the AVE service, before heading west to Madrid.

❶ Seville

Start your journey by getting tangled up in the labyrinthine alleyways of seductive Seville. Its historic centre is lorded over by an enormous Gothic cathedral built on the remains of the city mosque; climb to the top of the Giralda, the church's bell tower, to experience the panoramic views once seen by the muezzin who clambered up this repurposed minaret five times a day for the call to prayer. Nearby, the Real Alcázar is Seville's headline sight. The palace boasts mesmerising Mudéjar plasterwork, ceramic tiling and a series of peacefully enclosed courtyards.

🚇 **High-speed trains run about once an hour to Córdoba (0h45). www.renfe.com.**

Fact box

Carbon (kg per person) 10
Distance (km) 490km
Nights 10+
Transport budget (€) 150

The prayer hall in Córdoba's Mezquita

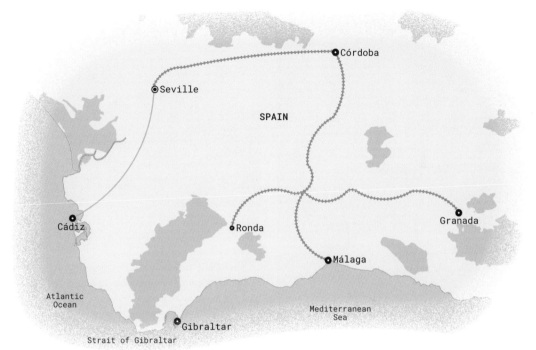

SPAIN

Córdoba

Seville

Cádiz

Ronda

Granada

Málaga

Atlantic
Ocean

Mediterranean
Sea

Gibraltar

Strait of Gibraltar

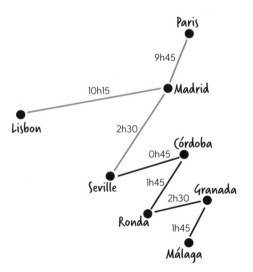

Paris

9h45

10h15   Madrid

2h30

Córdoba

0h45

Seville

1h45

Ronda

2h30   Granada

1h45

Málaga

Lisbon

⊕ Day trip

Cádiz

Cádiz might just be the oldest continuously inhabited settlement in Europe, and its ancient centre, now well into its fourth millennium, is a jumble of streets where waves crash against eroded sea walls, taverns fry up fresh fish and beaches teem with sun-worshippers. Despite the city's age, it's a good place to track down a more modern take on Moorish design, so seek out Gran Teatro Falla, built in 1884. With keyhole arches and alternating red-and-white bricks, this Neo-Mudéjar theatre hosts live performances as well as Cádiz's annual Carnaval competitions in February.

🚆 **Trains run approximately hourly between Seville and Cádiz (1h45).**

Left, sherry at a bodega in Andalucía; below, Cádiz; right, the Alhambra in Granada

❷ Córdoba

One building alone is enough reason to stop in Córdoba: the magnificent Mezquita, where more than 850 perfectly aligned stone columns hold red and white arches aloft in this pinnacle of Islamic architecture. Once the city's great mosque, the Mezquita had a Renaissance cathedral plonked into its heart in the 1500s, but even centuries ago, the city was known as a place where Muslims, Christians and Jews coexisted peacefully.

🚆 **Twice a day, high-speed trains travel between Córdoba and Ronda (1h40). www. renfe.com.**

❸ Ronda

Straddling a deep river-carved gorge, Ronda is the largest of Andalucía's whitewashed hill towns. Backing onto the water are the Baños Arabes, a 13th-century Moorish bathhouse complex, one of the best preserved in Andalucía that's complete with horseshoe arches perched atop brickwork columns and clearly designated hot and cold thermal areas following the Roman model. The nearby Puente Arabe isn't the bridge in Ronda that gets the most attention, but it was the first to span the Río Guadalevín and was built during the Moorish era.

🚆 **Three trains a day run from Ronda to Granada (2h30–3h). with www.renfe.com.**

❹ Granada

The Alhambra is Granada's – and Europe's – love letter to Moorish culture. Set against a backdrop of the peaks of the Sierra Nevada, this fortified palace complex started life as a walled citadel before becoming the opulent seat of Granada's Nasrid emirs. The palaces are among the finest Islamic buildings this side of the Mediterranean. Granada was the last stronghold of the Spanish Moors, and it's here that their influence is felt most strongly, best absorbed in the relaxed *teterías* (teahouses) in Albaicín,

the historic Arab quarter.

🚆 **Trains between Granada and Málaga (1h45) run approximately every two hours but require a change in Antequera. www. renfe.com.**

❺ Málaga

Designed to defend the town's port, Málaga's imposing 11th-century palace-fortress of Alcazaba has been extensively restored and is one of the best preserved in the entire country. Burbling fountains stand watch in the numerous courtyards that are accessed by distinctive Islamic-style arches.

Returning home

Direct trains from Málaga run approximately hourly to hustle you back to Madrid (2h40) and beyond.

Cultural capitals of Mitteleuropa

Paris · Cologne · Berlin · Wrocław · Kraków
Beginning in Paris, this adventure crosses the Rhine bound for some of Central Europe's cultural icons, with forests, rivers and little market towns rolling past the window.

Departure points

Paris is perfectly poised for access from across Western Europe – with direct trains from London St Pancras to Gare du Nord (2h30), and from Barcelona Sants to Gare de Lyon (6h30). It's also very easy to begin this itinerary in Brussels Midi/Zuid – around two hours from Cologne Hauptbahnhof.

❶ Paris

Gare du Nord is the terminus from which to begin your eastbound journey. Before stepping inside, glance up at the station facade – adorned with statues representing towns accessed by the railway. Shield in hand, Berlin looks down regally from the roof.

Fact box

Carbon (kg per person) 56
Distance (km) 2800
Nights 10+
Transport budget (€) 400

🚆 **Trains to Cologne Hauptbahnhof (3h30) run 36 times a day. www.thalys.com**

❷ Cologne

Perhaps Germany's most big-hearted city, Cologne is synonymous with lively beer halls, a crop of world-class galleries and a history as a frontier fortress of the Roman Empire. The town's greatest landmark, however, hits you the moment you exit the station: the soaring Kölner Dom – the Gothic cathedral-cum-skyscraper that

Berlin's TV Tower soars above the city's skyline

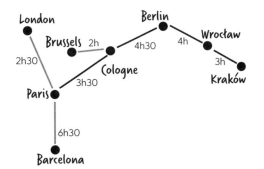

was once the tallest building in the world. Climb the 533 steps up the South Tower for a view of the Rhine, snaking its way out to the North Sea.

🚊 **Direct ICE services run from Cologne Hauptbahnhof to Berlin Hauptbahnhof roughly every hour (4h30). www.db.com**

❸ Berlin

Berlin was for much of the 20th century a city divided in two, and even today it's a place of pronounced contrasts. The formalities of Prussian Potsdam versus the hedonistic nightlife of Kreuzberg: the splendour of the Pergamonmuseum versus the irreverence of the East Side Gallery. It's worth a minimum of two days – not least because it's an easy place to escape the urban hubbub. Join a kayaking excursion into the serene channels of Spreewald, whose wooded waterways are a weekend retreat for Berliners.

🚊 **Direct trains connect Berlin Ostbahnhof to Wroclaw Główny (4h). www.bahn.com**
🛏 **Hotel tip: Hotel Zoo**

❹ Wrocław

One of Europe's most underrated cities,

Wrocław (pronounced vrots-wahf) ticks all the boxes for the perfect city break: a grand market square, lively cafes and bars aplenty. One of its more curious attractions, however, are its gnome population: tiny bronze figures dotted around the city, variously using tiny ATMs, riding pigeons, playing golf or snoozing on the street. Pick up a gnome map from the tourist information to spot them – at last count there were 200 (and rising).

🚊 **Roughly seven trains a day travel the Wrocław Główny–Kraków Główny route (3h). www.intercity.pl**

❺ Kraków

Arriving at the station, Kraków reveals its majesty by degrees: first the 14th-century

© Blue Jay Photo / Getty Images

Below, Kraków's Kazimierz district;
right, Wawel Royal Castle

Florian Gate and the battlements of the barbican loom into view, then the expanse of Rynek Główny – one of the largest medieval squares in Europe. And finally the town's crowning glory: Wawel Hill, adorned by a mighty castle and a royal cathedral, watching out over the rooftops of Kraków. For a different view of Polish history, board a rattling tram to Kazimierz – the city's old Jewish quarter, dotted with synagogues and museums chronicling the community's past.

🚲 Day trip

Wieliczka Salt Mine

Cathedrals and churches aren't lacking on this itinerary, however none are as unusual as the chapel inside the Wieliczka Salt Mine. With altars and figures hewn entirely from salt, it's part of a vast subterranean labyrinth excavated from the 13th century until the recent past, accessed on guided tours.

🚆🚌 **Wieliczka is 14km from Kraków, and easily reached on local trains and buses.**

Returning home

It's possible to get back to Paris in less than 24 hours. Overnight sleeper trains run to Berlin from Kraków: from Berlin, catch an early morning express service back to Paris (8h).

Slovenia to southern Germany

Ljubljana · Salzburg · Innsbruck · Munich
A thoroughly Teutonic train journey, taking in Mozart's birthplace, Hitler's hideout, the Austrian Alps and a bevy of Munich beer gardens.

Departure points

Slovenia is well connected by road and rail with its neighbours – Italy, Austria, Hungary and Croatia. Slovenian Railways (www.slo-zeleznice.si) links with the European railway network via Italy (Trieste), Germany (Munich, Frankfurt), Czech Republic (Prague), Croatia (Zagreb, Rijeka), Hungary (Budapest), Switzerland (Zürich) and Serbia (Belgrade).

❶ Ljubljana

You won't find a greener city in Europe than Ljubljana, Slovenia's delightful capital – a city of pavement cafes, riverside terraces and leafy streets, set along the banks of the emerald-green Ljubljanica River. The city's centre is pedestrianised, making it perfect for exploring on foot or by bike – you can rent bikes from Ljubljana Bike at the tourist office (www.visitljubljana.si) or from 38 Bicikelj (www.bicikelj.si) stations around the city.

Ⓡ **Österreichische Bundesbahnen (ÖBB, www.oebb.at) intercity trains run from Ljubljana's central station to Salzburg (4h50, three daily).**

Fact box

Carbon (kg per person) 15
Distance (km) 750
Nights 9+
Transport budget (€) 150

The Ljubljanica River flows through Ljubljana city

Salzburg's handsome
cityscape

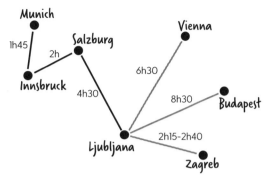

with scenic cycling trails heading off in all directions, including along the Salzach River. A'Velo (www.avelosalzburg.com) provides bike and e-bike rental.

🚆 **Direct trains run hourly to Innsbruck (2h).**

✈ **Day trip**

Salzwelten (Salt Works)

During Salzburg's heyday, the sale of salt (then known as 'white gold') filled its coffers. At Austria's biggest show mine you can slip into a boiler suit and descend to the bowels of the earth. The tour aboard a rickety train passes through a maze of claustrophobic passageways, over the border to Germany and down a 27m slide.

🚆🚌 **ÖBB trains run to Hallein (15-40 minutes, several per hour), from where buses leaves frequently for the mines; a combo ticket including admission and transport is available (http://kombitickets. railtours.at).**

✈ **Day trip**

Berchtesgaden

Framed by six mountain ranges, the Berchtesgadener Land is a corner of Bavaria steeped in legend. Much of the area is protected by law within the Berchtesgaden National Park, declared a

❷ Salzburg

Home of Mozart and *The Sound of Music*, princely Salzburg radiates baroque splendour, from the domes and spires of its churches to the sprawling grandeur of the Residenz, where the prince-archbishops resided. Other essential sights include Mozart's birthplace and the clifftop Festung Hohensalzburg, reached via a funicular for incredible views over the city. It's a very bike-friendly place,

© Franz Pritz / Picture Press / Getty Images

Left and below, Munich's
English Garden

Left and below, Munich's
English Garden

biosphere reserve by Unesco in 1990. But
the mountains here are most notorious for
their Nazi connections: the mountaintop
Eagle's Nest was a lodge built for Hitler and
is now a major dark-tourism destination.
The Dokumentation Obersalzberg
exhibition chronicles the region's Nazi past.
🚌 **RVO bus 840 (0h45), leaves from
Salzburg train station roughly hourly.**

---

❸ Innsbruck

Tyrol's capital is a sight to behold. The
jagged rock spires of the Nordkette
range are so close that within minutes
it's possible to travel from the city's heart
to alpine pastures where cowbells chime
more than 2000m above sea level. Its
late-medieval Altstadt (Old Town) is
picture-book stuff, presided over by a

grand Hapsburg palace and baroque
cathedral, while its Olympic ski jump with
big mountain views makes a spectacular
leap between the urban and the outdoors.
🚆 **Two-hourly trains serve Munich (1h45).**

❹ Munich

Tall tankards and high-tech cars, street
art and lederhosen – Munich is a city
where traditional and modern sit side by
side. It's long been known as the 'city of
art and beer', so allow at least a couple
of days to savour both facets of the city.
There are four major avenues to visit in
the Kunstareal, Munich's art quarter, and
literally scores of beer halls and gardens
where you can sip the local suds while
getting to know the locals. Try Schneider
Weisses Bräuhaus (www.schneider-
brauhaus.de) for classic Bavarian
atmosphere, complete with oompah band
and Weisswurst (veal sausage).

Returning home

There are numerous fast trains from
Munich to cities across Germany (including
Berlin, Frankfurt and Cologne) and around
Europe (including Zürich and Vienna).

Santiago to the Douro

Santiago de Compostela · Vigo and the Islas Cíes · Porto · Guimarães
This trip through northwestern Iberia takes in Spain's holiest city and Portugal's most hallowed vineyards with lively ports, Atlantic beaches and scenic railways en route.

Departure points

Direct trains run to Santiago de Compostela from Madrid Chamartín (5h). It's possible to travel by rail from Bilbao Abando, changing at Miranda de Ebro (12h), or travel direct by long distance bus with a similar journey time. From Bilbao, ferries connect with Portsmouth in the UK (24h).

❶ Santiago de Compostela

For some, Santiago represents the finishing line after an epic trek through northern Spain – for this itinerary, it's the start of a railway adventure to the south. Even if your walk only begins at Santiago station, make sure you follow pilgrims into the cathedral, an eclectic and elaborate mix of Romanesque, Gothic and baroque flourishes, currently undergoing internal restoration.

🚆 **Over 10 trains a day travel from Santiago to Vigo stations (1h). www.renfe.com**

❷ Vigo and the Islas Cíes

Vigo has something of a split personality. On the one hand it's a gritty industrial city, on the other it's a historic port with a proud past – evident in the sloping

Fact box

Carbon (kg per person) 9
Distance (km) 400
Nights 11
Transport budget (€) 200

Dusk in Santiago de Compostela

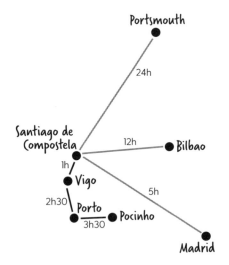

lanes of the old quarter, Casco Vello. Just beyond the port lie the Islas Cíes, a cluster of beautiful, car-free islands designated as a nature reserve. Through the summer months, numerous ferry companies operate the 45-minute route from Vigo to the sandy beaches of the archipelago.

🚆 Only one or two daily trains run from Vigo to Porto Campanhã (2h30) – note that Spain and Portugal are in different time zones when reading timetables. www.renfe.com

🏨 Hotel tip: Camping Islas Cíes

❸ Porto

Porto is the city that put the 'Port' in Portugal and it's a beautiful muddle of townhouses, palaces and churches cascading down the steep banks of the Douro. It's famous as the city that exported port wine to the world – some of that wealth shows in the Palácio da

Left, Porto's Passeio Alegre gardens; below, vineyards on the banks of the Douro

Bolsa, the city's historic stock exchange, while many historic port warehouses are open for tasting experiences. Trains for the Douro line depart from the magnificent São Bento station – arrive early to admire its surfaces swathed in *azulejos* (traditional hand-painted tiles), which depict episodes from Iberian history across some 20,000 tiles.

🚆 **Direct trains run hourly from Porto to Guimarães (1h30). www.cp.pt**

🔄 **Day trip**

Linha do Douro to Pocinho

The Linha do Douro is Portugal's most beautiful rail journey – following the course of the Douro River upstream towards the Spanish border. The best scenery comes east of the town of Pinhão, as vineyard terraces rise up

on both banks. The line is now a dead end after the final section towards Salamanca was closed some decades ago – catch a morning service to the current terminus at Pocinho and return to Porto in the afternoon.

🚆 **Five trains run daily from Porto along the Linha do Douro to the terminus at Pocinho (3h30). www.cp.pt**

---

❹ Guimarães

The birthplace of Portugal's first king, the university town of Guimarães is regarded as a crucible of Portuguese identity. Start exploring at the town's 10th-century castle, originally built to repel Moorish and Viking invasions, before losing an afternoon in the shady squares and rambling alleyways beyond.

Returning home

From Porto retrace your steps northward to Santiago de Compostela – or alternatively break up the journey at the beguiling Spanish city of Pontevedra, midway between Vigo and Santiago.

Croatian island-hopping

Zagreb · Split · Brač · Hvar · Korčula · Mljet · Dubrovnik

Spend two blissful weeks sampling the beaches, old towns, seafood and wine on this island-hopping adventure from Split to Dubrovnik along Croatia's Adriatic coast.

Departure points

This itinerary takes advantage of the extensive ferry network linking some of Croatia's most attractive islands with two major Dalmatian cities, Split and Dubrovnik. The starting point for the journey is the capital Zagreb, which can be reached by train from other Western European cities including Venice, Munich and Vienna.

❶ Zagreb

Spend a day enjoying the street life and cafe culture of the Croatian capital before catching your onward bus to Split.

🚌 From Zagreb bus station (www.akz.hr), there are frequent buses (more than one per half-hour) to Split each day (5h).

❷ Split

Croatia's second city is an excellent introduction to Dalmatian life. Explore the labyrinthine streets of ancient Diocletian's Palace, a lived-in Unesco World Heritage Site. Don't miss the Meštrović Gallery, a wonderful seaside villa exhibiting the works of Croatia's famous sculptor, and climb the pine-forest paths to Marjan Hill for extraordinary views over Split and the islands beyond. Taste superb local seafood

Fact box

Carbon (kg per person) 240

Distance (km) 1420

Nights 14

Transport budget (€) 115

Dubrovnik and the island of Lokrum

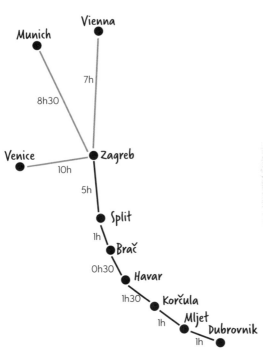

at Vela Varoš restaurants; come nightfall, hit the bars on the Riva.

🚢 **From June to September, Jadrolinija (www.jadrolinija.hr) and Kapetan Luka (www.krilo.hr) have daily high-speed catamaran services to Brač (1h).**

❸ Brač

The largest of central Dalmatia's islands, Brač is home to the poster child of Croatian tourism – the glorious Zlatni Rat beach at Bol. This white-pebble, tongue-shaped beach backed by pine trees is a windsurfing hotspot thanks to the maestral – a strong westerly wind that blows from April to October. Konoba Mali Raj, above the beach, serves delicious Dalmatian dishes such as grilled squid.

🚢 **Two daily Jadrolinija catamarans connect Brač with Hvar from June to**

September. Kapetan Luka has daily services between May and mid-October (0h30).

❹ Hvar

Officially Croatia's sunniest spot, Hvar is also its most glamorous island destination, attracting international yachties and crowds of partygoers. Away from Hvar Town you can explore lavender fields, ancient vineyards and isolated coves. Taxi boats serve the nearby chain of wooded isles known as the Pakleni Islands. Make sure you try *hvarska gregada* (a traditional fish stew).

🚢 **Jadrolinija operates daily catamarans to**

Korčula from June to September. Kapetan Luka runs a daily service from May to mid-October, with another between June and September (1h30).

❺ Korčula

Purported to have been Marco Polo's home, Korčula Town impresses with imposing towers and city walls, marble streets and Gothic-Renaissance architecture including the magnificent St Mark's Cathedral. The island's interior offers great hiking and biking trails. Korčula also attracts wine lovers, with excellent whites produced from the indigenous grapes pošip and grk.

😊 From May to mid-October, Kapetan Luka runs a daily catamaran to Mljet island, with another between June and September. In July and August, G&V Line (www.gv-line.hr) catamarans go to Mljet four times a week (1h).

❻ Mljet

Tranquil Mljet is home to a verdant national park with two gorgeous saltwater lakes and shady walking and cycling paths. It also offers interesting

Below left, St Mary Benedictine Monastery in Mljet; below, Dubrovnik's Old Town; right, Veliko Lake in Mljet National Park

dives, including a German WWII torpedo boat and a 3rd-century Roman wreck. Memorable meals include *brodet* (fish stew) and lamb cooked under hot coals.

😊 G&V Line has daily catamarans to Dubrovnik. Kapetan Luka runs a daily service from May to mid-October, and an additional one between June and September (1h).

❼ Dubrovnik

The marvellous Old Town, with its ancient walls and inevitable *Game of Thrones* associations, is worth a trip in its own right. Stroll the limestone streets, popping in and out of churches, museums and palaces, then catch a cable car up to Mt Srđ for panoramic views or take a 10-minute ferry ride to the rocky beaches of forested Lokrum island. At night, choose between the sophisticated wine bars of the Old Town and sunset drinks at beach bars clinging to a cliff.

🚌 From Dubrovnik bus station (www.libertasdubrovnik.hr), catch one of the frequent daily buses back to Zagreb (11h30) for train connections north and west to Austria, Germany and Italy.

The Black Forest and beyond

Baden Baden · Freiburg · Gengenbach · Triberg · Konstanz
Straight from a Grimm Brothers tale, the brooding Black Forest and its valleys are perfect for slow travel by rail, with half-timbered villages where time seems paused.

Departure points

Baden-Baden is easily reachable from many of Western Europe's major cities, including Paris Gare de l'Est (3h) on SNCF, Brussels Midi/Zuid (5h) on Deutsche Bahn or Thalys, Amsterdam Centraal (5h) on Deutsche Bahn, and Berlin Hauptbahnhof (6h) on Deutsche Bahn. Trains starting outside Germany require a change in a German city.

❶ Baden-Baden

The clue's baked into the name: baden means 'to bathe' in German. Baden-Baden's curative waters and air of old-world luxury have attracted royals, the rich and famous for centuries. Friedrichsbad, a palatial 19th-century marble-and-mosaic-adorned spa, makes for an atmospheric spot to rejuvenate. It's just steps away from the remains of one of the oldest and best-preserved ancient Roman bathing complexes left in the country.

🚄 **Fast, direct ICE trains run approximately hourly between Baden-Baden and Freiburg (0h45; www.bahn.de).**

❷ Freiburg

At the foot of the Black Forest, Freiburg is Germany's sunniest city – a fact that is clearly reflected in the mood of this

Fact box

Carbon (kg per person) 5.5
Distance (km) 270km
Nights 10+
Transport budget €90

The pump house in Baden-Baden's Kurhaus spa complex

cheerful university town. The medieval Altstadt (Old Town) is a story-book tableau of gabled townhouses, cobbled lanes and cafe-rimmed plazas, ideal for sipping a glass of white wine from a local vineyard. Freiburg has impressive eco-credentials too, with strict urban design guidelines to reduce car usage and maximise green space. Solar panels top the roofs of many neighbourhoods.

🚆 **Trains from Freiburg to Gengenbach (1h) require a change in Offenburg to reach the start of the scenic Black Forest Railway that continues to Singen.**

✦ Day trip

Schauinsland

The 1284m peak of Schauinsland looms above Freiburg and is topped by a lookout tower with fabulous views to the Rhine Valley and Alps at what has to be the most soul-stirring vantage point in the Black Forest. Walking, cross-country and cycling trails allow visitors to capture the scenery from every angle. You can hoof it up the hill or take a cable car,

commissioned in 1930 as the world's first, which glides to the top in 20 minutes.

🚆 **Take tram line 2 to Freiburg Dorfstrasse, and then catch bus 21 to Horben Schauinslandbahn, the location of the lower station of the cable car.**

❸ Gengenbach

If ever a Black Forest town could be described as chocolate box, it

Opposite, the Old Town of
Gengenbach; left, Triberg Waterfalls;
below, the town of Triberg

House of 1000 Clocks, where you can pick
out a traditional or trendy bird of your
own to take home.

🚆 **You'll chug along the final stretch of the
beautiful Black Forest Railway, until the line
ends in Konstanz (1h30). Trains run every
hour.**

❺ Konstanz

Central Europe's third-largest lake, Lake
Constance straddles three countries:
Germany, Austria and Switzerland. Sidling
up to the Swiss border, bisected by the
Rhine and outlined by the Alps, the city
of Konstanz sits prettily on the lake's
northwestern shore. Konstanz is a feel-
good university town with a lively buzz
and upbeat bar scene, particularly in the
cobbled Altstadt and around the harbour.
In summer, the locals head outdoors to
the leafy promenade and enjoy lazy days
in lakefront lidos.

Returning home

Konstanz' train station has a direct line
to Zürich (1h15), which then has nonstop
routes to Paris (4h).

would surely be Gengenbach, with its
scrumptious Old Town of half-timbered
houses framed by vineyards and orchards.
Every December, the village rekindles
childhood memories of opening tiny
windows when the town hall morphs into
the world's biggest Advent calendar. At
6pm daily, one of 24 windows is opened
to reveal a festive scene.

🚆 **Hop back on the Black Forest Railway to
Triberg (0h40). Direct trains depart every
two hours.**

❹ Triberg

Triberg is home to Germany's highest
waterfall, and it's the heir to the original
Black Forest gateau recipe. It's also the
kitschy nesting ground of the world's
biggest cuckoos. Here you'll find the
so-called 'world's oldest-largest cuckoo
clock', which took a local clockmaker
three years to build by hand. Visit the

Adriatic adventure

Paris · Munich · Zagreb · Belgrade · Bar

With trains ranging from lightning fast French TGVs to the trundling services of the Balkans, this route passes through eight countries to the blue shallows of the Adriatic.

Departure points

Paris is at a crossroads for Western European rail services – direct trains run from London St Pancras (2h30), Amsterdam Centraal (3h30) and Toulouse Matabiau (4h). Low Countries passengers who want to make tracks south straight away can skip Paris, and instead make directly for Munich via Thalys services to Cologne, before changing for southbound ICE trains to the Bavarian capital.

❶ Paris

Gare de L'Est is the terminus where this journey begins – it's also in a prime spot for easy Métro trips to some of Paris' major landmarks. Board Line 4 direct to Cité to see reconstruction work on Notre Dame, or disembark at Les Halles to take a short walk to the Centre Pompidou.
🚆 **Board one of about 20 services a day to Munich Hauptbahnhof (6h). www.sncf.com**

❷ Munich

The Bavarian capital is a powerhouse of precision engineering and a bastion of tradition: you can see both elements at play at the Glockenspiel in the 19th-century town hall, where 32 figures perform clockwork dances to crowds below. Fast forward to the present at the excellent Deutsches Museum – the

Fact box

Carbon (kg per person) 38
Distance (km) 1900
Nights 12+
Transport budget (€) 450

The Bay of Kotor on the Adriatic Coast

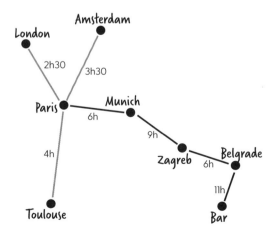

world's largest museum of science and technology.

🚆 **From Munich Hauptbahnhof, daily sleeper trains depart at 11.35pm, crossing Austria and Slovenia and arriving in Zagreb Glavni Kolodvor at 8.35am the following morning (9h; www.hzpp.hr)**

❸ Zagreb

Part Yugoslav metropolis, part Hapsburg capital, the handsome city of Zagreb sees a fraction of the visitors of the Croatian coast, but it's worth an overnight stay on the journey south. Alongside churches, galleries and cobbled squares, the Museum of Broken Relationships has emerged as one of the main attractions here – inside you'll find mementos from

A sunset river-barge cruise in
Belgrade

**Topcider station at 9am, reaching Bar on
the Montenegrin coast at 8pm. A sleeper
service also runs. No online bookings.**

❺ Bar

The industrial port of Bar, Montenegro,
is where the rails finally run out on the
shore of the Adriatic. The town isn't much
to write home about, but it's the perfect
base for forays along the Montenegrin
coast – to the southeast are the sunny
beaches and ethnic-Albanian culture of
Ulcinj. Alternatively, head north to the
village of Virpazar to take a boat trip on
the waters of Lake Skadar, where green
hills rise over the reedy expanse.

✈ Day trip

Bay of Kotor
Looking not unlike a Norwegian fjord
transplanted to the Mediterranean, the
Bay of Kotor is the Adriatic coast at its
most sublime. A few towns cluster around
the bay, but Kotor itself is the highlight:
a jumble of churches, battlements and
piazzas, sandwiched between limestone
cliffs and the sea.
**🚌 Numerous local bus companies travel to
Kotor from Bar bus station 1h45).**

lost loves, donated from all over the world.
**🚆 From Zagreb, a daily train departs for
Belgrade – it's not possible to book online,
but spaces are normally available (6h).
Check times at www.bahn.de.**

❹ Belgrade

Huddled around a mighty citadel on the
banks of the Danube, gritty Belgrade is
one of Europe's most underrated capital
cities. It's also the starting point for the
spectacular Belgrade-Bar railway – a
masterpiece of Yugslav engineering
that traverses the Dinaric Alps, passing
through Bosnia and into Montenegro,
following turquoise rivers and rattling over
lofty spans. Look out for the spectacular
Mala Rijeka viaduct, which was once the
world's highest railway bridge.
🚆 A single daytime train leaves Belgrade

Returning home

An alternative route back to Paris would
be to board a ferry from Bar to Bari in
Italy, followed by a direct train to Milan
and another direct train to the French
capital. Another option is to catch local
buses up the Montenegrin and Croatian
Coasts, reconnecting with the Italian rail
network around Trieste.

Rome, Naples and Sardinia by Ferry

Rome · Naples · Cagliari · Olbia · Civitavecchia
This itinerary takes in two shores of the Tyrrhenian Sea, from the volcanic drama of the Bay of Naples to the idyllic beaches and captivating landscapes of Sardinia.

Departure points

Rome is the starting point for this adventure. It's accessible from Milan Centrale on high-speed Frecciarossa services (3h). Milan stations can be reached by onward connections to Munich Hauptbahnhof (10h total to Rome), or direct TGV services from Paris Gare de Lyon (10h total to Rome).

❶ Rome

Rome is a city deserving a lifetime's exploration – it's also compact enough to see many of its defining sights in a day or two, such as the soaring columns of St Peter's and the ruins of the Forum. To see a quieter side of the city, rent a bike and cycle along the cobbles of the Appian Way – the old Roman road that extends out of the city into glorious countryside beyond.

🚆 **From Rome Termini, board a Frecciarossa service to Naples Centrale – there are roughly two departures every hour (1h). www.trenitalia.com**
🛏 **Hotel tip: Ecohotel Roma**

❷ Naples

Like Rome today, Naples was also once a major European capital with a swagger that's still evident in its baroque chapels

Fact box

Carbon (kg per person) 124
Distance (km) 1200
Nights 10+
Transport budget (€) 300

Rome's Trevi Fountain

and monasteries, striding boulevards and in glorious Neapolitan pizza. It's also the gateway for the attractions of the Gulf of Naples – among them Sorrento, the myth-steeped island of Capri and the vertiginous slopes of the Amalfi Coast.

There are up to two sailings a week from Naples to Cagliari (14h). www.tirrenia.it

Day trip

Pompeii & Herculaneum

The twin sites of Pompeii and Herculaneum are a testament to the power of Vesuvius. See the Roman frescoes, bathhouses and temples frozen in time from the AD79 eruption.

Pompeii and Herculaneum are respectively a 30-minute and a 20-minute metro ride from Naples' Piazza Garibaldi. www.pompeiisites.org

Italy's Amalfi Coast is peppered with stunning views, like this one at Ravello

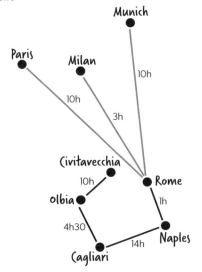

❸ Cagliari

Arriving by sea is the perfect introduction to Sardinia's spirited capital – rising above the rooftops is Il Castello, a fortified quarter of crumbling battlements and winding lanes. Down below are the seafood restaurants of the quayside Marina district. In between are enough museums, architecture and gastronomic highlights to keep you occupied for a few days.

🚆 **From Cagliari, there are direct departures for Olbia – be warned, it's a slow stopping service (4h30). www. trenitalia.com**

❹ Olbia

Olbia is often regarded as a staging post for the stellar beaches of Sardinia's northeast coast, but it's a charming city in its own right, with a small *centro storico*,

(historic centre) and shady vineyards to explore on the edge of town.

⛴ **From Olbia's port, Stazione Marittima, there are multiple ferries to Civitavecchia daily, taking just under 10 hours. www. tirrenia.it**

❻ Day trip

Costa Smeralda

There's no shortage of competition, but the Costa Smeralda is one of Italy's most hallowed coastlines, with fjord-like inlets of Caribbean-hued waters, and exclusive resorts beloved of billionaire jetsetters. The coastline starts 17km north of Olbia, but its hub is the town of Porto Cervo, reached on a one-hour bus ride from Olbia. Ask the driver to stop en route so you can hop off at sublime beaches like Spiaggia Liscia Ruja and Spiaggia Romazzino.

Crystal waters on the Sardinian coast

❺ Civitavecchia

Civitavecchia is the mainland cruise ship port serving Rome, and is visited mostly as a transit point for the capital. From the docks, it's an easy 20-minute walk to the station, passing the 17th-century battlements of Forte Michelangelo.

Returning home

From Civitavecchia, thrice hourly trains leave for Rome stations, taking roughly one hour. From Rome, onward connections lead to Paris and Munich. For an alternate end point or an adventurous extension to this itinerary, board a ferry at Porto Torres on Sardinia's northwestern coast to Barcelona, taking around 12 hours.

Provence and Languedoc by rail

Aix-en-Provence · Avignon · Nîmes · Montpellier · Sète
Roman history, great food and fine art fill the senses on this leisurely train hop through France's sunny south.

Departure points

You can start this trip in Paris, which can be reached from Berlin Hauptbahnhof (8h30), Amsterdam Centraal (3h) and London St Pancras (2h30) with ease. Around 10 TGVs a day connect Paris Gare de Lyon with Aix-en-Provence (3h30). Tickets for the service (and every route mentioned in this itinerary) can be booked with https://en.oui.sncf. Aix's TGV station is a 15-minute bus trip from the city centre.

❶ Aix-en-Provence

Chi-chi but relaxed Aix is a lovely city for gentle exploration. Churches, galleries, boutiques, cafes and fountains dot its intimate alleys and grand boulevards. The engrossing Musée Granet is the city's artistic highlight, and contains nine works by local master Paul Cézanne.
🚄 **TGVs run from Aix to Avignon (0h25) roughly hourly. Avignon's TGV station is a 10-minute bus trip from the centre.**

❷ Avignon

Home to imposing medieval walls, an iconic bridge and the enormous Palais des Papes – the world's largest Gothic palace – Avignon's headline sights take the breath

Fact box

Carbon (kg per person) 5
Distance (km) 250
Nights 10+
Transport budget (€) 150

Avignon Bridge with the Palais des Papes beyond

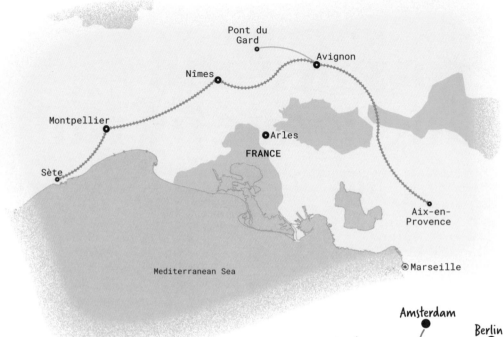

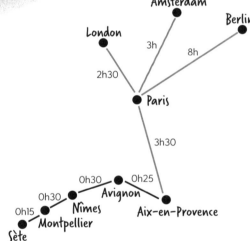

away. But you're likely to have as much fun away from the main streets, getting lost down cobbled hillsides or digging up fine food on Rue des Teinturiers, which manages to be hip and picturesque at the same time.

🚉 **From Avignon Centre station, trains run roughly hourly to Nîmes (0h30).**

✈ Day trip

Pont Du Gard

Roman remains are plentiful in Provence, but this awe-inspiring aqueduct is the pick of the bunch. The statistics (50m high, 275m long) are impressive and the views from the banks of the River Gard are phenomenal. It looks even better from the water – you can swim right by the aqueduct itself.

🚌 **Bus B21 (from Nîmes) and A15 (from Avignon) run several times a day, both taking around 50 minutes – it's easy to get a bus there in the morning and return the same afternoon. www.edgard-transport.fr**

Left, the Palais de Justice in Montpellier; below, the magnificent Pont du Gard

❸ Nîmes

One of the great cities of Roman Gaul, Nîmes boasts a vast Roman arena and a two-thousand-year-old Temple of Diana, while its 19th-century cotton production gave denim ("de Nîmes") its name. But these remnants of empire have been re-clothed: modern architecture and contemporary art galleries helped lift the city from its 20th-century doldrums, and the Musée de la Romanité houses some of the region's finest archaeological finds in a gleaming carapace of steel and glass.

🚆 **Several trains per hour run from Nîmes to Montpellier (0h30).**

❹ Montpellier

It's a substantial city – Languedoc's largest – but Montpellier can feel a little off the main tourist trail, which makes this easy-going place all the more enjoyable. The Musée Fabre offers a rich collection of Old Masters and Impressionists, while elsewhere France's oldest botanic gardens, lovely squares and courtyard restaurants – their atmosphere made lively by the large student population – await.

🚆 **Trains from Montpellier Saint-Roch to Sète (0h15) leave several times an hour. Local buses run to the beaches.**

❺ Sète

The cranes and warehouses of this busy port might not scream Mediterranean charm, but that's part of the point: Sète is a lively city with a buzzing fish market and a year-round population. There's good food to be had, alongside 20km of rather lovely beaches and water-jousting (just what it sounds like) festivals in summer. The Canal du Midi ends here, emptying into a great lagoon, and a stroll along the shore is a fitting finale to the trip.

Returning home

From Sète, around four direct trains a day go to Paris Gare de Lyon (4h): change in Montpellier for more services.

Via Dinarica hike

Zagreb · Split · Biokovo Nature Park · Herceg Novi · Durmitor National Park · Sutjeska National Park · Sarajevo

Experience thrilling mountain landscapes as you hike the rugged peaks of the Dinaric Alps and explore three national parks along this trans-Balkans mega trail.

Departure points

This itinerary takes advantage of the waymarked hiking paths that cross the mountains of Croatia, Montenegro and Bosnia and Hercegovina along the cross-border Via Dinarica route. The journey begins in Zagreb, which can be reached by train from other Western European cities including Venice, Munich and Vienna.

❶ Zagreb

Spend a day discovering the art, cuisine and nightlife of the vibrant Croatian capital before catching the onward bus to Split.

🚌 From Zagreb bus station (www.akz.hr), there are frequent services (more than one per half-hour) to Split each day (5h).

❷ Split

Dalmatia's largest city, Split is home to the extraordinary Diocletian's Palace – a lived-in ancient Roman complex whose tangled alleys are packed with bars, shops and restaurants. Its highlight is the splendid medieval Cathedral of St Dominus. To get a taste of the hiking adventure that awaits, climb Marjan Hill's shady paths for sweeping views over the city and the surrounding Adriatic islands.

Market huts in Zagreb's Old Town

Fact box

Carbon (kg per person) 123.5

Distance (km) 1643

Nights 10+

Transport budget (€) 110

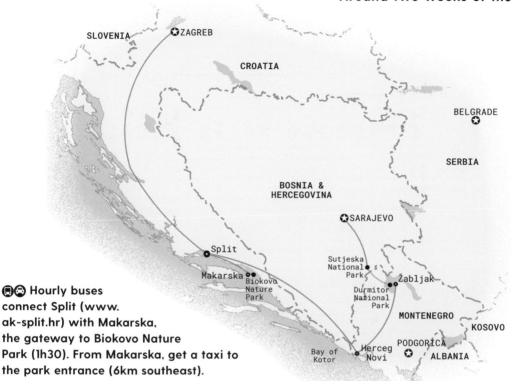

🚌 **Hourly buses connect Split (www. ak-split.hr) with Makarska, the gateway to Biokovo Nature Park (1h30). From Makarska, get a taxi to the park entrance (6km southeast).**

❸ Biokovo Nature Park

The popular beach resort of Makarska is backed by the glorious Biokovo mountain range, which makes it the perfect base for day hikes and other active pursuits such as paragliding. Various agencies offer guided walks in the Biokovo massif. The climb to the highest peak, Sveti Jure (1762m), takes about seven hours – you'll be rewarded with fantastic views over the Makarska riviera.

🚌 **From Makarska, head back to Split to catch a bus to Herceg Novi in Montenegro; there are two daily services (6h).**

❹ Herceg Novi

Welcome to the Bay of Kotor! Herceg Novi's Old Town rises uphill from the coastal promenade; its sturdy forts,

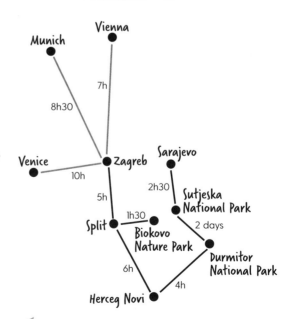

Opposite, Đurđevića Tara Bridge in Montenegro; left, Durmitor National Park

🚶 Herceg Novi's Black Mountain and Sarajevo-based Green Visions (www.greenvisions.ba) organise cross-border hikes along this stretch of the Via Dinarica, including all the logistics. The hike takes about two days.

❻ Sutjeska National Park

On the Bosnian side of the Via Dinarica trail, the wilderness of majestic Sutjeska National Park awaits. The park has a network of hiking trails; the highlight is the climb to Bosnia's highest peak, Maglić (2386m), and another popular trail winds among the upland lakes of Zelengora. For the strictly protected reserve of Perućica, one of the few remaining European rainforests, you'll need to arrange a guide through the information centre (www.npsutjeska.info).

🚌 **The only settlement within the park, with several accommodation options, is Tjentište. Buses run daily between Tjentište and Sarajevo (2h30).**

❼ Sarajevo

The beating heart of Bosnia's capital is the charming Baščaršija quarter, with its historical courtyards and traditional crafts stores. Strolling its cobblestoned alleys reveals Sarajevo's multicultural heritage, including Ottoman-era mosques, synagogues and churches. As a final thrill, take the cable car up Mt Trebević for panoramic views and to check out the abandoned Olympic bobsled track.

🚌 **From Sarajevo's central bus station, catch one of the several daily buses back to Zagreb (6h30) for train connections north and west to Austria, Germany and Italy.**

picturesque churches, fragrant parks and pebbly beaches merit at least a day's exploration. This is also the best place in Montenegro for arranging outdoor activities; Black Mountain (www.montenegroholiday.com) is an excellent agency offering anything from diving to mountain biking.

🚌 **Buses run daily from Herceg Novi to Žabljak (4h), a resort town in Durmitor National Park with plenty of accommodation options.**

❺ Durmitor National Park

The rugged Durmitor mountain range, with its canyons, glacial lakes and limestone peaks (the highest is Bobotov Kuk at 2523m), is prime hiking territory. The visitor centre (www.nparkovi.me) can help with maps and advice. Rewarding hikes through magnificent scenery include the route to Škrčka Lakes and another from the Black Lake to the Ice Cave. The cross-border hike to Sutjeska National Park in Bosnia is the Via Dinarica's classic leg.

Canals & bicycles

Amsterdam · Rotterdam · Antwerp · Bruges · Antwerp · Amsterdam
Zipping between the Netherlands and Belgium by train is a breeze, and these pan-flat neighbours are perfect for exploring by bike or boat.

Departure points

High-speed Thalys services connect Amsterdam with Brussels and Paris; direct Eurostars travel to London (via Brussels and Rotterdam) in under four hours. German ICE trains run six times daily between Amsterdam and Cologne; many continue to Frankfurt.

❶ Amsterdam

The city of canals makes a dreamy start. It's eminently walkable – most of the major sights and museums can be reached on foot – but the best idea is to follow the locals' lead and explore by bike: rental companies are dotted all over the city. Whatever you do, don't miss a cruise on a canal boat, ideally at sunset.

Fact box
Carbon (kg per person) 11
Distance (km) 560
Nights 10+
Transport budget (€) 160

🚲 **GVB (www.gvb.nl) tickets cover all Amsterdam's public transport, including buses, metros and trams. Rental bikes cost about €12 daily.**
🚆 **NS Intercity trains (www.ns.nl) run four times an hour to Rotterdam, a journey of 40 to 75 minutes. Many Eurostars also stop in Rotterdam en route to Brussels.**

❷ Rotterdam

The Netherlands' second city is all about innovation and cutting-edge design.

Canal life in Amsterdam

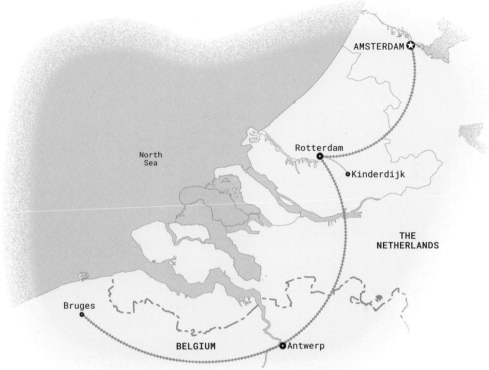

North
Sea

AMSTERDAM ✪

Rotterdam

● Kinderdijk

THE
NETHERLANDS

Bruges ○

BELGIUM   ○ Antwerp

Brilliant buildings include the Erasmus
Bridge, De Rotterdam tower, the eye-
popping Markthal (Market Hall) and the
redeveloped docklands at Kop van Zuid
(South Bank). Rotterdam is also known for
its lively cafe culture and, of course, for its
canals. Well, this is Holland after all.

🚊 **Frequent high-speed Thalys trains run
from Rotterdam to Antwerp (0h30) but you
need an advance booking (www.thalys.
com). Slower NS IC trains run hourly and
don't need reservations (1h).**

🕑 Day trip

Kinderdijk

Few landscapes look more quintessentially
Dutch than Kinderdijk, where 19 historic

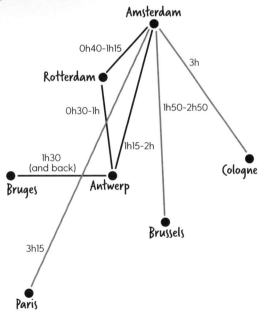

Amsterdam

0h40-1h15

3h

Rotterdam

1h50-2h50

0h30-1h

1h15-2h

Cologne

1h30
(and back)

Bruges   Antwerp

Brussels

3h15

Paris

windmills spin over a vista of canals, marshes and wetlands. Some are still operating, others are now private homes; a network of lovely cycle paths meanders between them.

🚲😊 **Kinderdijk is close enough to Rotterdam to cycle (16km), or you can catch the Waterbus fast ferry from Rotterdam Erasmusbrug (eight daily, www.waterbus. nl). Bikes are carried for free.**

---

❸ Antwerp

Antwerp is Belgium's biggest port and capital of cool. Famous as the home of Peter Paul Rubens, it's stuffed with art museums – factor in the artist's former studio at Rubenshuis, the collection at Museum Mayer van den Bergh and the Museum Plantin-Moretus, home to the world's oldest printing press. Wherever you wander, the 123m-high spire of Onze-Lieve-Vrouwekathedraal, Antwerp's 14th-century cathedral, is impossible to miss.

🚲 **Antwerp's red-bike system, Velo-Antwerpen (www.velo-antwerpen.be) has more than 100 stations around the city.**
🚆 **Two trains an hour shuttle direct to Bruges (1h30).**

❹ Bruges

Medieval Bruges (Brugge in Dutch) looks like it's dropped from the pages of a fairy tale – a photogenic confection of cobbled lanes, canals, market squares and whitewashed almshouses. Snap a selfie in the Markt and Burg, the city's public spaces, then another at the top of the

Right, Antwerp's fashion district; opposite, the Belfort belfry in Bruges

13th-century Belfort belfry.
🚆 **Catch a return train back to Antwerp (1h15-2h).**

❺ Antwerp

A second stop in Antwerp gives time to delve into cafe and beer culture: head for 't Zuid for cocktails, Zurenborg for terrace cafes, and Borgerhout for hipster bars.
🚆 **Return to Amsterdam by train (1h15-2h, three per hour).**

❻ Amsterdam

Back in Amsterdam, explore museums, including the vast Rijksmuseum and excellent Van Gogh Museum, then take day trips into outer neighbourhoods: trendy Jordaan, hip de Pijp and up-and-coming Oost.

© Michael Jacobs / Getty Images. © Alyaksandr Stzhalkouski / 500px

A circuit of Sicily

Palermo • Taormina • Catania • Syracuse • Agrigento

Take slow trains around the crossroads of the Mediterranean, disembarking to see modern cities and ancient ruins, glorious beaches and smouldering volcanoes.

Departure points

Coming from the Italian mainland, Palermo might be easiest accessed by long distance ferry – GNV has sailings from Naples (10h) and Civitavecchia outside Rome (14h). Ferries to Palermo also run from Cagliari, Sardinia (12h), which can connect with Barcelona via another ferry that leaves from Porto Torres on the northern coast of Sardinia (12h).

❶ Palermo

As charming as it is chaotic, the Sicilian capital Palermo is where Sicily's cultural stew is spiciest – from neoclassical porticos to oriental domes and glittering Byzantine mosaics to souk-like markets that whisper of the island's Arab past. Head to the boisterous Mercato di Ballarò to taste fresh olives, charcuterie and cheeses.

From Palermo, catch a train to Taormina Giardini; it'll involve a change either at Catania Centrale or Messina Centrale to follow the coastline (4h). www.trenitalia.com

❷ Taormina

Taormina's Greek theatre is arguably the most dramatically sited in the world,

Fact box

Carbon (kg per person) 14

Distance (km) 700

Nights 10+

Transport budget (€) 200

Mercato Ballaro in Palermo

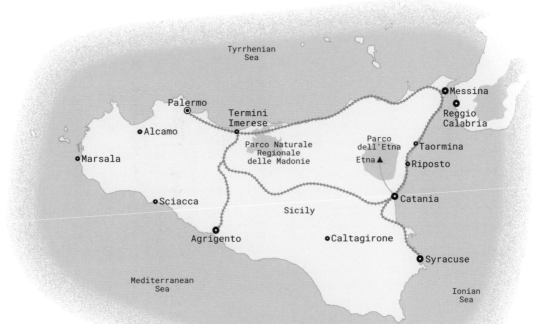

perched on
a hillside with
Etna smouldering above
and the Ionian sea shimmering
below. Wander the streets of this sometime writers' retreat, or cool off from the
Sicilian heat with a dip at Lido Mazzarò
– a crescent-shaped beach accessed by a
short cable car ride from Taormina.
🚆 **From Taormina, board one of up to 30
southbound services to Catania Centrale
(1h).**

✈ Day trip

Ferrovia Circumetnea
Europe's biggest and most active
volcano, Etna lures no shortage of
determined hikers to its slopes. For a
lazier (and possibly safer) perspective
on the mountain, catch the Ferrovia
Circumetnea – a narrow-gauge railway
that loops around Etna, trundling through

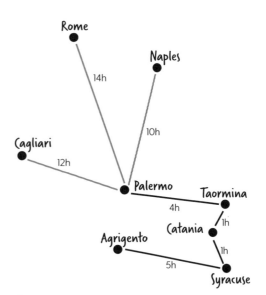

© f.sco 81 / 500 px

A roadside granita stall

lush vineyards, olive groves and barren lava fields. This trip also makes a good diversion en route to Catania as Riposto, the departure point for the Ferrovia Circumetnea, is also on the line from Taormina to Catania.

🚆 It's a 20-minute train ride from Taormina Giardini to Giarre-Riposto, from where the Ferrovia Circumetnea departs for Catania Borgo (3h). www.circumetnea.it

❸ Catania

Catania is Sicily's second city, and worth a day or two's exploration thanks to its baroque palaces, lively piazze and busy fish market. It's also the hometown of pasta alla norma (a dish made with aubergine, tomatoes and pecorino) – Nuova Trattoria del Forestiero serves one of the best in town.

🚆 Around 10 daily direct trains connect Catania with Syracuse (1hr). www.trenitalia.com

❹ Syracuse

Stepping over the channel separating the island of Ortygia from the Sicilian mainland, Syracuse quickly evokes swoons from newcomers. Its streets are a study in the baroque, with rambling alleys leading to the Piazza del Duomo. It's easy to forget this was once the biggest city in the ancient world: the Parco Archeologico della Neapolis on the city outskirts preserves remnants of its Grecian past.

🚆🚆 Getting from Syracuse to Agrigento Centrale by train is famously slow, potentially involving changes at Catania and Termini Imerese (5h). Expect a similar journey time if you catch a bus from Syracuse to Catania airport, changing for another bus to Agrigento (www.trenitalia.com).

❺ Agrigento

There's nowhere more stirring to conclude a Sicilian odyssey than Agrigento's Valley of the Temples – the ruins of the ancient Greek city of Akragas. The highlight is the magnificently preserved 5th-century BC Temple of Concordia – built in tribute to the goddess of harmony and sited on a ridge so it could be visible to sailors far out on the Mediterranean swells.

Returning home

Direct trains run from Agrigento Centrale to Palermo Centrale (1h).

Paris to Copenhagen

Paris · Strasbourg · Frankfurt am Main · Bremen · Hamburg · Copenhagen
Strike out from the City of Light to Scandinavia, stopping in fairy-tale German towns and boarding one of Europe's last rail ferries across the Baltic.

Departure points

Paris Gare du Nord has Eurostar connections to London (2h30) and fast TGV services Barcelona (6h30), which in turn has onward connections to Madrid (2h30). If you'd rather do the itinerary in reverse, Copenhagen is served by direct trains from Stockholm (5h).

❶ Paris

Originally called 'Strasbourg Platform', the glorious Gare de L'Est is the starting point for the trip east. A 10-minute walk from the station is Du Pain et Des Idées – arguably Paris' best loved bakery, and the perfect place to stock up on pain au chocolat and croissants ahead of your train journey.

Ⓡ Roughly 15 trains run daily from Paris to Strasbourg-Ville (2h). www.sncf.com

❷ Strasbourg

Perched on the easternmost frontier of France, Strasbourg has an unmistakably Teutonic feel to it, from its half-timbered houses to its *winstubs* – rustic taverns serving Alsatian wine by the carafe. The sense of cultural disorientation continues ambling the Grande Île, the island

Strasbourg's half-timbered houses at dusk

Fact box

Carbon (kg per person) 28

Distance (km) 1400

Nights 10+

Transport budget (€) 400

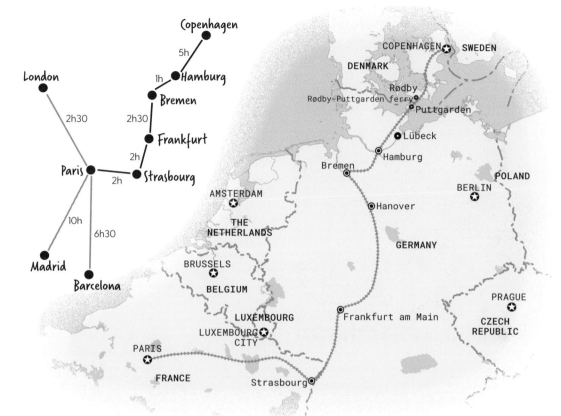

at the heart of the city. Here buildings back on to the River Ill, and the city's Gothic cathedral soars over the rooftops. 🚆 **Around 15 trains a day travel from Strasbourg-Ville to Frankfurt Hauptbahnhof (2h), some direct and some requiring changes at Offenburg or Karlsruhe (www. sncf.com).**

❸ Frankfurt am Main

Unfairly synonymous with finance, high-rise buildings and trade fairs, Frankfurt has plenty to occupy visitors for a day or two, from its pretty Altstadt (Old Town) to its Museumsufer, a collection of stellar

museums and galleries on the banks of the River Main. One landmark with a fascinating and tumultuous history is the IG Farben Building – a chemical weapons hub for the Nazis and later the post-war Allied HQ in Germany, it's now a university building containing quirky paternoster lifts. 🚆 **Around 30 trains a day link Frankfurt Hauptbahnhof with Bremen (2h30; www. bahn.de).**

❹ Bremen

You might have heard of Bremen from the Brothers Grimm story *Town Musicians of Bremen* – and on first glance its fairy-

Left, a beach bar at Hamburg's harbour; right, Carcassonne; previous page, the Eiffel Tower

shaped like a hoisted sail, perched atop a 1960s warehouse.

🚇 **Take the train to Copenhagen (5h), which involves the train boarding the Rødby-Puttgarden ferry. Tickets can be booked online at www.bahn.de**

➤ Day trip

Lübeck

A city of the Hanseatic League like Hamburg, Lübeck has a more sedate feel than its bigger neighbour. Arriving from the station, enter the town via its biggest landmark, the Holstentor, a giant medieval gate crowned by pointy towers that resemble witches' hats.

🚇 **Up to 40 trains a day travel from Hamburg Hauptbahnhof to Lübeck Hauptbahnhof (1h). www.bahn.de**

tale credentials seem legit. The town has a gabled town hall and a fishers' quarter, Schnoor, with quaint cottages. That being said, it's also a forward-facing city, evident in the Universum, a futuristic science museum shaped like a silver UFO.

🚇 **Up to 40 trains a day connect Bremen with Hamburg Hauptbahnhof (1h). www.bahn.de**

❺ Hamburg

Germany's biggest port, Hamburg has been a city defined by the sea since the heyday of the Hanseatic League. Recent times have brought big changes to its waterfront, namely HafenCity, a new district featuring bold contemporary architecture south of Speicherstadt. At the vanguard of the changes is the Elbphilharmonie, a new concert hall

❻ Copenhagen

Copenhagen is a pioneer in urban planning. Its latest masterstroke is CopenHill, a waste management plant that doubles as an 'urban mountain sports centre', with a ski slope on the roof and Europe's highest climbing wall scaling its facade. Ascend its dizzy heights for views west to the wharves and towers of the Danish capital, and east to the Øresund Strait.

Returning home

To return to Paris, you'll need to travel back to Hamburg. From here, the fastest way to the French capital is a train to Karlsruhe, followed by a TGV from Karlsruhe to Gare de L'Est (8hr30 in total).

French connection to Tunisia

Montpellier · Nice · Marseille · Tunis
Explore the many moods of the Mediterranean on this jaunt that takes in France's sun-drenched southern cities before crossing over the sea for a taste of North Africa.

Departure points

High-speed SNCF train services connect Montpellier to Paris Gare de Lyon (3h30). A direct Renfe/SNCF line also connects Madrid and Montpellier in under seven hours. The journey from Rome Termini (11h40) is more arduous, requiring a handful of changes from Frecciarossa trains to France's TGV, but is possible in half a day.

❶ Montpellier

One of France's most multicultural cities, laidback Montpellier is a student town with a stylish streak. A jumble of narrow pedestrianised lanes forms the beating heart of the city, and grand 17th-century *hôtels particuliers* (private mansions) show off the success of Montpellier's old merchants.

🚆 **Trains to Nice (5h) require at least one change, usually in Marseille. Buses take just an hour longer but are direct and significantly less expensive.**

❸ Day trip

Carcassonne

Fairy-tale Carcassonne is perched on a rocky hilltop and bristles with zigzag battlements, stout walls and spiky turrets.

Fact box

Carbon (kg per person) 111

Distance (km) 1265

Nights 12+

Transport budget (€) 300

LOW-CARBON EUROPE

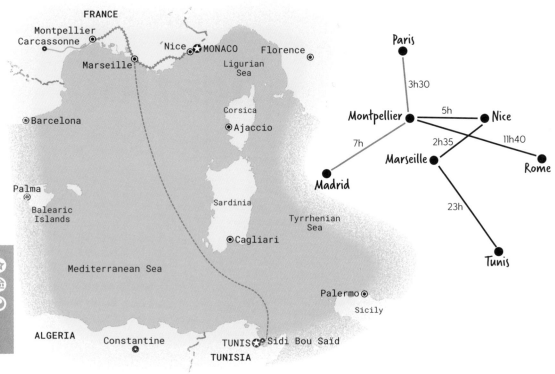

FRANCE
Montpellier
Carcassonne
Nice · MONACO
Florence
Marseille
Ligurian
Sea

Barcelona
Corsica
Ajaccio

Palma
Balearic
Islands
Sardinia
Tyrrhenian
Sea
Cagliari

Mediterranean Sea

Palermo
Sicily

ALGERIA   Constantine   TUNIS · Sidi Bou Saïd
TUNISIA

Paris
3h30
Montpellier — 5h — Nice
7h   2h35   11h40
Marseille   Rome
Madrid
23h
Tunis

A Unesco World Heritage Site since 1997, Cité Médiévale, as the old walled town is called, is most people's idea of the perfect medieval castle.

🚉 **Direct trains run nearly hourly between Montpellier and Carcassonne (1h30). www. sncf.com.**

❷ Nice

Nice has been a tourist magnet since the 1700s, and the same attractions that drew Europe's belle-époque aristocrats still exert their pull today: the sea, the sun and that perfect Mediterranean climate. Nothing compares to the simple joy of a balmy beach day punctuated with a spot of people-watching from the Promenade des Anglais' famous blue chairs.

🚉 **Direct train services operate**

approximately hourly between Nice and Marseille (2h35).

⊕ Day trip

Monaco

A draw for high-rollers and hedonists, Monaco is renowned as a playground for the prosperous. It's also the world's second-smallest country. Squeezed into just 200 hectares are the famous Monte Carlo casino, a stack of high-rise hotels and a port full of super-sized yachts.

🚉 **Trains to Monaco leave every 20 minutes from Nice Ville station (0h20).**

❸ Marseille

Grit and grandeur coexist seamlessly in Marseille, an exuberantly diverse port city. Once the black sheep of the Provençal

Below, Nice's Promenade des Anglais; right, Sidi Bou Saïd

coastline, the city has blossomed in cultural confidence since its stint as the European Capital of Culture in 2013. Marseille's core is the vibrant Vieux Port (Old Port), mast-to-mast with yachts and pleasure boats. Thanks to renovations and new construction, the city's galleries and museums are flourishing.

🚢 **A daily ferry runs between Marseille and Tunis (23h) in summer, and leaves one or two times a week the rest of the year.**

❹ Tunis

In Tunisia's capital, the term 'living history' really does apply. Waves of colonisation have made the city's fabric complex and created an intoxicatingly rich culture. Take the magnificent medieval medina, previously sidelined by the French but now coming into its own as boutique hotels open and arty cafes lure locals back to the neighbourhoods their grandparents grew up in. To the north is the historic settlement of Carthage, once occupied by Phoenicians and Romans but now the province of upwardly mobile residents.

⊕ Day trip

Sidi Bou Saïd

With its blue-and-white colour scheme, cobbled streets and glimpses of azure waters, the cliff-top village of Sidi Bou Saïd is one of the prettiest spots in Tunisia. Its distinctive architecture is a mix of Ottoman and Andalusian, a result of the influx of Spanish Muslims in the 16th century, and has long been a haven for Western artists, philosophers and eccentrics.

🚆 **The suburban TGM train line runs between Tunis Marine station and Sidi Bou Saïd (0h35).**

Returning home

Returning to Europe means hopping back on the overnight ferry and then a TGV train to Paris (3h20) and beyond.

Baltic to the Mediterranean

Copenhagen · Hamburg · Cologne · Paris · Marseille · Île de Porquerolles
This epic route slices from the blustery straits of Denmark to the balmy shores of the French Riviera, using high-speed railways on a truly Trans-European adventure.

Departure points

Copenhagen is the starting point for this adventure – it's served by regular direct trains from Swedish hubs, including Gothenburg (3h30) and Stockholm (5h), as well as overnight ferries from Oslo (17h).

❶ Copenhagen

Copenhagen has long set a blueprint for sustainable cities, with an ever-evolving network of cycle lanes, organic restaurants and eco-hotels. Its intentions to become the first carbon-neutral capital city by 2025 make it the perfect place to embark on a low-carbon odyssey. Board a direct southbound service to Hamburg, and look out the window as your train rattles onto the Rødby-Puttgarden ferry –

it's one of the few routes in Europe where the trains travel by sea.

🚆 **Deutsche Bahn operates overnight services from Copenhagen to Hamburg (7h). www.bahn.de**

🏨 **Hotel tip: Admiral Hotel**

❷ Hamburg

A seafaring city like Copenhagen, Hamburg has a salty charm of its own – evident wandering the canals and neo-

Copenhagen's Tivoli Gardens

Fact box

Carbon (kg per person) 80
Distance (km) 4000
Nights 14+
Transport budget (€) 600

Oslo
17h
Stockholm
Gothenburg
5h
3h30
Copenhagen
7h
Hamburg
4h
Cologne
3h30
Paris
3h
Marseille — 2h — Île de Porquerolles

Gothic warehouses of the Speicherstadt district. If you've not had enough of trains at this point, visit Miniatur Wunderland – the world's biggest model railway, in which tiny trains traverse all corners of the continent, from the Alps to the Mediterranean.

🚆 **From Hamburg, around 20 services a day connect with Cologne (4h). www.bahn.de**

❸ Cologne

A supersized cathedral, cavernous beer halls and a fine setting on the banks of the Rhine all make Cologne a mandatory stop for a night or two before dashing to warmer climes. Set next to the main station, the Museum Ludwig houses one of Europe's preeminent collections of Pop Art.

🚆 **From Cologne Hauptbahnhof, around 30 direct services run to Paris Gare du Nord (3h30), or connect at Mannheim or Frankfurt for trains running into Paris Gare**

de l'Est with a similar journey time. www. bahn.de

❹ Paris

Crossing from Gare de L'Est to Gare de Lyon takes you past some of Paris' liveliest neighbourhoods – the leafy squares of the Marais district, and the bistros that line the Canal St Martin. As luck would have it, the most opulent restaurant in all of Paris is actually housed inside Gare de Lyon. Le Train Bleu is a mini-Versailles where the great and the good would dine before boarding sleeper services to the Riviera. If the prices on the menu look a

Left, Île de Porquerolles; below,
Marseille; right, Canal St-Martin, Paris

bit frightening, nip in for a quick coffee before catching 300kph TGV Sud-Est services to Marseille.

🚄 **Around 20 direct services connect Gare de Lyon with Marseille St-Charles (3h). www.sncf.com**

❺ Marseille

Marseille is where you'll catch your first sight of the sea since Hamburg. Rather like Hamburg, it's a second city whose waterfront has been wholly reinvented in recent times. Leading the charge is the excellent Mucem – a museum of Mediterranean civilisations through the ages, housed inside a 13th-century fort meshed with a futuristic cubic structure.

🚄⛴ **Over 40 trains per day connect Marseille with Toulon (1h), www.sncf.com. From Toulon, ferries depart for the island of Porquerolles from May to September (1h). www.bateliersdelacotedazur.com**

✛ Day trip

Les Calanques

On first impressions, Marseille may be an unpolished port, but at its southern fringe you'll find the pristine Parc National des

Calanques – a 20km stretch of rocky promontories, where limestone cliffs drop down to azure beaches. Catch a 15-minute train from Marseilles Saint Charles to Cassis on the edge of the park, where it's possible to join kayaking tours, or walk to the three nearest *calanques*.

❻ Île de Porquerolles

The largest of the Îles d'Hyères, Porquerolles sits at the eastern edge of the Riviera and has everything you could want from a Mediterranean island, from remote rocky coves to shady forests of pine and eucalyptus. Lazing on its sandy beaches or cycling its car-free lanes is the perfect way to end your Baltic to Mediterranean adventure.

Returning home

The fastest way back to Copenhagen will likely involve returning to the mainline at Toulon and retracing your steps on TGV and ICE services. Alternatively, return via the Alps, connecting at Milan, Zürich, Munich and onward through Germany towards Hamburg.

Snow train to the Alps

London · Bourg St-Maurice · Grenoble · Annecy · Chamonix
In less than a day, you can rocket from central London right into the heart of the French Alps. Pack your snowboard or skis and goggles and hit the slopes.

Departure points

The Eurostar makes train travel between London, Paris, Lille, Brussels and Amsterdam fast and easy, with a huge network of further connections across Europe. Manchester is just over two hours by train from London; Edinburgh is between 4h and 5h, depending on which service you catch.

❶ London

Limber up with an afternoon rambling around London's greatest outdoor space. Hampstead Heath, with its rolling woodlands and meadows, feels a million miles away from central London (although it's actually only four). It's a wonderful place to stroll: Parliament Hill offers perhaps the finest view of London's skyline. It's easy to get to by tube: take the northern line to Hampstead Heath.

🚆 **On weekends from mid-December to early April, Eurostar (www.eurostar.com) operates direct daytime and overnight services between London St Pancras and Bourg St-Maurice (7h30 to 9h).**

❷ Bourg St-Maurice & Val d'Isère

The combined terrain of Val d'Isère and the lakeside commune of Tignes form one enormous ski area, Espace

The ponds at London's Hampstead Heath

Fact box

Carbon (kg per person) 22
Distance (km) 1080
Nights 10
Transport budget (€) 180

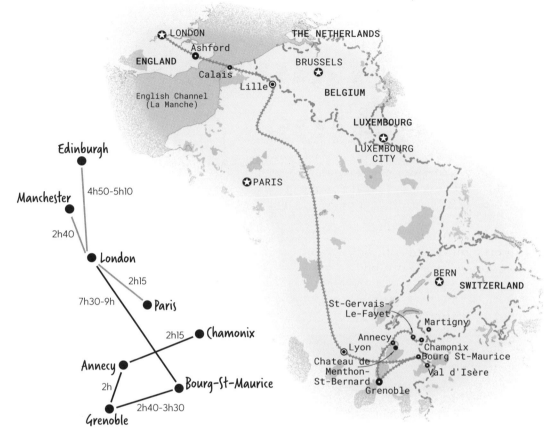

Killy, named after the Olympic downhill champion Jean-Claude Killy who grew up here. It has something for everyone, from beginner-friendly slopes to wild off-piste skiing. From the station at Bourg St-Maurice, buses travel up to Val d'Isère; once you're there, free shuttles link the main skiing areas.

🚇 **Trains run approximately hourly to Grenoble (2h40 to 3h30), mostly requiring a change at Montmelian. Grenoble's train station is about 1km west of the centre, linked by tram lines A and B.**

❸ Grenoble

Haloed by mountains, the self-styled 'Capital of the Alps' unites city pleasures and breathtaking nature. The Isère River slices through the centre, girding the clifftop Bastille, several cutting-edge galleries and riverside museums. The city is also home to the world's first urban cable car, the Téléphérique Grenoble-Bastille, whose spherical pods (known as 'les bulles', or the bubbles) give dreamy views of the mountains. A futuristic tram system makes getting around a breeze.

Left, Mont Blanc and the cable
cars ascending from Grenoble

⊕ Day trip

Château de Menthon-St-Bernard
Twenty-three generations of the De
Menthon family have lived within this
grand chateau, 12km south of Annecy. The
birthplace of St Bernard in 1008, it's also
supposedly one of the inspirations for
Walt Disney's Sleeping Beauty castle. Tours
of the medieval interior take in tapestry-
adorned salons and a magnificent library.
**🚌 Buses run from Annecy (25 minutes, five
to eight services Monday to Saturday).**

**🚌 Regular trains go from Grenoble to
Annecy (2h, at least hourly); there's a direct
service every couple of hours, or an hourly
service if you don't mind changing at
Chambery or Aix-les-Bains.**

❹ Annecy

Nestled on its namesake lake, Annecy
is the jewel of the Haute-Savoie. From
its crowning Château d'Annecy down to
its gurgling canals, Annecy's Vieille Ville
(Old Town) is infused with antique charm.
Canals trickle through town, earning
Annecy its reputation as an 'Alpine
Venice'. Biking and blading are big here,
with 46km of cycling track encircling the
lake: rent from Cyclable (www.cyclable.
com) or Roul Ma' Poule (www.annecy-
location-velo.com).
**🚆🚌 Trains and buses serve Chamonix
throughout the ski season. To get there by
train (2h15, hourly), you'll need to change at
St-Gervais-Le-Fayet.**

❺ Chamonix

The Alps loom over Chamonix, not least
France's highest peak, Mont Blanc (4808m).
The classic view is from the Aiguille du Midi
(3842m), reached via téléphérique (cable
car) year-round. France's largest glacier,
the Mer de Glace, can be reached via the
historic Train du Montenvers, a 5km-long
cog railway opened in 1909. It rattles up to
Montenvers (1913m), from where another
cable car descends to the glacier, which
flows 7km down the crevasse-scarred side
of Mont Blanc. Four hundred steps lead
to an ice cave that is refilled with glacial
sculptures seasonally. From Chamonix,
excursions on the narrow-gauge Mont
Blanc Express (www.mont-blanc-express.
ch) go to the Swiss town of Martigny, via
Argentière and Vallorcine.

Returning home

Backtrack to St-Gervais-Le-Fayet, then
change for Lyon or Paris, from where you
can head to other European cities.

Germany's Romantic Road

Würzburg • Rothenburg ob der Tauber • Nördlingen • Augsburg • Füssen

This train ride along Bavaria's Romantic Road takes a headfirst dive into the Germany of many a fairy tale, with castles, half-timbered towns and Alps galore.

Departure points

Unfurling through Bavaria, Germany's fabled Romantic Road kicks off in Würzburg in the north. The stops en route can get swamped in summer, making shoulder season travel preferable. Direct trains link Würzburg to Berlin (4h) or Frankfurt am Main (1h10). From Frankfurt, high-speed connections head to Paris Est (a further 4h). Alternatively, rent an e-car in Frankfurt or an e-bike in Würzburg to explore the route at your own pace.

❶ Würzburg

Sitting astride the Main River, Würzburg packs a historic punch with a medieval fortress rising above the gables and lanes of its Altstadt, the HQ of prince-bishops for 500 years. Top billing goes to the Unesco-listed Residenz, a baroque palace with a zigzag staircase topped by the world's largest fresco. Veitshöchheim, the summer palace and gardens of the Würzburg prince-bishops, is another highlight a short train ride away. The city has medieval looks but a youthful spirit, with an array of wine taverns, beer gardens and bars.

Regional trains run hourly to Rothenburg ob der Tauber (1h10). www.bahn.de

Fact box

Carbon (kg per person) 7

Distance (km) 350

Nights 8

Transport budget (€) 92

Würzburg is the capital of Bavaria's wine country

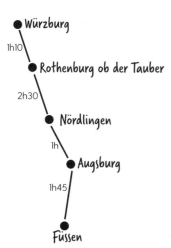

Würzburg

1h10

Rothenburg ob der Tauber

2h30

Nördlingen

1h

Augsburg

1h45

Füssen

❷ Rothenburg ob der Tauber

After the tour buses have departed, you'll fall head-over-heels in love with this medieval honeypot of higgledy-piggledy lanes, half-timbered houses and towered walls – it's pure bedtime-story stuff. Walk the 2.5km circular trail along the city walls, poke around hidden alleys where coopers, cobblers and potters once plied their trades, and gawp in wonder at the Marktplatz, which looks like a Christmas card in December.

🚆 **Regional trains serve Nördlingen (2h30), involving up to three changes.**

❸ Nördlingen

A lower-key vibe makes for an altogether more authentic medieval feel in this charmingly ring-walled, alley-woven town. It sits in the Ries Basin, a massive impact crater gouged out by a meteorite more than 15 million years ago, which you can find out more about at the Rieskrater Museum. Déjà vu? You perhaps recognise these pretty gabled houses from the final

great glass elevator scene in the film *Willy Wonka & the Chocolate Factory* (1971).

🚆 **Regional trains run about every hour between here and Augsburg (1h).**

❸ Day trip

Schloss Harburg

The castle of every kid's wildest medieval

Left, Augsburg's Christmas market; below, Rothenburg ob der Tauber; right, Neuschwanstein

dreams, turreted Schloss Harburg is a 15-minute hike up from the cute, half-timbered town of the same name.

🚇 **Hourly trains run to Schloss Harburg from Nördlingen (0h19).**

❹ Augsburg

A much-adored stop, this Roman-rooted city, founded in 15 BC, was named after Emperor Augustus. Its medieval wealth as a textile hub is mirrored in its historic heart today. Most striking is the Rathausplatz, overlooked by the onion-domed spires of the Renaissance town hall (visit to see its frescoed banquet hall). A backstreet stroll takes in hidden courtyards, patrician houses and rustic Bavarian taverns where dirndl-clad waitresses deliver beers, giant schnitzels and pork knuckles.

🚇 **Hourly local trains run to Füssen (1h45).**

❺ Füssen

The Romantic Road saves the best for last. Wooded hills give way to pop-up views of the Alps as you approach Füssen. While the town is lovely in itself, you'll be itching to head out to the fantastical castles of 'Mad' King Ludwig II. The old romantic put his ever-so-eccentric stamp on Schloss Neuschwanstein, the possible blueprint for Disney's Sleeping Beauty castle. The Alpine backdrop is best admired from the gorge-spanning Marienbrücke bridge.

✈ Day trip

Tegelberg

Give the crowds the slip with an Alpine hike at 1720m-high Tegelberg. Bus 78 runs roughly twice hourly from Füssen train station to the bottom station of the Tegelbergbahn cable station.

Returning home

Direct trains run from Füssen to Munich (2h) every two hours, for connections such as Paris (6h) and Berlin (5h30).

© Michael Thaler / Shutterstock. © Zoom-Zoom / Shutterstock. © Zoom-Zoom / Getty Images. © Samot / Shutterstock

Ionian islands hop

Venice · Corfu · Paxos · Lefkada · Ithaki · Kefallonia
Explore the Venetian towns, lusciously forested mountains and hidden coves of Greece's Ionian Islands by taking a high-speed train to Venice then a scenic ferry.

Departure points

There's a magic about reaching Greece by ferry from Italy, and the Ionian Islands are the first port at which to call. High-speed trains connect northern European cities like Paris (10h), Munich (7h30) and Vienna (8h) to Venice. From here, it's a day-long ferry journey to Corfu, taking in the mountainous coast of Croatia and Albania.

❶ Venice

After the train ride south, you'll want to devote a day to this lagoon city of marble palaces, world-class art and mazy canals. Tick off big-hitters like the golden mosaic-domed Basilica San Marco, Gothic Palazzo Ducale and the outstanding Galleria dell'Accademia,

festooned with original works by Titian, Tintoretto and Canaletto.

🚢 **May to September, there are early morning sailings to Corfu (25h30) every Wednesday and Thursday. www.minoan.gr.**

⊕ Day trip

Venetian islands

From Venice, boat across to one of the more peaceful outlying islands: glass-making Murano, pastel-painted Burano

Melissani Lake (and cave) on Kefallonia

Fact box

Carbon (kg per person) 211

Distance (km) 1100

Nights 10-14+

Transport budget (€) 125

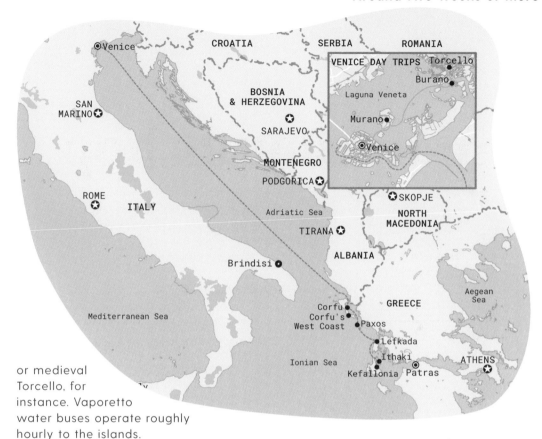

or medieval Torcello, for instance. Vaporetto water buses operate roughly hourly to the islands.

❷ Corfu

Head up on deck as the ferry docks in Corfu Town (Kerkyra) at sunrise. This vivacious town is ideal for a saunter in back alleys lined with chalk-coloured townhouses, pausing for an iced coffee and people-watching at the Liston arcade. Or make for the rocky headland topped by a 14th-century Venetian fortress. Stay overnight to see the city bathed in a soft light once the crowds have subsided.

🚢 **Three daily hydrofoil ferries link Corfu's port to Paxos (1h30) from June to September (one daily May and October).**

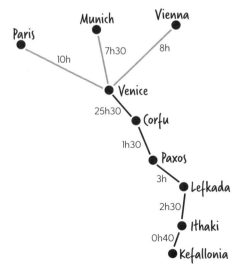

Left, a cove on Antipaxos, just south of Paxos; above, the village of Longos on Paxos

🔄 Day trip

Paleokastritsa

Corfu's west coast is draped with olive and cypress trees, which drop abruptly to bays pummeled by inky-blue water. Take an hour's bus ride to Paleokastritsa for views from its Byzantine monastery.

🚌 **Buses run approximately hourly from Corfu Town's Green Bus station.**

---

❸ Paxos

A vision of the Greek islands before tourism got a grip, small, sleepy Paxos reclines off Corfu's south coast. Allow a day or two on this tiny isle to hike through cicada-filled olive groves to bays where limestone cliffs sheer into azure water, or hang out at piazza-side tavernas. Fine hikes head to Tripitos Arch in the south and Erimitis Beach in the west.

⚓ **The Azimut ferry runs Monday, Wednesday and Friday morning to Lefkada Town (3h) from mid-April to September.**

❹ Lefkada

Mountainous Lefkada has an enticingly wild interior full of villages and centuries-old olive groves. Guarded by a fortress, its harbourside main town makes a relaxed pit stop before you head on to Ithaki.

⚓ **The same ferry (operating on the same days) continues to Pissaetos on Ithaki (2h30)**

❺ Ithaki

The home of Odysseus in Homeric legend, lost-in-time Ithaki is rugged, romantic and largely unscathed by tourism. It has been a yacht-set secret for years, but the hiking is decent too, with mule trails crisscrossing hills to harbour villages, ruins and the occasional beautiful beach suchas cliff-backed Gidaki, a white-pebble crescent slipping into near-luminous water.

⚓ **The Azimut ferry continues on to Sami on Kefallonia (0h40).**

❻ Kefallonia

Wild, mountainous Kefallonia is the largest of the Ionians so getting off the beaten track here is a breeze. With a couple of days, you can visit the likes of stunning Myrtos beach and the harbour town Fiskardo, with its crop of Venetian villas. Or rent a bike to pedal through oak forests, vineyards and olive groves. You'll dock in the cheerful port of Sami, where an ancient acropolis crowns the hillside.

Returning home

From Kefallonia, ferries serve Patras (3h30), where you can board an overnight ferry to Brindisi in Italy (16h). From here you can connect to train services heading north, such as Venice (8h45) and Munich (18h, usually involving several train changes).

Italian lakes & canals

Milan · Lake Garda · Verona · Padua · Venice
From Italian high fashion via lakeside towns to the storied city of canals, this trip across northern Italy shows you the very best of la dolce vita.

Departure points

Milan is a major European rail hub. High-speed trains serve cities such as Geneva (4h), Zürich (3h40), Nice (4h50), Lyon (5h30 with a change in Turin) and Munich (7h30, change in Verona).

❶ Milan

Italian design is world renowned, and its roots lie in 1930s Milan. A visit to the Triennale design museum is a wonderful way to pay homage to the work of Italy's best and brightest designers. After seeing Leonardo da Vinci's *The Last Supper* (Il Cenacolo), there's plenty more art at the Pinacoteca di Brera, including Italian masters like Titian, Tintoretto, Botticelli, Raphael, Caravaggio and the Bellini

Fact box

Carbon (kg per person) 5
Distance (km) 244
Nights 10
Transport budget (€) 100-120

The town of Malcesine on the banks of Lake Garda

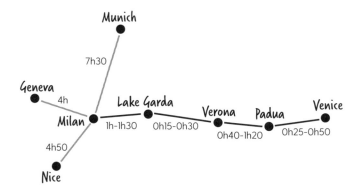

brothers. Otherwise, a spot of shopping around the Quadrilatero d'Oro – one of the world's most famous retail district – is definitely on the agenda.

🚊 **The main Milan–Venice train line runs direct to Lake Garda's principal towns, Desenzano del Garda and Peschiera del Garda (1h to 1h30, twice hourly).**

⟲ Day trip

Como

Eighteenth-century Austrian rule gave Como an orderly, central European air and a cafe culture, while the silk industry paid for dozens of palazzi and Stile Liberty (Italian art nouveau) villas. Navigazione Lago di Como (www.navigazionelaghi.it)

operates ferries and hydrofoils on the lake.

🚊 **Como's train station, Como San Giovanni, is served by trains from Milan's Stazione Centrale or Porta Garibaldi (0h37 to 1h30, at least hourly).**

❷ Lake Garda

Covering 370 sq km, Lake Garda is the largest of the Italian lakes. Like the best Italian lunches, exploring this region can't be rushed. Mitteleuropeans colonise northern resorts such as Riva del Garda and Torbole, where restaurants serve air-dried ham and Austrian-style *carne salada* (salted beef), while in the south, French and Italian families bed down in

Above, the town of Verona; left, the thriving waterways of Venice

Valtenesi farmhouses and family-friendly thermal spa towns such as Sirmione and Bardolino. Round-the-lake ferries are run by Navigazione Lago di Garda (www. navigazionelaghi.it).

🚆 **Verona is 15 minutes by train from Peschiera del Garda, 20 to 30 minutes from Desenzano del Garda. Trains run at least hourly.**

❸ Verona

Best known for its Shakespeare associations, Verona amounts to much more than Renaissance romance. Its heart is dominated by a mammoth 1st-century amphitheatre, the venue for the city's annual summer opera festival – but it's the handsome churches, attractive bridges over the Adige and delicious wine and food from the Veneto hinterland that really steal your heart.

🚆 **There are up to four trains an hour from Verona to Padua (0h40 to 1h20). Padua's station is north of the historic centre, linked by a monorail-bus.**

❹ Padua

As a medieval city-state and home to Italy's second-oldest university, Padua once challenged both Venice and Verona in importance. A series of extraordinary frescoes recall this golden age – including those in Giotto's blockbuster Cappella degli Scrovegni, Menabuoi's heavenly gathering in the Baptistery of St John and Titian's St Anthony in the Scoletta del Santo.

🚆 **Frequent trains serve Venice (0h25 to 0h50, one to nine per hour).**

© Javen / Shutterstock. © Matt Munro / Lonely Planet (2x)

❺ Venice

Pity the trippers with a mere three hours to take in Venice. That's about enough time for one long gasp at the show-stopper that is Piazza San Marco, but not nearly enough time to see what else Venice is hiding. Glimmering with iconic palazzi, glorious galleries and landmark churches, it's a city defined by water. You can take a classic gondola trip, of course, but better yet, why not learn how to row a traditional *batellina coda di gambero* (shrimp-tailed boat) with Row Venice (www.rowvenice.org).

Returning home

Direct intercity services operate out of Venice to most major Italian cities, as well as various points in France, Germany, Austria, Switzerland, Slovenia and Croatia.

Naples and the Amalfi Coast

Naples · Minori

Pick off the best of Naples' sights before using the Amalfi Coast's laid-back ferry network to enjoy a gentle week of beaches, culture and walking.

Departure points

Be as energetic or laid-back as you prefer on this two-stop break, using Trenitalia's high-speed service to whip you down to Salerno's ferry with a stop at Naples. Services from the northwest (Turin) meet up with high-speed trains from France, while services from the northeast (Verona) allow access from Germany.

❶ Naples

The centro storico – Naples' World Heritage-listed historic core – can be as high- or low-brow as you make it, mixing operatic palazzi and cultish shrines with bellowing baristas and deep-fried pizza. Spend at least a day exploring, or book an Elena Ferrante-inspired walking tour with

Looking For Lila (www.lookingforlila.com) 🚆😊 **Hop on the morning or lunchtime high-speed train to Salerno (0h40). From the train station it's just a 7-minute walk to the Travelmar ferry dock at Piazza Concordia (six departures daily from April to October). It's a very picturesque 30-minute ride to Minori.**

The town of Amalfi on Italy's Amalfi Coast

Fact box

Carbon (kg per person) 33
Distance (km) 325
Nights 10
Transport budget (€) 125

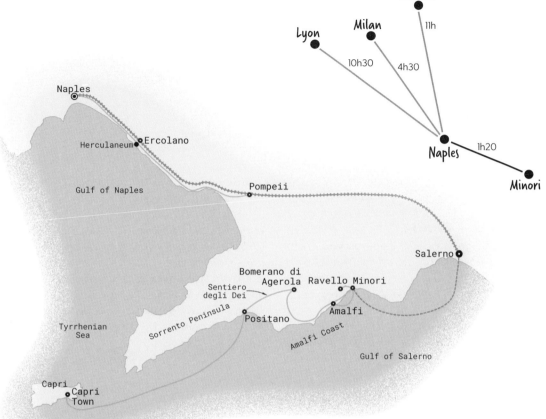

Around two weeks or more

Munich

Milan

Lyon

11h

10h30

4h30

Naples

1h20

Minori

Naples

Herculaneum • Ercolano

Gulf of Naples

Pompeii

Salerno

Bomerano di
Agerola   Ravello Minori
Sentiero
degli Dei
Tyrrhenian
Sea
Sorrento Peninsula   Positano   Amalfi
Amalfi Coast
Gulf of Salerno

Capri
Capri
Town

⚡ Day trip

Pompeii or Herculaneum

The ruins buried under the ashes of Mt
Vesuvius in AD 79 need no introduction.
The only choice is which site to visit.
Pompeii is huge and still being uncovered,
whereas Herculaneum is more intimate in
scale and, in terms of what survived the
eruption, displays a more domestic side to
ancient life.

🚆 **The metropolitan Circumvesuviana line
services both sites with several departures**
per hour. For Herculaneum, get off at
Ercolano-Scavi; for Pompeii, use Pompeii
Scavi – Villa dei Misteri.

❷ Minori

The Travelmar ferry (www.travelmar.
it/en) touches in at every village along
the Amalfi Coast, meaning you can base
yourself anywhere – if your wallet is deep
enough. The more affordable choice is
Minori. It may be a little scrappier than its
chichi neighbours, but it's central, small

Opposite, sparkling seas off Capri;
left, traditional Italian cooking

and less crowded. With a small sand beach, some great walks and a handful of bars and restaurants, it makes a perfect base for a week.

🚶 **From here, you can walk the delightful Sentiero dei Limoni (Footpath of the Lemon-trees) to resorty Maiori, 2.5km to the east, or climb the steps to cliff-top Ravello, with its villas, gardens and piazzas, 2km to the west.**

✈ Day trip

Amalfi

It's hard to believe that little Amalfi, hemmed in by its huge cliffs, was a maritime superpower of 70,000 people a millennium ago. Today, enjoy the cathedral, cloisters and buzzy town square. Or hike from the centre up the Valle delle Ferriere, a surprisingly wild forested walk past ruined paper mills up to a mossy, Jurassic-feeling waterfall.

⛴ **Just 10 minutes on the ferry gets you to Amalfi.**

✈ Day trip

Sentiero degli Dei & Positano

One of the most famous short hikes in Italy, the Footpath of the Gods traverses a balcony high above the Mediterranean with jaw-dropping views at every turn, slowly losing height before it plummets down to the restaurants, boutiques and wisteria-draped streets of Positano after 7km. Here, succour is at hand for the thirsty hiker, with bars and people-watching galore.

🚌⛴ **Take the 9.45am ferry or 9am bus to Amalfi, from where buses on weekdays at 10.15am for the climb up to Bomerano di Agerola, from where the hike is sign-posted. Ferry back from Positano to Minori via Amalfi at the end of the day (0h35).**

✈ Day trip

Isle of Capri

Capri has been synonymous with beauty since the time of Emperor Tiberius, who built 12 villas here. Spend a day exploring its towns, trails and villas.

⛴ **Regular ferries to Capri depart Positano from 9am returning until 7pm. Take the Travelmar service Minori to Amalfi, then Amalfi to Positano to link up with them.**

Returning home

From Minori, catch the Travelmar ferry back to Salerno (0h40). Six trains daily head north to Milan via Naples, Rome, Florence and Bologna. But only the ferries at 11.35am, 1.15pm and 2.30pm get you to Salerno in good time for trains at 1.30pm, 3.30pm and 5.37pm respectively.

A Corsican & Alpine escape

Paris · Nice · Bastia · Genoa · Turin · Chambéry · Lyon · Paris
This ferry-train combo takes in the sun-drenched Côte d'Azur, the craggy island of Corsica and the mountains of northern Italy before crossing the Alps back to France.

Departure points

Since the French capital has a fast, direct TGV service to Nice and Marseille, it's easy to access the trip from anywhere in Europe that has a train link to Paris.

❶ Paris

Begin with a day in Paris. With limited time, it's best to just focus on one arrondissement rather than trying to pack too much in. The Marais is a great place to start, with many of the capital's coolest cafes, bistros and bars: try the Breton-themed Breizh Café (www.breizhcafe.com) for Cancale oysters and buckwheat galettes, or La Maison Plisson (www.lamaisonplisson.com) for a smorgasbord of fabulous French produce.

🚆 Hop on a TGV at Paris' Gare du Lyon, and just under six hours later you'll be basking on Nice's pebble beaches (four to six daily).

❷ Nice

With a day in Nice, concentrate on the tangled alleys of the Old Town: browse the market stalls on Cours Saleya, cycle or rollerblade along the Promenade des Anglais, or hike up Colline du Château for

Fact box

Carbon (kg per person) 85
Distance (km) 2398
Nights 14
Transport budget (€) 500–550

❸ Bastia
Crumbling tenements, a lovely old town and a photogenic harbour make the lived-in city of Bastia a perfect introduction to Corsica. The Terra Nova, the high-walled citadel above the harbour, was built as the stronghold of Bastia's Genoese overlords. Dine on superb seafood at the harbourside restaurants, then overnight at a family-run hotel.

⚓ **Moby Lines sail from Bastia twice a day in summer to Genoa in Italy (6h).**
🏨 **Hotel tip: Hotel Central (www. hotelcentral.fr)**

✈ Day trip

Ajaccio
Corsica's only train line shuttles over the mountains via the island's one-time capital, Corte, to Ajaccio, birthplace of Napoleon Bonaparte. It's a spectacular ride.

views over the city's rooftops. Snack on Niçois specialities like *socca* (chickpea pancakes), *pissaladière* (onion tart) and, of course, salade Niçoise.
⚓ **Corsica Ferries (www.corsicaferries.com) and Moby Lines (www.mobylines.fr) run several ferries a day in summer from Nice to Bastia (quickest journey time 5h30).**
🏨 **Hotel tip: Nice Garden Hotel (www. nicegardenhotel.com)**

© Pete Seaward / Lonely Planet

century Palazzo Reale, admire the grand architecture of Piazza Castello and feast on gourmet Piedmont produce at Eataly Torino Lingotto, home of the Slow Food movement.

Ⓜ **Take the metro to Torino Porta Susa, from where TGVs cross the Franco-Italian border to Chambéry (2h40, three daily).**

🛏 **Hotel tip: DuParc Contemporary Suites (www.duparcsuites.com) is a stylish overnight option.**

❻ Chambéry

The attractive Alpine town of Chambéry was Savoy's capital from the 13th century until 1563, when the Dukes relocated to Turin. Past centuries have enriched the town with elaborate *hôtels particuliers* (grand townhouses), a medieval château and a one-of-a-kind trompe l'œil-decorated cathedral.

🚆 **Trains run almost hourly to Lyon Part-Dieu (1h30).**

❼ Lyon

At the foot of the Alps, Lyon is renowned for the richness of its food – traditional

🚆 **Timetables for Chemin de Fer de la Corse can be found at www.cf-corse.corsica. The trip is 3h45 each way.**

❹ Genoa

Italy's largest sea port, Genoa has a medieval heart with a twisting maze of largely intact *caruggi* (narrow streets), while the splendid Unesco-listed Palazzi dei Rolli is the city's most impressive architectural landmark.

🚆 **Spend a few hours exploring, then catch a train from Genoa to Turin (2h, hourly).**

❺ Turin

The elegant Alp-fringed city of Turin (Torino) has echoes of Vienna with its art nouveau cafes and stately architecture. Take in the dazzling 17th-

check-clothed bistros known as *bouchons* serve hearty dishes like *quenelles de brochet* (pike dumplings served in creamy crayfish sauce) and *poulet au vinaigre* (chicken cooked in vinegar). Allow a day for Lyon's Unesco-listed Old Town, with its narrow streets, medieval and Renaissance houses and impressive cathedral, and another two if you want to explore hilltop Fourvière and the redeveloped

area around Confluence. Bikes, trams, a four-line metro and two funiculars make getting around easy.

🚄 **It's two hours back to Paris Gare de Lyon by TGV: some depart from Gare de la Part-Dieu, 1.5km east of the Rhône, others from Gare de Perrache.**

🛏 **Hotel tip: The trendy, design-driven Mob Hotel (www.mobhotel.com) favours local sourcing wherever possible.**

Poitou-Charentes: boats, bikes, beaches

Coulon • Arçais • Île de Ré

Explore the marshes, cycleways and beaches around La Rochelle in a lazy itinerary that's as much fun with kids as it is without.

Departure points

Regular, direct SNCF services leave Paris Montparnasse for Niort every couple of hours throughout the day, taking 2h10. Once in Niort, buses and trains get you everywhere you need to be, although distances are such that you could easily do the whole itinerary by bike given an extra day. To reach the first night's stop in Coulon, take bus 22 from Niort station (0h30, no service on Sundays, prebook online on Saturdays at www.tanlib.com).

❶ Coulon

The Poitevin Marshlands are known in French as La Venise Verte (Green Venice). This dense network of canals and channels is second only to the Camargue in size and is best explored at a lazy pace from the saddle of a bike, or in one of the region's flat-bottomed boats. It's bucolic and languid – willows dip into the water, birds dart from the poplars and cows munch the grass, staring as you glide by. Learn about the marshlands at Coulon's eco-museum before taking a guided tour (if you can find an English-speaking guide) of the canals by boat. Bikes are available for hire too, with plenty of towpaths making for relaxed cycling.

The Île de Ré is paradise for pedallers

Fact box

Carbon (kg per person) 14

Distance (km) 182

Nights 4-10+

Transport budget (€) 74

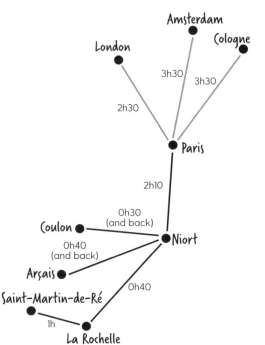

📍 Take the 22 bus back to Niort (0h30, six daily, reduced service at weekends), then change for the 21 to Arçais (0h40, 5 daily, reduced service at weekends). Call ahead or book online to ensure the bus stops in the town centre (www.tanlib.com).

❷ Arçais

This tiny village is one of the marshlands' most seductive, with the wooden cranes of its 'grand port' surviving from the days before rail took over. It's just big enough to have all you need for a day or two of exploring, with a village shop and a couple of restaurants. Hire a boat here without a guide – a canoe for activity, or a flat-bottomed punt to pole at a slower pace. Bikes are also for hire, with recommendations on the best canal-side routes to take.

📍 Catch the bus back to Niort train station, from where hourly trains take you to La Rochelle in 0h40. From La Rochelle station, take the 3 or 3E bus across the 3km

Left and below, Saint-Martin-de-Ré; right, boardwalk at Le Blois Plage

with a bike you can choose a different beach every day and along the way explore the salt pans and marshes of the north, the markets of Le Bois Plage, the huge citadel of Saint-Martin-de-Ré itself and the views from the Phare des Baleines lighthouse at the far tip of the island.

bridge linking Île de Ré with the mainland (1h, hourly, reduced service Sundays and holidays).

❸ Île de Ré

Despite having a bridge to the mainland since 1988, Île de Ré remains somehow a place apart from the rest of France. Here, the pace of life slows. Roads are replaced by rose-lined lanes. Cars are replaced by bikes. The harbour villages, dunes and pine forests are best explored on two wheels, and every village has hire shops where you can find tandems, electric bikes or trailers for kids. The island is small enough that you can stay anywhere. Choose somewhere on the sand if you have kids, or the pretty fortified capital of Saint-Martin-de-Ré if you don't.

🚲 **The beach is the main activity here, but**

⊕ Day trip

La Rochelle

If there's a rainy day, or if you just fancy some shopping, La Rochelle lies just across the bridge. It's known for historic buildings, seafood restaurants and smart boutiques, so a day here is easily spent. For those who prefer their seafood unharmed, it also has an aquarium that will please any kids and most adults too.

🚌😊 **Take the bus as you did to get here, or (April to September) take the ferry from Saint-Martin-de-Ré direct (1h10, irregular daily departures, check www.iledere-larochelle.fr).**

Returning home

From La Rochelle, trains head direct to Paris Montparnasse (via Niort) in under 3h.

© Justin Foulkes / Lonely Planet

An Atlantic Vélodyssée

Bordeaux · Lacanau-Océan · Mimizan · Biarritz · Bayonne · Bordeaux

Combine wine, water and easy-going cycling with a tour of Bordeaux then a flat, family-friendly bike ride south to the resort town of Biarritz via Atlantic surf beaches.

Departure points

TGV services connect Paris with Bordeaux in about 2h, making Paris the most sensible hub for anybody starting north or northeast of Bordeaux (including London). There's also a fast direct rail link between Bordeaux and Montpellier to the southeast, taking about 4h30. Note that reservations are required for bicycles on TGV services if you plan to pedal La Vélodyssée bike path.

❶ Bordeaux

Bringing your own bicycle (or renting then returning one in Bordeaux) on this itinerary means that several wineries are within reach without any need for a car. The grand chateaux around the town of Margaux in the Médoc region

are about 30km northwest, along the Garonne river. Closer still is the Pessac-Léognan appellation to the southeast. Château Haut-Brion is within the city limits in Pessac, but Château Bardins is only 12km from Bordeaux's centre and offers a guided cycle tour of the surrounding chateaux and vineyards. Be sure to explore the river, including the city's Chartrons quarter along the waterfront. From Bordeaux, the goal is to cycle to

Fact box

Carbon (kg per person) 4

Distance (km) 300km cycling, 200km train

Nights 5-10+

Transport budget (€) 50

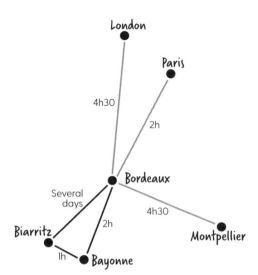

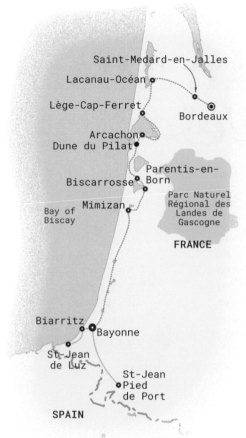

the coast while avoiding the busiest roads. One route is the *voie verte* (green way) along a disused railway line from Bordeaux to Lacanau-Océan.

🚲 **This is a ride of about 70km so stock up on pastries in Saint-Medard-en-Jalles on the outskirts of the city. Depending on your experience (or if you are travelling with children) you may wish to break the journey in half (or thirds) over one night or two along the route.**

❷ Lacanau-Océan

Surf and sand await at this seaside town, with plenty of places to eat and sleep, either in a hotel, B&B or campsite. This is where you will pick up La Vélodyssée, the long-distance cycle route that is signposted all the way from the Spanish border along France's Atlantic coast to Brittany (it's part of the epic EuroVelo 1 route). Bike riders can follow the green signposts at their own pace with towns

and villages at regular intervals providing pit stops. South from Lacanau-Océan, it's 36km to Lège-Cap-Ferret and another 42km to Arcachon, the chic weekend escape for the Bordelais. Fuelled by seafood, explore the bay and the giant sand dune at Pilat.

🚲 **From Arcachon La Vélodyssée travels 26km to Biscarrosse Plage, another 26km to Parentis-en-Born and then 32km to Mimizan Plage. If you're travelling with children you can stop or camp as required. The bike path is suitable for bike trailers.**

Left, the Atlantic coast, the Musée de la Mer in Biarritz; Pont Saint-Esprit in Bayonne; previous page, Bordeaux vineyards

❸ Mimizan

La Vélodyssée (www.cycling-lavelodyssee.com) recommends cycle-friendly accommodation along the route and Mimizan makes for a convenient stop. From this town you can hop southward between beaches with the Landes forest ever-present on your left and the Atlantic on your right. Your destination is Biarritz, the elegant beach and spa resort that was an R&R retreat of Napoleon.

Stronger solo cyclists can make the ride from Mimizan to Biarritz (about 125km) in a day, with the only gradients appearing as you enter Biarritz. But as always, there are places to overnight at regular intervals if you wish.

❹ Biarritz

Take a break in Biarritz. The town revolves around the sea, with plenty of walks, seawater spas and a lighthouse overlooking the Bay of Biscay. You can continue another 15km to the fishing port and holiday town of Saint-Jean-de-Luz or take a train from Bayonne to pilgrim-packed Saint-Jean-Pied-de-Port for some more hilly cycling or hiking in the foothills of the Basque Pyrenees.

It's less than 10km north from Biarritz to Bayonne on the bike path.

❺ Bayonne

The capital of France's Basque Country has great food and rich history so explore the cobbled town centre and the riverside restaurants for a day before taking the train back to Bordeaux.

There are typically 12 train departures daily from Bayonne for Bordeaux, taking about 2h (you don't lose much time taking the TER local train and there's no need to reserve a bike place, though arrive early to be sure of availability).

Returning home

From Bordeaux retrace your steps to your starting point.

Moroccan meander

Málaga · Melilla · Fez · Meknes · Tangier · Algeciras
Use Spain's high-speed trains and take an overnight ferry from Málaga to Morocco for a tour of imperial cities with day trips to intoxicating mountain villages.

Departure points

This trip begins in Málaga, easily reached by high-speed train from Barcelona, Madrid and other cities in Spain and France thanks to the Renfe-SNCF pact that provides high-speed train services between France and Spain. The ferry to Morocco leaves from Málaga and you return to Algeciras just across the strait of Gibraltar.

❶ Málaga

Spain's southern city buzzes with youthful energy and ambition. Recent openings of outposts of Russia's Hermitage museum and France's Pompidou Centre have put it firmly on the art circuit. Take a night or two here to sample tapas and wines.
🚢 **Take an overnight ferry (6hr) from**

Málaga to Melilla (www.balearia.com or www.trasmediterranea.es).

❷ Melilla

Who would expect to find hundreds of Modernist buildings, the second-largest collection outside Barcelona, in North Africa? Yet here they are, along with one perfectly preserved medieval fortress, several fascinating museums and a lot of

Heri es-Souani in Meknes

Fact box
Carbon (kg per person) 45
Distance (km) 1015
Nights 10
Transport budget (€) 150

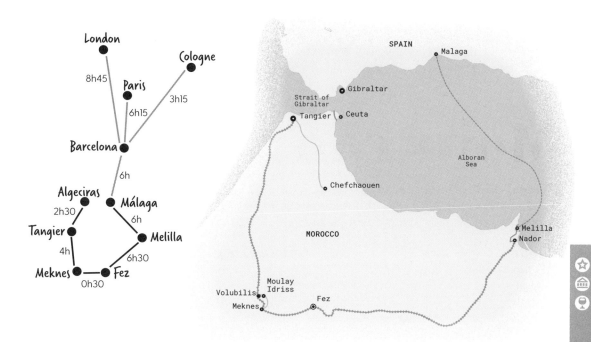

tapas bars, making Melilla a great place to explore. Along with Ceuta, multicultural Melilla is one of two autonomous Spanish cities on the Moroccan coast. Tourist infrastructure is excellent.

🚕 **Take a taxi from Melilla to Nador (0h35).**

🚉 **Trains depart from Nador to Fez twice daily (6hr; see www.oncf-voyages.ma).**

❸ Fez

Fez's historical and cultural lineage beguiles visitors. There's something raw about a place where 70,000 people choose to live in the maelstrom of a medina so dark and dilapidated that it remains the world's largest urban car-free zone.

🚉 **There are five train departures daily from Fez to Meknes; the journey takes about 30 minutes.**

🏨 **Hotel tip: Riad Tizwa Fes**

❹ Meknes

Laid-back Meknes is the most understated of Morocco's four imperial cities but no less enthralling. The Berber tribe Meknassis settled here in the 10th century, but Meknes came into its own in the 17th century when Moulay Ismail of the Alawite dynasty endowed the city with 25km of walls, monumental gates and a palace complex. Today, it's a great base for visiting the Roman ruins of Volubilis and the holy town of Moulay Idriss.

🚉 **From Meknes trains run five times a day to Tangier and take about four hours.**

✪ Day trip

Volubilis & Moulay Idriss

Morocco's best-preserved archaeological site, the Roman ruins of Volubilis, lies 33km north of Meknes. Most visitors combine a

Left, Bou Inania Madrasa in Fes's medina; a date farmer; below, Chefchaouen

day trip with a visit to the whitewashed town of Moulay Idriss, 5km away.

🚌 **There are no buses to Volubilis so share a taxi from Meknes to the site for a half or full-day excursion.**

---

❺ Tangier

Tangier wears many faces, from dissolute post-war Beat Generation hangout to redeveloped tourist-friendly city. Its medina, a labyrinth of alleys within a 15th-century Portuguese fort, offers a glimpse of another way of life. Lose yourself here for a day.

⛴ **From the port of Tangier Med, reached by taxi from Tangier Ville (1h, or a less predictably punctual bus), take the frequent ferry to Algeciras (1h30, or a high-speed 30-minute option).**

➕ Day trip

Chefchaouen

Morocco's famously blue town is perched beneath the peaks of the Rif. The old medina is a delight of Moroccan and Andalusian influence with red-tiled roofs, bright-blue buildings and narrow lanes converging on busy Plaza Uta El Hammam and its restored kasbah. Stay as long as you like and explore more of the surrounding hills.

🚌🚕 **Buses and taxis reach Chefchaouen from Tangier in about three hours so it's possible to plan a day trip or a longer stay.**

Returning home

Once in Spain, the high-speed rail hubs of Málaga or Madrid are accessible by standard trains from Algeciras.

A Balearic break

Barcelona · Alcúdia · Pollença · Palma · Ibiza · Valencia
Tour the beautiful Balearic islands of Mallorca and Ibiza from northern Europe by taking high-speed trains to Barcelona and a fast ferry to Alcúdia and then Ibiza.

Departure points

This itinerary takes advantage of Renfe-SNCF's high-speed train services between France and Spain. The ferry to Mallorca leaves from Barcelona, which can be reached by high-speed train from Paris in 6h15. Fast trains also link Paris with such cities as London, Cologne, Frankfurt, Geneva and Brussels.

❶ Barcelona

Take a day to discover Barcelona's art and architecture before catching your onward ferry to Mallorca.
🐟🚌 There are up to 19 sailings weekly from Barcelona to Alcúdia (6h) with www.balearia.com or www.trasmediterranea.es, including overnight options. There's a bus every 20 minutes from Port d'Alcúdia to Port de Pollença (taking about 40m). Or share a taxi.

❷ Pollença

Pollença and its associated port are popular bases for people wishing to explore the Tramuntana range – with its monasteries and mountain villages – and also have access to the beaches of the north and east coasts. The handsome

Fact box

Carbon (kg per person) 72
Distance (km) 600
Nights 12
Transport budget (€) 220

Mediterranean
Sea

SPAIN

Balearic
Sea

Costa del
Azahar

Barcelona

Menorca

Cap de
Formentor

Pollença

Sa Calobra

Alcúdia

Parc Natural
de S'Albufera

Palma

Mallorca

Valencia

Ibiza
Ibiza Town

Balearic Islands

Formentera

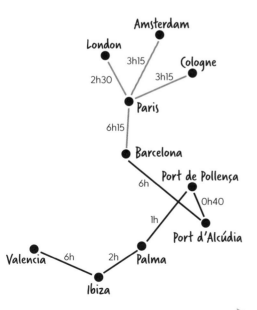

Amsterdam

London

3h15

Cologne

2h30

3h15

Paris

6h15

Barcelona

Port de Pollença

6h

0h40

1h

Port d'Alcúdia

Valencia

6h

2h

Palma

Ibiza

town has a broad range of hotels and holiday properties with more generic options available in Port de Pollença. Three to four days is just enough to experience the best of island's north.

🚌 **Take a bus (16 each weekday, nine on weekends, taking about an hour) or rent an electric car to head south to the capital, Palma.**

⏱ Day trip

Cycle ride

Mallorca is famously cycle-friendly with lots of quiet signposted routes plus easy availability of bike hire. Choose anything from mountainous explorations of the Tramuntana for experienced cyclists to gentle pedals around the flat interior and coast to the east. Some suggestions:

Left, Ibizan prawns with garlic; right, Cala d'en Serra, Ibiza; previous page, the Palau Nacional in Barcelona

the Balearics' party-hard sister. In summer the cream of the world's DJs arrive, but outside the nightclubs and during the rest of the year, there are wellness retreats and peaceful beaches. Base yourself in the capital or head for an ecofriendly agriturismo in the countryside. Nowhere does sunset chilling like the White Isle.

⚓ **From Ibiza Town, take the ferry to Valencia (6h), sailing 12 times weekly.**

⊕ Day trip

Yoga

In secluded, whitewashed villas or on quiet beaches, yoga devotees find that Ibiza offers the perfect environment for practising their pranayama. Local instructors offer a variety of classes to suit your preferences.

℗ **Book a class or one-to-one instruction: try a hatha workshop at Almond Blossom or a vegan retreat at Supersoulyoga.**

for hillier routes from Pollença consider cycling to the Cap de Formentor or Sa Calobra; for easier routes, try the S'Albufera nature reserve from Alcúdia.

🚲 **Rent a bicycle from Pollença or Alcúdia.**

❸ Palma

Petite, sun-splashed Palma is one of Europe's most underrated regional capitals, with museums the match of Barcelona, an amazing Gothic cathedral and an Old Town crammed with Moorish marvels.

⚓ **There are daily ferry departures from Palma to Ibiza, taking about 2h.**
🏨 **Hotel tip: Convent de la Missió**

❹ Ibiza

All-night raver, boho-cool hippy, blissed-out beach lover – Ibiza is all this and more to the many fans who have a soft spot for

❺ Valencia

Vibrant Valencia has thriving cultural, eating and nightlife scenes. The architecture is futuristic – check out the Ciudad de las Artes y las Ciencias plus the collection of modernista buildings, including the vast Mercado Central in the historic heart of the city. Rest awhile here before beginning your return rail journey.

Returning home

From Valencia, take a train to Madrid or Barcelona to connect with fast services north to France, Germany and the UK.

© Annapurna Mellor / Lonely Planet

Tour de Mont Blanc

Paris · Chamonix · Courmayeur · Chamonix · Paris
Circumnavigate Western Europe's tallest mountain by foot or bicycle on this world-class trekking route.

Departure points

With many people setting off for Chamonix by train from Paris, this trip is easily accessible from such northern European cities as London, Amsterdam and Munich. From Italy or the south of Europe, it may be quicker to take a bus from Turin to Courmayeur (2h30) and start the Tour de Mont Blanc from there.

❶ Paris

Leave the urban adventures of Paris for another trip and get on the first TGV to the Alps. If you're planning to mountain bike the route, check the latest information on reserving a space for a bike bag on the TGV Lyria trains (not necessary at the time of writing). As the train glides

through the French countryside, which becomes progressively more vertiginous, you can mull over the question of why attempt the Tour de Mont Blanc, a popular 170km circuit through the Alps? There are a couple of good logistical reasons: firstly, it's a loop, meaning that travel arrangements are easier. And secondly, it's an accessible hike through three countries (France, Italy, Switzerland) with huts roughly every 15km — these will likely

Fact box

Carbon (kg per person) 11
Distance (km) 800
Nights 7-12
Transport budget (€) 200

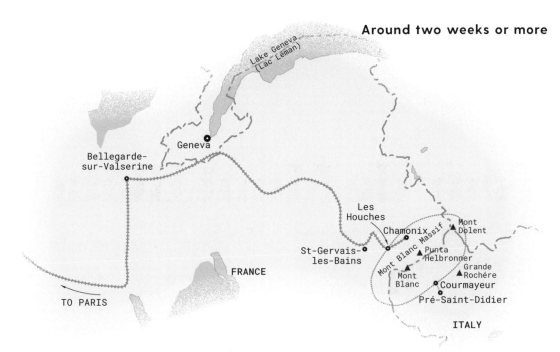

need to be booked in advance during the peak season of July and August. Most people hike it anticlockwise from the small town of Les Houches, taking 10 days or more (the very fittest and fastest trail runners can complete it in 24h). And it can be mountain biked in around five days, depending on the weather and how crowded the trail is (try September to avoid summer hikers). From December to May, the Mont Blanc range is the domain of ski tourers.

🚆 **TGVs depart Gare de Lyon for Chamonix about six times daily, with two changes at Bellegarde sur Valserine and Saint-Gervais-Les-Bains onto local trains, taking from 5h30 in total.**

❷ Chamonix

When you arrive in Chamonix it's clear that you're in one of the world's classic mountain towns: there are trip outfitters everywhere, including mountain-bike

rentals. If you haven't done so already, gather the kit you'll need: a stove for heating dried food, snacks, water bottles and purification filter (although there's no shortage of *eau potable* – drinkable

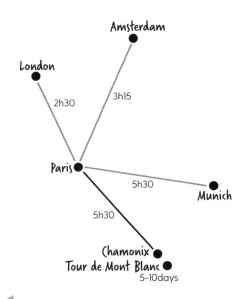

Previous page, Lac Blanc and the Mont Blanc Massif; left, a chalet in Courmayeur; right, mountain bikers in Chamonix

with unavoidable hike-a-bike sections. The reward will be epic scenery and the sense of being far above your worldly worries. Although this is high country, you won't be far from company, sharing the trail and huts with many other users. And if something does go wrong, there are bail-out options along the route back to civilisation.

From Les Houches, your fate depends on your two feet (or tyres). Most hikers average up to 20km per day and mountain bikers double that.

❸ Courmayeur

About halfway round, you'll come to the old Italian mountain town of Courmayeur in the Aosta Valley: wash sweaty clothes, drink beer, eat food and rest awhile. Courmayeur, like Chamonix, is close to cable cars for panoramas of the mountain range with minimal effort. Or take to the spa at Pré-Saint-Didier, enjoyed since Roman times and reached by a 30-minute bus journey. Then continue your way around Mont Blanc: you'll cross the border from Italy to Switzerland next and pass by villages such as Issert and Champex, accompanied by the bells of the cattle and sheep roaming the mountain meadows.

In theory, you're halfway back to Chamonix now. Keep going!

Returning home

From Chamonix, take the train back to Paris and then onward to your home town or city.

water – signs along the route).

For the hikers each day generally involves the ascent of a high pass before descending to habitation lower down the valleys. The elevation gain on this trek is greater than the height of Everest (at 10,000m or more) so gaining fitness over the six months before the trip will make the experience much more enjoyable. The same applies to cyclists – for bike riders this is definitely a challenge and will better suit experienced and fit riders who can manage rough and exposed descents on a laden mountain bike and long climbs

Paris to London by bike

Paris · Chaussy · Gisors · Dieppe · London
A largely traffic-free cycling route, the Avenue Verte (Green Way) links these two capitals in a week with castles, rolling farmland, and a ferry across the Channel.

Departure points

Travel to Paris from many European cities, including London, via train with your bicycle. On the Paris-bound Eurostar from Brussels (1h30) or London (2h30) you need to pre-book and pay for your bike. Only two bikes per train can travel pre-assembled so be ready to pack it in a bike bag or box. Check-in 90 minutes before departure. There are two routes from Paris to London – this is the less hilly Normandy option, it's easier for families. The 460km ride is fairly flat. The super-fit can attempt it in three days, those looking to take in the scenery – and food and wine pit stops – should allow a week, not including exploring Paris, London or Chaussy. You can do the route in reverse too.

❶ Paris

Where better to kick off your city-to-city journey than outside the spiritual heart of Paris: Notre-Dame. The Avenue Verte takes you through the oak and beech trees of the Saint-Germain-en-Laye forest, past the outskirts of Conflans-Ste-Honorine and through the picturesque Vexin Français Regional Nature Park. Pre-book accommodation with a flexible estimated time of arrival (just in case you venture off

Fact box

Carbon 14.5

Distance (km) 400

Nights 5-10

Transport budget (€) 24 (Channel ferry)

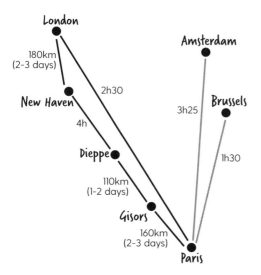

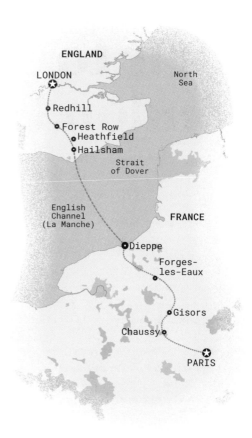

the path or take a picturesque detour!).

🚲 **The signposted route to Canal St-Martin eventually joins the Seine valley for a 45km ride out of the city towards Gisors (160km from central Paris, two to three days).**

⟳ Day trip

Domaine de Villarceaux

Take a day out from journeying to explore Domaine de Villarceaux at Chaussy. Beyond the manicured gardens and fairy-tale castle you can also learn about the sustainable rural development work of the Center Ecodevelopment Villarceaux (CEV). Accommodation is available here too in eco-conscious renovated farmhouses at La Bergerie de Villarceaux (Sheepfold of Villarceaux; http://bergerie-villarceaux. org), with seasonal rural meals at the organic restaurant on-site. Booking ahead is recommended.

🚲 **On the road to Gisors you'll cycle through Chaussy, which is 12km north of the Seine.**

➋ Gisors

Heading for the medieval castle town of Gisors and the Epte Valley next, you'll find signposts are regular enough, but you may get lost among the quiet country lanes, orchards and hills of rural Normandy, so take a good map and ideally a GPS. After several days meandering through French countryside, the final push from the spa city of Forges-les-Eaux to Dieppe (50km) is along a former railway line, where the idea for the Avenue Verte began.

© StockBrunet / Shutterstock

Left, the forest of Saint-Germain-en-Laye; below, St Paul's Cathedral; right, Domaine de Villarceaux; previous page, pedalling through Paris

two to three days with a few hilly climbs before you finally see the capital on the horizon. For symmetry, finish your trip at St Paul's Cathedral just north of the Thames, then take a day or two to explore London by bike (though be aware bike theft is rampant, a really good lock is essential and remove any panniers).

Returning home
If you're returning via Paris pre-book your bike on the Eurostar back from St Pancras International.

🚉😊 Local SNCF train runs from Dieppe to Paris every hour (2h30) if you want to turn back now. Otherwise join the ferry queue: cyclists await embarking with cars and motorcycles and once your passport and papers are checked, you'll be asked to walk your bike on board where bike racks are available to secure your trusty steed for the crossing (4h; twice daily).

❸ London
For those crossing the Channel by ferry, the route in England follows the National Cycle Network, though the Avenue Verte logo is being added to help navigation. From Newhaven head to the East Sussex village of Hailsham on Routes 20 and 21 then continue on to Forest Row, Red Hill and London over several days. The England section, at 180km, usually takes

Book a barge on Canal du Nivernais

Auxerre · Mailly-le-Château · Clamecy
Explore regional France – forests, castles, vineyards – but travelling at a gentler pace by boating and bicycling along the Canal du Nivernais.

Departure points

Your launching point to cruise the Canal du Nivernais is the medieval city of Auxerre, a 1h30 train journey from Paris (www.sncf.com) and also accessible from Brussels (4h15) and Zürich (6h). Choose between an all-inclusive boat hotel (with full board, wine and bicycles to explore further afield; www.edgecharter.com); or the more affordable option of self-navigating (it's a canal, there's not much to it) in a four-berth vessel (www.leboat.co.uk), picking up bicycles independently in Auxerre to take with you. To read more about the history of the Canal du Nivernais (it was originally used to transport firewood), see www.france.fr and http://burgundy-waterways.com.

❶ Auxerre

The Canal du Nivernais wends 174km through Burgundy from Auxerre via Clamecy and on to Decize on the Loire River. Between Auxerre and Clamecy the cut is entirely man-made. You'll cruise past wineries and through a gorge of striking limestone cliffs, paralleling the meandering river Yonne. Lock-keepers are on hand to help with the locks (of which there are 116 staggered along the canal's entire length).

Fact box

Carbon (kg per person) Depends on boat
Distance (km) 65
Nights 6-10
Transport budget (€) 1000-3500

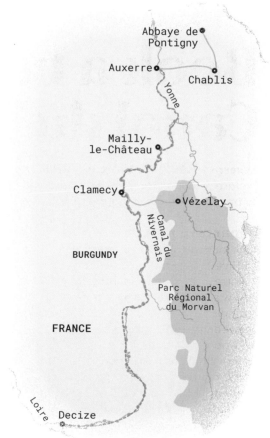

Take a few days to get to Mailly-le-Château
(27km; 6h cruising).

⊕ Day trip

Cycling Chablis

Plan for at least a day cycling in the
picturesque region of Chablis, exploring its
ancient villages, water meadows, forests
and wineries. The development of the
Chablis wine industry is credited to the
monks of Pontigny. For confident road
cyclists, don't miss the spectacular Abbaye
de Pontigny, 15km north of Chablis. It's
one of the last surviving examples of
Cistercian architecture in Burgundy, with
stone white walls contrasting with the
green countryside around.

⊗ **Cycle on back roads to Chablis (20km, 1h
one-way) from anywhere along the canal
until Champs-sur-Yonne. You'll need a local
map or a GPS.**

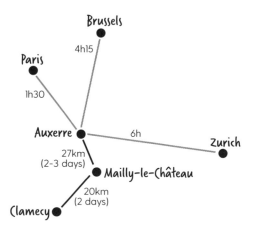

Left, swimming at Mailly-le-Chateau; Librairie L'Or des Etoiles bookshop in Vézelay; Chablis; previous page, the locks at La Colancelle

❷ Mailly-le-Château

Break up the first long stretch to Mailly-le-Château, with its old bridge adorned the chapel of Saint-Nicolas, at Ecluse des Dames – a great option for children with an adventure playground and restaurant. It's impossible not to feel your cares slip away when gliding along the calm flat water of the canal, watching the bow break the reflection of trees. For nature lovers, besides the occasional cyclist or walker, your only other company is families of mallards, herons, swans and butterflies.
➜ The next major stop is the village of Clamecy (20km).

❸ Clamecy

Clamecy is a 13th-century town embraced by both the rivers Yonne and Le Beuvron, with flower-filled medieval streets to see.

❤ Day trip

Vézelay

The hilltop village of Vézelay is a Unesco World Heritage site and one of France's architectural gems. Perched on a rocky spur crowned by a medieval basilica and surrounded by a patchwork of vineyards, sunflower fields and cows, Vézelay seems to have been lifted from another age. One of the main pilgrimage routes to Santiago de Compostela in Spain starts here.
🚲 From Clamecy it's a 20km cycle (about 1hr) to Vézelay and back.

Returning home

Though you've only travelled about 45km to Clamecy, time slows down at this pace. If time allows you can keep heading towards Decize, or find a winding spot to turn around and see the canal from the other perspective, as you head north back to Auxerre. If you're taking a one-way journey, the train line follows the canal so you can return to Paris from any main village along the canal (boat-hire agreements dependent).

Walk Portugal's Atlantic coast

Lisbon · Santiago do Cacém · Porto Côvo · Odeceixe · Cabo de São Vincente
Slow-travel the Alentejo coast on the Rota Vicentina, a network of trails combining the Historical Way and the coastal paths of the Fishermen's Trail.

Departure points

From Paris take the TGV from Gare Montparnasse to Hendaye on the Spanish border (5h) before swapping to the overnight Sud Expresso train to Lisbon (13h30). Overnight trains also run from Madrid (9-10h), and there are shorter connections from Seville (3h20). From Lisbon it's easy to access the Historical Way at Santiago do Cacém to walk the three days to Porto Côvo. The Fishermen's Trail is a nine-day hike from there to Cabo de São Vincente in the Algarve, but you can peel off anytime and get a local bus back to Lisbon if time is short.

❶ Lisbon

Before beginning your hike, spend a day or two soaking up Libson's art and architecture, join a foodie walking tour and get over to Belém to visit Jerónimos Monastery.

🚌 **To get to the Historical Way, book the short bus ride with Rede Expressos from Sete Rios Coach Station to Santiago do Cacém (2h, every three hours).**

❷ Santiago do Cacém

Begin your hiking adventure in the sleepy

Fact box

Carbon 16
Distance (km) 264
Nights 8-14
Transport budget (€) 33.30

orange-treed town of Santiago do Cacém, heading southwest to the Atlantic coast via Cercal do Alentejo. Some budget travellers take camping gear, but most pre-book accommodation, or make use of commercial operators who can organise guesthouses and luggage transfers for you. Accommodation on this section is plentiful thanks to a host of websites.

⚡ **The three-day, 57km walk to Porto Côvo takes you through a mosaic of cork groves, pine forests and farmland, punctuated with sun-bleached hilly villages.**

❸ Porto Côvo

Here the Historical Way gives way to the Fishermen's Trail. For the next three days or so you'll be walking on beaches and sometimes sand dunes, so allow plenty of time (and patience) – this is perhaps the definition of sloooooow travel! Take plenty of water and food on these days as this is pretty remote coastal country. When you're not tramping along deserted

beaches, you'll be following fishermen's tracks along the craggy clifftops of Southwest Alentejo and Vicentine Coast Natural Park, which sometimes lead down to secret coves. This section is not so fun if you suffer from a serious fear of heights.

⚡ **From Porto Côvo to Vila Nova de Milfontes it's only 16km but allow plenty of time. The next major village is Cavaleiro (20km) then Odeceixe (24 km).**

Above, Cabo de São Vincente; right, Odeceixe; previous page, hiking through Porto Côvo

❹ Odeceixe

Overlooking the mouth of the Ribeira de Seixe, which divides the region from its southern neighbour, the Faro District, Odeceixe is a great spot for canoeing, birdwatching and surf lessons; if you need a rest from walking consider booking a couple of days here. The beach is busy in summer with Portuguese holiday-makers but fairly quiet the rest of the year.

🥾 **The next four to six days' walk on the Fishermen's Trail to Cabo de São Vincente (60km) continues to be broken into 20km stretches between villages.**

❺ Cabo de São Vincente

This wind-whipped cape, Europe's southwestern-most point, is a dramatic spot from which to watch the sun set.

It was once the last view of Europe for explorers as their ships launched into the unknown beyond the horizon during the Age of Discovery. The lighthouse here is home to a small museum on Portugal's maritime history.

Returning home

Buses leave from Sagres (a 1h walk from Cabo de São Vicente) back to Lisbon (4h15, daily). If you want to finish up earlier, buses service the villages in the area and timetables and tickets are available online with Rede Expressos (www.rede-expressos.pt).

Danube Cycle Path

Passau · Schlögener Loop · Linz · Grein · Melk · Krems · Vienna

Take the Danube Cycle Path for a joyous pedal between vineyards, orchards and castle-topped villages, tracing the course of one of Europe's mightiest rivers.

Departure points

Passau can be reached by high-speed train from Munich (2h45) and Salzburg (2h30). From Paris Est, the journey by TGV/ICE (9h) involves at least one change. The cycle path is easiest to cycle west-east, going downstream and downhill. Avoid July and August if you can. Bikes and e-bikes can be hired at numerous outlets in Passau and returned in Vienna for a small extra fee (around €35).

❶ Passau

Nudging the Austrian and Czech borders, Passau was built high on the riches of it once being the largest bishopric in the Holy Roman Empire. Its proud baroque Altstadt (old town) perches on a peninsula

above the confluence of three rivers: the Danube, the Inn and the Ilz. Its web of lanes, tunnels and archways wrap around an opulent, Italianate cathedral.

⚲ From Passau, the first section of the ride heads through gentle countryside into Austria towards Schlögen (45km).

⊕ Pit stop

Engelhartszell

Stop off at Engelhartszell, a 13th-century

Fact box

Carbon (kg per person) 0.1

Distance (km) 315

Nights 9+

Transport budget (€) €130-235

Trappist abbey, where you can sample monk-made brews, liqueurs and cheeses.
🚲 **Engelhartszell is roughly 30km into the ride from Passau to Schlögener**

---

❷ Schlögener Loop

The icing on the scenic cake in this uplifting stretch of the Danube Valley is the Schlögener Loop, where the river makes a complete 180-degree turn, unspooling like a ribbon through wooded granite hills. For sensational views, hike 30 minutes above the village of Schlögen to Schlögener Blick.
🚲 **Small passenger ferries chug from Schlögen village to the other side of the**

river, where the ride continues to Linz (46km).

❸ Linz

The Danube Valley broadens as you roll on through fertile plains towards Linz. Winging you into the 21st century, this culture-crammed town has its sights firmly set on the future. With a day to explore, check out Lentos Kunstmuseum for modern art wonders and the hands-on Ars Electronica Center for new technology, science and digital media. Alternatively, go for a mooch in the baroque and Renaissance Altstadt, which fans out from the cafe-rimmed Hauptplatz. It's another 60km from Linz to Grein.

⊕ Pit stop

Enns
Factor in time to see medieval Enns en

Follow the signs for EuroVelo 6 along the Danube

© Julian Love / Lonely Planet

Passau — 3h — Schlögener Loop — 2h45 — Linz — 3h15 — Grein — 2h45 — Melk — 2h15 — Krems — 4h30 — Vienna

AUSTRIA
Dürnstein · Krems an der Donau
Spitz
Melk · Tulln · Wienerwald Woods
Ybbs
VIENNA

route. Founded in 1212, it's one of Austria's oldest towns.

🚲 **Enns is approximately 23km into your ride from Linz to Grein.**

❸ Grein

Many cyclists rave about Grein being their favourite part of the ride and it's a beauty for sure. Jutting above the village, its whimsically turreted baroque castle hides an impressive late-Renaissance arcaded inner courtyard. The 18th-century theatre in the former granary is the oldest still in operation in Austria.

🚲 **It's a 44km pedal from Grein to Melk via Ybbs (a good lunch stop).**

❹ Melk

Few sights lift spirits like the Benedictine abbey-fortress of Melk, high on a hill above the Danube, where you can tour the baroque-gone-mad church, library and Marmorsaal (Marble Hall). The next leg of the ride takes you deep into the Unesco-listed Wachau region, where the river carves a path past terraced vineyards, apricot orchards, forested slopes and castles on almost every bend.

🚲 **You won't want to hurry the 35km ride from Melk to Krems.**

✪ Pit stop

Spitz & Dürnstein

Allow time in vine-swathed Spitz to taste local wines in Heurigen (wine taverns). Dürnstein ramps up the romance with its eyrie-like castle where Richard the Lionheart was once imprisoned.

🚲 **Spitz is about 18km from Melk; Dürnstein**

is at about the 29km marker on your cycle to Krems.

❺ Krems an der Donau

Krems entices with a laid-back historic centre to stroll, Grüner Veltliner and Riesling white wines from local vineyards to sample, and plenty of atmospheric places to eat and stay. The gallery-crammed Kunstmeile area and lavishly baroque Stift Göttweig abbey are also worth checking out.

🚲 **From here, pedal on to Vienna, via Tulln and the wooded Wienerwald (80km).**

✪ Pit stop

Tulln

Austrian Expressionist Egon Schiele (1890-1918) was born in Tulln and his hometown has two museums devoted to his life and work (one of which was his birthplace).

🚲 **Tulln is about 45km into the ride to Vienna.**

❻ Vienna

A fittingly grand end to one heck of a bike ride, the Austrian capital reels you in every time with its magnificent ensemble of palaces, galleries, parks, concert halls and coffee houses. Spend at least a day or two resting and exploring here before the journey home.

Returning home

Frequent high-speed trains connect Vienna with cities to the north and east, including Munich (4h15), Paris (10h30), Bratislava (1h) and Prague (4h).

Mallorca to Madrid

Barcelona · Palma · Sóller · Sa Pobla · Petra · Manacor · Valencia · Madrid
Look beyond the beaches and Spain's holiday isle will reveal its mountains,
monasteries and unique local culture. Then explore the Spanish capital's art and dining.

Departure points
Barcelona can be reached on high-speed rail lines from Madrid, Paris (6h30), London (10h), Geneva (8h30) and beyond.

❶ Barcelona
Acquaint yourself with Catalan culture in the home of Joan Miró and Ferran Adrià. Barcelona remains a city of cutting-edge cuisine even after the closure of Adrià's El Bulli restaurant. From classic tapas at Pinotxa Bar in La Boqueria (the city's food market) to Michelin cooking from an Adrià alumnus at Disfrutar, there's something for every taste in Barcelona. Now feed your creativity with a visit to the Fundació Joan Miró, as complete a collection of the work of the city's favourite son as you could hope for, displayed in a light and airy building on a hilltop in Parc de Montjuïc. .

⚓ **From Barcelona, ferries operated by Balearia (www.balearia.com) and Trasmediterránea (www. trasmediterránea. com) depart daily for Palma, taking about 7h30 (including the overnight options).**

❷ Palma
Almost a miniature Barcelona, the Mallorcan capital was where Joan Miró

Fact box
Carbon (kg per person) 133
Distance (km) 1083
Nights 10-15
Transport budget (€) 160

Terraces along the Tramuntana at Banyalbufar

lived out his days. Visit the Fundació Pilar i Joan Miró for more of his work. Get a sense of the city's Islamic history at the Museu de Mallorca and the Palau de l'Almudaina.

🚂 **Take the tiny train from Palma to Sóller (www.trendesoller.com), which runs six times per day from April to October (1h) and less frequently in winter.**

❸ Sóller

The town lies in a valley in the Tramuntana range that is fragrant with citrus blossom. Spend a few days exploring the region on public transport. A tram runs to the Port de Sóller (noted for its seafood restaurants). Take local buses to visit Deià and Valldemossa to the south (the 210 service) and the pretty village of Fornalutx and beyond Puig Major to Lluc monastery to the north (the 354 service). There are superb hiking routes in the hills, including the Ruta de Pedra en Sec (Dry Stone Route) that traces cobbled paths along the range from Port d'Andratx to Pollença. Take a bus in one direction and walk the way back.

🚌 **Take the 354 bus (www.tib.org) to Pollença (1h30) with a morning or an**

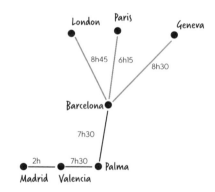

afternoon departure Monday to Saturday (summer only; if after October, return to Palma and take the 340 bus).

❹ Pollença

Dive deeper into island culture by climbing the 365 steps from the town square to the simple and serene hilltop chapel Església del Calvari. Continuing the active theme, there are bikes available (including electric bikes) for rent so you could explore the back roads or embark on an adventure to Cap de Formentor.

🚌 **From Pollença, take the 340 bus to Sa Pobla, which stops on the town ring** road. The train station is 2km away on the opposite side of town.

❺ Sa Pobla

This is a transition point, for transport but also from the Tramuntana to Es Pla, the fertile plains to the east. Vineyards and almond orchards start appearing.

🚆 **Take the T2 train from Sa Pobla to Inca and change to the T3 line for Petra and Manacor (www.tib.org). Journeys take a few minutes.**

❻ Petra

There are two big reasons to stop at Petra: to check out the Ermita de la Mare de Déu de Bonany, where Franciscan monk and missionary Juníper Serra gave his final sermons before founding California in the New World. And to buy some wine at Bodegas Miquel Oliver.

🚆 **Continue to Manacor on the T3 train.**

❼ Manacor

Like Sa Pobla, this is a transit point, not a place to linger. Hop on one of several buses to the east coast of Mallorca and stop at Porto Cristo for the amazing (and crowded) Coves (caves) del Drac. South of Porto Cristo lie quiet coves (beaches), accessible by a couple of bus services.

🚆⛴ **Return to Palma on the train and then take a ferry to Valencia. The route is operated by the same two companies and also takes about 7h30.**

❻ Valencia

Cool, contemporary Valencia merits at least a couple of days to absorb Santiago

Live music at Mercado do Motores in Madrid

Calatrava's Ciudad de las Artes y las Ciencas, the fishing port of El Cabanyal and the countless bars and restaurants. .

🚆 **Trains from Valencia's Joaquin Sorolla station reach Madrid Puerta de Atocha in less than 2h. There are about 15 high-speed departures daily plus stopping options.**

❻ Madrid

In a country of beguiling coastal cities, Spain's landlocked capital sometimes misses deserved acclaim. But it is home to one of the world's great art galleries museums, the Museo del Prado, where Goya and Velázquez shine a light on the Spanish soul.

Returning home

Madrid has high-speed train connections north to France and beyond via Barcelona.

Liguria Loop

Nice · Menton · Genoa · La Spezia · Genoa · Milan
Pack a pair of hiking points for this journey around the coast of the Ligurian Sea to the villages of Cinque Terre where some amazing clifftop trails await.

Departure points

Nice is readily accessible by TGV from Paris (and therefore London and Brussels) and is also on high-speed train routes from Montpellier, Marseille and Milan.

❶ Nice

Nice reigns over the French Riviera, bestowing its charms – the light, the opulence, the glittering sea – upon the visitors who come to pay homage. There's no secret hinterland to this most paparazzi-ed part of the Mediterranean coast but it does pay to explore beyond the justly famed Promenade des Anglais, the Musée Matisse and the markets of Nice's Old Town. The reclusive peninsula of Saint-Jean-Cap-Ferrat has long attracted

the stars and the waterfront town of Villefranche-sur-Mer just to the east offers a relaxing retreat from the city.
🚄 **Hop on a local train for the half-hourly 0h40 ride along the coast to Menton.**

❷ Menton

Menton was once owned by the princes of Monaco (who taxed the town's prized lemons) but, thankfully, by the 19th century it was a French resort with which future generations, from Queen Victoria and

Fact box

Carbon (kg) 17

Distance (km) 547

Nights 10+

Transport budget (€) 55

Milan

Turin

ITALY

Genoa

Gulf of Genoa

FRANCE

Cinque Terre

La Spezia

Sainte Agnes

Ligurian
Sea

MONACO

Nice

Menton

London   Paris   Stuttgart

8h   5h30   10h30

Nice

0h30   Milan

1h30

3h   1h

Menton   Genoa   La Spezia

Winston Churchill to Aubrey Beardsley and Jean Cocteau (check out his museum), would fall in love. Backed by the Alps, its climate is supposedly the finest along the Riviera: sit back among the citrus trees in Jardins Biovès to test that theory.

🚆 **Around 50 trains depart daily for Genoa, the fastest taking 2h30 (changes required).**

✛ Day trip

Sainte-Agnès

The Alps rise suddenly behind Menton and 10km inland lies the enchanting medieval village Sainte-Agnès, which makes for a perfect day trip. Some of the restaurants have terraces from which to enjoy views of the sea.

🚌 **The line 10 bus departs Menton bus station six times daily for Sainte-Agnès (0h45, www.zestbus.fr). Or if you're feeling very athletic, Bike Trip has rental bicycles.**

From left, Vernazza; hiking the Cinque Terre coast; local lemons; previous page, Gare de Nice-Ville, Menton icecream

© Justin Foulkes/ Lonely Planet

❸ Genoa

The birthplace of Christopher Columbus retains its seafaring connections, with ferries setting off across the Mediterranean. The city's maritime wealth is apparent in the former palaces of its most powerful families, collectively known as the Palazzi dei Rolli, many of which are open to the public. Head for the Via Garibaldi to see the art collections of three palazzi at the Musei di Strada Nuova. Then collect supplies for the hiking ahead at the Mercato Orientale.
🚇 **Intercity trains from the Piazza Principe station take 1h30 to reach La Spezia (2-3 trains hourly; www.trenitalia.com).**

❹ Cinque Terre

The gateway to Cinque Terre, a precipitous stretch of the Ligurian coast, is La Spezia, southeast of the five famous villages.

From La Spezia, heading west, they are Riomaggiore (about 15km from La Spezia), Manarola, Corniglia, Vernazza, Monterosso. Scenic footpaths link all five (as do train services), known as the 11km Blue Trail. From Riomaggiore the Via dell'Amore follows the cliffs to Manarola (about a 0h30 walk) and so on. If you plan to hike the length of Cinque Terre consider leaving heavier luggage in Genoa to await your return. Note also that the Parco Nazionale delle Cinque Terre and the villages get very busy in the high season (May to September) so try shoulder season travel and book accommodation in advance. There are less crowded hikes in the park that you can explore from a base in one of the villages.
🚇 **Intercity trains return to Genoa's Piazza Principe from Monterosso every two hours (1h20). Frequent, direct trains take a further 1h30-2h to reach Milan from Genoa.**

❺ Milan

From Genoa, the closest major transport hub is Milan, which may offer speedier links to your home than returning to Nice. Before leaving, spend a day or more in this dynamic city, seeing the Duomo, the boutiques of the Quadrilatero d'Oro and *The Last Supper.*

Classical East Mediterranean

Rome · Naples · Bari · Dubrovnik · Sarandë · Corfu · Athens · Samos · Kuşadası
Take a month or more to uncover many of the relics and ruins of Classical antiquity from the Roman and Greek empires on this tour of the Eastern Mediterranean.

Departure points

Options for reaching Rome by train include a Thello sleeper train from Paris to Milan then a fast train to Rome (3h) or a TGV via Turin from Paris from 10h (and by extension London, 2h30). From Munich, take a EuroCity train to Verona (5h) and then change for Rome (3h).

❶ Rome

Start this itinerary in the capital of the Roman Empire. Ancient Rome's sites are in a compact area in the southeast of the city. For four centuries the Colosseum was an entertainment venue for Romans and a place of death for gladiators and wild animals. A more civilised centre was the Roman Forum, now a group of ruined temples, basilicas and public spaces.
🚆 **Frequent fast trains to Naples (www. trenitalia.com) take about 1h.**

❷ Naples

For a detailed insight into Roman culture, visit Naples' Museo Archeologico Nazionale, one of the world's greatest collections of Graeco-Roman artefacts.
🚆 **Fast trains to Bari Centrale take about 4h with a change at Caserta.**

❹ Day trip

Pompeii

The Roman port of Pompeii was buried in ash during the eruption of Mt Vesuvius in AD 79, preserving astonishing details of the thriving town, from frescoes, bathhouses and temples to the places where people perished.
🚆 **Trains from Naples Piazza Garibaldi depart half hourly for Pompei. taking 0h45.**

❸ Bari

Puglia's capital is the departure point for ferries across the Adriatic and although it may not have much in the way of Roman

---

Fact box

Carbon 451

Distance (km) 2915

Nights 30+

Transport budget (€) 360

---

sites, it does offer an exceptionally handsome 12th-century basilica in the centre of the Old Town (where you can also pick up snacks for the journey).

⚫ The ferry company Jadrolinija (www. jadrolinija.hr) has overnight crossings to Dubrovnik (two to four departures weekly, depending on the month).

Left, the Roman Forum

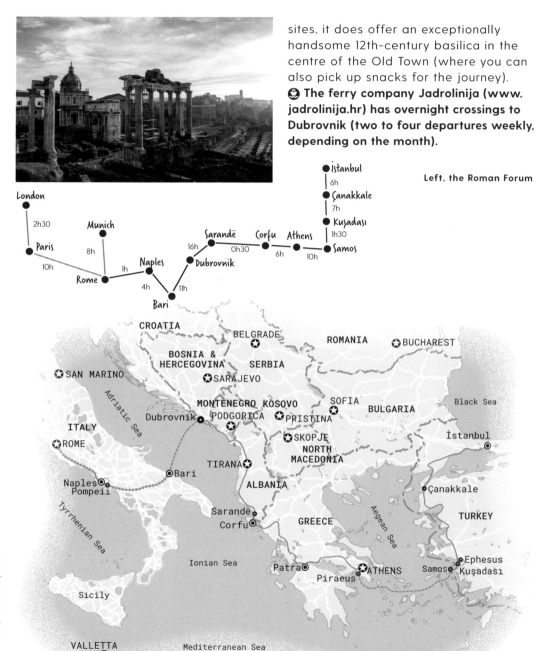

④ Dubrovnik

Dubrovnik's 14th-century city walls enclose an utterly absorbing Old Town, despite the number of visitors in the high season. Snap a photo from Srd hill, reached by cable car. If you're feeling claustrophobic, take a 10-minute ferry ride to Lokrum, a small island with swimming spots and forests.

🚍 **The next stage of your odyssey is the most adventurous. Follow the coast road through Montenegro then Albania to the southern city of Sarandë. It's not as daunting as it sounds: there are direct buses to Kotor from Dubrovnik (about 2h, www. buscroatia.com) and travel agencies offer bus rides from Kotor to the Albania capital Tirana (5h30). From Tirana there are about eight buses daily to Sarandë (8h).**

⑤ Sarandë

From this popular resort city, you can relax at some of the beaches along the Albanian Riviera.

⛴ **Next take a ferry to Corfu. The frequency varies according to season: there's typically at least one or two daily (www.sarrislines. gr; www.finikas-lines.com), taking 0h30.**

⑥ Corfu

Having come this far, take a break on the island where Odysseus sought refuge. The beaches, wild scenery and good food are still beguiling. You can get around the island by local bus (www.greenbuses.gr). Bicycles are available to rent at several shops in Corfu Town.

🚍 **From Corfu take the X1 bus to Athens (www.greenbuses.gr), at least 6h, not including a ferry crossing to the mainland.**

⑦ Athens

The Acropolis and its excellent museum are just two of the essential sights of the Greek capital. For a deeper grounding in Ancient Greece, visit the National Archaeological Museum and the Temple of Olympian Zeus.

⛴ **Next take a ferry from Athens' port Piraeus to Vathy on Samos (10h, www. hellenicseaways.gr) or you can take an indirect route island-hopping through the Cyclades via Mykonos, Paros and more.**

⑧ Samos

Greece's easternmost island was an important centre of Hellenic culture, being the birthplace of Hera, wife of Zeus, as well as philosopher Pythagoras. The striking capital is Vathy.

⛴ **The ferry from Vathy to Kuşadası in Turkey takes 1h30 (www.meandertravel. com; timings vary).**

⑨ Kuşadası

From this rambunctious resort and port, visit mind-blowing Ephesus then make your way up the coast to Çanakkale.

🚍 **Buses run to İzmir (1h) then change to a bus north to Çanakkale (6h).**

Left, the beaches of Corfu;
above, the ruins of Ephesus

😊 Day trip

Ephesus

Europe's most complete classical ruins have taken more than 150 years to excavate and that's revealed only 20% of the city. Ephesus was the capital of Roman Asia Minor, vibrant, educated city of traders, sailors and pilgrims to the Temple of Artemis, one of the Seven Wonders of the Ancient World. A visit brings the Graeco-Roman world alive.

🚌 **Minibuses go to Ephesus or you can book a tour with an agency like Meander or take a taxi there and back.**

⑩ Çanakkale

This smart and sociable university city is close to the location of the legendary city of Troy. Just remember that's there's no mention of a wooden horse in *The Iliad*, the chronicle of the Trojan War.

🚌 **Buses take about 6h to reach İstanbul.**

Returning home

From İstanbul, one way west is to follow the route of the Orient Express (p173).

Index

Low-Carbon Europe

May 2020

Published by Lonely Planet Global Limited

CRN 554153

www.lonelyplanet.com

10 9 8 7 6 5 4 3 2 1

Printed in Malaysia

ISBN 9781838691080

© Lonely Planet 2020

© photographers as indicated 2020

Managing Director, Publishing Piers Pickard

Associate Publisher Robin Barton

Editors Bridget Blair, Lorna Parkes,
Polly Thomas, Clifton Wilkinson

Art Director Daniel Di Paolo

Layout Jo Dovey

Cover Illustration Eiko Ojala (http://ploom.tv)

Cartography James Leversha, Wayne Murphy

Print Production Nigel Longuet

Thanks to Jessica Cole

Written by Oliver Berry, Oliver Smith, Kerry Christiani, Brana Vladisavljevic, Tasmin Waby, James Smart, Tom Hall, Lauren Keith

Lonely Planet Offices

STAY IN TOUCH lonelyplanet.com/contact

Australia

The Malt Store, Level 3,
551 Swanston St, Carlton, Victoria 3053
T: 03 8379 8000

USA

Suite 208, 155 Filbert St,
Oakland, CA 94607
T: 510 250 6400

Ireland

Digital Depot, Roe Lane (Off Thomas Street)
The Digital Hub,
Dublin 8, D08 TCV4

UK

240 Blackfriars Rd,
London SE1 8NW
T: 020 3771 5100